Women Entrepreneurs Across Racial Lines

NEW HORIZONS IN ENTREPRENEURSHIP

Series Editor: Sankaran Venkataraman
*Darden Graduate School of Business
Administration, University of Virginia*

This important series is designed to make a significant contribution to the development of Entrepreneurship Studies. As this field has expanded dramatically in recent years, the series will provide an invaluable forum for the publication of high-quality works of scholarship and show the diversity of issues and practices around the world.

The main emphasis of the series is on the development and application of new and original ideas in Entrepreneurship. Global in its approach, it includes some of the best theoretical and empirical work with contributions to fundamental principles, rigorous evaluations of existing concepts and competing theories, historical surveys and future visions. Titles include original monographs, edited collections, and texts.

Titles in the series include:

A General Theory of Entrepreneurship
The Individual–Opportunity Nexus
Scott Shane

Academic Entrepreneurship
University Spinoffs and Wealth Creation
Scott Shane

Economic Development Through Entrepreneurship
Government, University and Business Linkages
Edited by Scott Shane

Growth Oriented Women Entrepreneurs and their Businesses
A Global Research Perspective
*Edited by Candida G. Brush, Nancy M. Carter, Elizabeth J. Gatewood,
Patricia G. Greene and Myra M. Hart*

Women Entrepreneurs Across Racial Lines
Issues of Human Capital, Financial Capital and Network Structures
Andrea E. Smith-Hunter

Women Entrepreneurs Across Racial Lines

Issues of Human Capital, Financial Capital and Network Structures

Andrea E. Smith-Hunter

Associate Professor of Marketing and Management at Siena College, USA

NEW HORIZONS IN ENTREPRENEURSHIP

Edward Elgar
Cheltenham, UK • Northampton, MA, USA

Published by
Edward Elgar Publishing Limited
Glensanda House
Montpellier Parade
Cheltenham
Glos GL50 1UA
UK

Edward Elgar Publishing, Inc.
136 West Street
Suite 202
Northampton
Massachusetts 01060
USA

A catalogue record for this book
is available from the British Library

Library of Congress Cataloguing in Publication Data
Smith-Hunter, Andrea.
    Women entrepreneurs across racial lines : issues of human capital,
financial capital and network structures / Andrea E. Smith-Hunter.
        p. cm. -- (New horizons in entrepreneurship series)
    Includes bibliographical references and index.
    1. Women-owned business enterprises--United States. 2. Minority
business enterprises--United States. 3. Businesswomen--United
States. I. Title. II. Series: New horizons in entrepreneurship.
    HD2358.5.U6S65 2006
    338.6'420820973--dc22

2005031677

ISBN-13: 978 1 84376 416 8
ISBN-10: 1 84376 416 4

Typeset by Manton Typesetters, Louth, Lincolnshire, UK.
Printed and bound in Great Britain by MPG Books Ltd, Bodmin, Cornwall.

This book is dedicated to
Andrew C. Hunter
Daphne Heslop Smith

and to

Jared Meshak
Gabrielle Elizabeth
Jacob Asiah
Joshua Emmanuel

Contents

Preface

The growth in the number of women entrepreneurs over the past three decades has been described by some as an unbelievable phenomenon. Intricately contributing to this growth phenomenon are the increases in the number of minority women entrepreneurs, whose growth has been described as critical to the overall contributions of women entrepreneurs in the marketplace.

The women business owners in this study are also in the purest sense entrepreneurs. That is, they were involved in the original development of their business or of the current state of their business. The basic thrust of this book is to hold gender constant and analyze the state of a national sample of women entrepreneurs across racial lines. A total of 263 women entrepreneurs (124 minority women entrepreneurs and 139 white women entrepreneurs) responded to the call to participate in this study.

Each woman entrepreneur was initially contacted by mail with a letter to garner her participation in this study. The names and addresses for the women entrepreneurs were obtained from Dun and Bradstreet, a nationally recognized database firm. The company sells information on businesses nationwide to interested parties, including: individuals, private and public organizations, government agencies and institutions. Dun and Bradstreet obtains the information from the businesses themselves, who contact, or are contacted by, Dun and Bradstreet in order to be listed with this database firm. Dun and Bradstreet was instructed on the number of women entrepreneurs needed in each racial stratum. The racial minority categories were over-sampled, to ensure that an adequate response rate was obtained for this sector of business owners.

Women entrepreneurs responded affirmatively to the request to participate by completing a quantitative questionnaire and returning it in a self-addressed stamped envelope. Follow-up in-depth interviews were conducted by use of a qualitative questionnaire with 20% of the original respondents from each group (25 of the minority women entrepreneurs and 26 of the white women entrepreneurs). This was done to clarify, explain and expand on the responses to the original questionnaire.

The book begins with an examination of the place of women in the current marketplace, after taking a look back at the historical contribution of women in the labor market. This is followed by a look at literature related to women entrepreneurs, with a special emphasis on issues related to human capital, networks and financial capital. The next four chapters analyze the findings from the current study, taking critical and in-depth looks at the two groups of women entrepreneurs. The quantitative findings are interwoven with qualitative explanations and clarifications to form a rich tapestry representing the total perspective of women entrepreneurs in the study.

Later chapters look at the status of women entrepreneurs in the national sphere, followed by various studies which look at women entrepreneurs' position in the global marketplace. The book concludes with a linking of the study's current findings to theoretical perspectives, national and international data. In addition, policy implications for improving women's entrepreneurial position in the marketplace are also provided.

Acknowledgements

I would like to thank all who assisted in the completion of this book, among them Alan Sturmer, Nep Elverd, Tara Gorvine, David Vince and the rest of the staff at Edward Elgar Publishing: their patience in the writing of this book was greatly appreciated. I would also like to thank the Coleman Foundation and the Hughes Charitable Foundation who provided the funds to conduct the survey for the book. Sincere thanks to Ahimsa Teabout, who was involved in the editing of this work and for her dedication to this project. Thanks to the following students who worked on different stages of this book: Amanda Fucci, Lisa Diblasi, Hope Gause and Michael Kolns. I am also very appreciative of the recommendations, encouragement and support I received from Robert Boyd at Mississippi State University and Margaret Hannay at Siena College. A heartfelt thanks to all the women business owners who participated in the completion of this project: their generosity goes beyond words. Their actions, work and dedication to women's development continue to contribute to the historical place of women in the marketplace.

Thanks to Linda Cary for the commitment and kindness she has shown towards my kids. Her presence in their lives has given me the extra time I have needed over the years to pursue my passion for writing and has kept and continues to keep me sane. A big thanks to my immediate family members for their love and continuous support towards all of my endeavors over the years. A special thanks to my sister, Marlene, who constantly reminds me that I am capable of great things. Thanks also to my children, Jared Meshak, Gabrielle Elizabeth, Jacob Asiah and Joshua Emmanuel, whose presence is a reminder of what I really live for. Thanks to lifelong friends Valrie Brown-McIntyre (29 years), Everton Reid (27 years), Willard Brown (17 years) and Jacqueline King (13 years) for always, always being there.

A final thanks to Andrew Hunter, my husband, whose support and commitment over the years remains steadfast and consistent, regardless of where the wind blows or where the tides take us.

1. The rise of women entrepreneurs

INTRODUCTION

The last half-century has witnessed monumental changes for women as income earners (Abelda and Tully, 1997; Bennett, 1917; Berger, 1989; Bielby and Baron, 1986). These changes included the influx of women into the mainstream labor market, the revolution of the Women's Movement and the Civil Rights Movement, which propelled women into non-traditional roles, and the explosion in the number of women entrepreneurs particularly over the last two decades (Bregger, 1996; Buttner and Moore, 1997). This latter phenomenon has given rise to countless books, articles and reports informing the public on the various aspects of the seemingly never-ending kaleidoscope of women as entrepreneurs.

Statistically, there is no doubt that women entrepreneurs are holding a commanding presence on the national and international level (Clark and James, 1992; Fried, 1989; Haynes and Helms, 2000). Figures from the United States indicate that women own 10.6 million firms or 48% of all United States-owned companies (The Center, 2004a). In addition, from 1987 to 1999, the number of women-owned businesses in the United States increased by 103%; employment of workers by female-owned companies grew by 436% during the same period (Coughlin and Thomas, 2002). Between 1975 and 2000, the number of women operating their own businesses in the United States more than doubled (Coughlin and Thomas, 2002). During the same period, the female self-employment rate increased by 63% as women started businesses at more than twice the rate than men (National Association of Women Business Owners' Annual Report, 2000). By 2000, the data showed that one out of every ten women over the age of 35 was self-employed, or owned her own business (The Center, 2004a). The impact of the number of women entrepreneurs on the national economy is staggering. According to The Center for Women's Business Research, 10.6 million women-owned businesses in the United States employ approximately 19.1 million people and generate over $2.46 trillion in sales annually.

On a global level, the data are just as impressive, with women entrepreneurs making significant contributions to their home countries' economies (Cromie, 1987; Cromie and Hayes, 1988; DeLollis, 1997). The World Bank states that approximately half of the world's economic growth in the last decade can be attributed to the contributions of female entrepreneurs (Coughlin and Thomas,

1

2002). In Southeast Asia, the number of women entrepreneurs is more than 50% of all entrepreneurs (Coughlin and Thomas, 2002). Women entrepreneurs in Hungary, Russia, Romania and Poland have made and continue to make significant contributions to previously stagnating economies (Coughlin and Thomas, 2002). The turnaround of such countries' economies is said to be primarily attributable to the opportunities provided by women owning and operating their own businesses. A recent Kaufman Center for Entrepreneurial Leadership study of 21 countries revealed that current women entrepreneurs and their ever increasing numbers are key to the long-term economic growth of any country that wishes to operate effectively in the current global marketplace.

WOMEN AND WORK

The last half-century has witnessed unprecedented improvements in women's inroads into the world of work in general, and entrepreneurship in particular (King, 1988; Kerber and Matthews, 1982; Jessup and Chippe, 1976; Kroll, 1998; Kean et al., 1993). Coleman and Pencavel (1993) indicated that factors such as the multiplication of the world's population primarily through the doubling of life expectancy contributed to the increase in numbers in the labor force, and that women's entry into the mainstream labor market would remain a key component of this increase. However, before the progress of women in the workplace can be tracked and their accomplishments highlighted, it is best to review the progress of women in the labor market and as income earners.

Before the late 1800s women's primary roles as wives and mothers relegated them to tasks performed in and around the home. If they worked outside this sphere, it was generally in the context of assistant – albeit almost always unpaid – to their husband in the latter's main labor market occupation. The 1890s showed significant changes with women moving outside the home to take jobs as factory workers. These changes were attributed to two key factors. Women were giving birth to fewer children, which allowed them more time to explore income opportunities outside the home (Kessler-Harris, 1982). In addition, technological advances were being used by wives and mothers to make their household tasks easier, again allowing more time to pursue other opportunities (Kessler-Harris, 1982).

This influx of women into the labor market remained approximately constant until World War II when women responded to patriotic appeals to contribute their labor. This contribution was to fill the employment gaps in two major sectors. Women went to war to work primarily as nurses in hospital-like settings with wounded soldiers who had misfortunes on the battlefields (Kessler-Harris, 1982). Second, women were asked to replace their husbands, brothers and fathers in the jobs they had left vacant (Kessler-Harris, 1982). In addition, there was an increase in jobs in aluminum, steel and weapons manufacturing, as a response to the increased demand for such products because of the war. The potential of women as a labor source became a lynchpin on which the labor force in various sectors could be maintained. Women entered the labor force without expectations of upward mobility, justifying their participation in terms of patriotic duty or a need to obtain income to compensate for the void left by the absence of male income earners.

The Women's Movement, which started in the early 1960s, laid new groundwork for the increased participation of women in the labor market. However, unlike the previous increase, where women had no expectations of career mobility, women who participated in the labor market during this period expected to be treated as equals to their male counterparts. They expected to be promoted, to receive equal accolades and to earn similar wages for comparable work. While white women represented the first entrants to the professional sector, their minority counterparts and especially black counterparts were not far behind.

Historically, black women have moved into jobs and occupations left vacant by white women, as the latter group moved forward and upward into the labor market (Malveaux and Wallace, 1987; Alderman-Swain and Battle, 2000; Benjamin, 1991; Blackwell and Hart, 1982; Higginbotham, 1995). Black women moved from private household work (which they performed for mostly white women who had entered the mainstream labor market), into female-dominated clerical work as white women, in turn, left for higher positions in management (Garland, 2000). In addition, as black women rose in management and professions in the inner city and public sector, white women deserted these positions for plusher positions in the private sector, in the suburbs and office parks (Garland, 2000). In a similar vein, black women have lagged behind white women in upper level management positions (Jenkins, 1985; Collins, 1993).

Overall, regardless of race, the female workforce in the current mainstream labor market faces a number of key issues. Research shows that women's earnings lagged consistently behind men's earnings at a rate of 72–76 cents in the dollar (Jones and George, 2003; Anker, 2001). At the same time, there is a growing debate in the literature about undervaluing and at times non-valuing of work done by women in the home. That argument will not be conducted here, but its mention serves to highlight the inequity in work value that is awarded to women's labor contributions to a nation's economy, whether inside or outside the home. Instead, the focus of this section will be on women performing the same work as men, in the same occupation, industry and oftentimes organization and consistently receiving lower returns than their male counterparts (DiPrete and Sourle, 1988).

Studies have continuously supported the notion that women continue to engage in approximately the same amount of household duties, regardless of whether they work inside or outside the home (Loscocco, 1997). Such unfairly apportioned household responsibilities have led to women being said to experience a work–family conflict issue when navigating the world of income earning (Greenwood, 2001).

The picture for female earnings in 2001 was approximately the same throughout the world, with average female–male pay ratios being approximately 60–70% based on monthly reference periods; 70–75% based on daily and weekly reference periods and 75–80% based on hourly reference periods (Anker, 2001). A look at Table 1.1 gives the ratios from the various regions worldwide.

Gunderson (1994) identified the following five sources as the key reasons for male–female pay differentials:

- differences in human capital endowments such as education and experience (caused mainly by non-labor market factors);
- differences in pay within the same occupation (caused by direct discrimination and dual labor markets);
- differences in pay for work of 'equal value' (caused by the relationship between pay level in an occupation and the degree to which it is feminized);
- differences in job desire;
- differences in the jobs available.

In addition to the wage gap, a second issue facing women is that they are stymied into lower level positions in the labor market. This stagnation results in a glass ceiling effect, which is a term originally used to describe women's exclusion from higher level management positions in the labor market (Jones and George, 2003).

Another issue is occupations where there is a traditional concentration of women and these occupations have lower wages attached to them. Fostering the concept that women are gendered into feminized occupations that offer lower returns, when compared to their male counterparts (Anker, 2001; Herring et al., 1993), Figure 1.1 shows that occupations such as nursing, teaching and waitressing have lower pay rates as opposed to plumbing, construction and engineering that offer higher pay rates. See also Table 1.2.

Another area of male/female differentiation is the allocation of household responsibilities. Studies have supported the notion that women continue to engage in approximately the same amount of household duties, regardless of whether they worked inside/outside the home (Loscocco, 2001). Such unfairly apportioned household responsibilities have led women to experience work–family conflict (Greenwoood, 2001).

The 1980s saw an increase in the number of women embracing entrepreneurship as an alternative to the mainstream labor market as a source of income. This

Table 1.1   Female–Male Ratios in the World – 1990

Region/Country Average Unweighted	Female–Male Ratio Non-Agricultural	Female–Male Ratio Manufacturing
OECD Countries – Hourly Rates		
Australia	88.2	82.5
Belgium	75.1	74.5
Denmark	82.6	84.6
Finland		77.3
France	80.8	78.9
Germany (Federal Republic of)	73.2	72.7
Greece		78.4
Iceland	87.0	
Luxemberg		69.2
Netherlands	67.8	62.2
New Zealand	77.5	75.0
Netherlands	80.6	74.9
Norway		86.4
Portugal	69.1	69.0
Sweden		88.9
Switzerland	67.6	68.0
United Kingdom	70.5	68.4
Developing Areas – Hourly Rates		
Sri Lanka	91.2	
Other Countries – Daily/Weekly Rates		
Cyprus	59.0	58.0
Turkey	84.5	81.0
Egypt	80.7	68.0
Hong Kong, China	69.5	69.0
Sri Lanka	89.8	88.0
All Types – Monthly Rates		
Costa Rica	66.0	74.0
Japan	49.6	41.0
Kenya	78.3	73.0
Korea (Republic of)	53.5	50.0
Malaysia		50.1
Paraguay	76.0	66.0
Singapore	71.1	55.0
Swaziland	106.6	88.0
World Averages (Unweighted)		
Hourly	77.8	75.7
Daily/Weekly	76.7	71.2
Monthly	71.6	62.1

Source: Anker (2001).

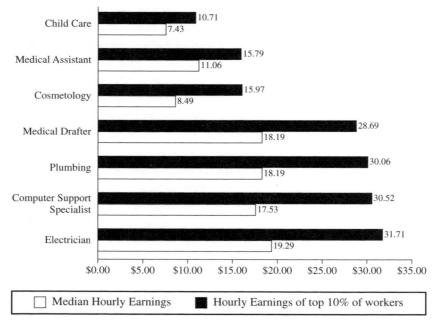

Source: Bureau of Labor Statistics.

Figure 1.1   Predominantly Female Occupations produce lower Earnings Than Predominantly Male Occupations

increase began to mushroom in the late 1980s and continued into the twenty-first century, with more women preferring to operate their own businesses as a viable alternative to earning income. The women who entered entrepreneurship are from all racial backgrounds and they were entering the market at a faster rate than any other group in the United States (The Center, 2004a).

WOMEN AS BUSINESS OWNERS

The rise of women as business owners in the last two decades is seen as unprecedented and impressive. However, women as entrepreneurs are not a new phenomenon. In fact, the earliest documentation of a woman operating her own business dates back to 1795 (Oppedisano, 2000).

The mushrooming of women's enterprises began earnestly in the 1970s, grew tremendously since then and has been called 'one of the most significant economic and social developments in the world' (Coughlin and Thomas, 2002).

Table 1.2   Full-Time Wage and Salary Workers – 2000

Occupation	Number of Workers (1,000) Male	Number of Workers (1,000) Female	Median Weekly Earnings Male	Median Weekly Earnings Female
Technical, Sales & Administrative Support	*10,828*	*17,424*	*655*	*452*
Tech. and related support	1,882	1,769	761	541
Sales	5,583	4,550	684	407
Admin. support, including clerical	3,363	11,105	563	449
Service	*5,284*	*5,736*	*414*	*316*
Private household	20	348	(B)	261
Protective	1,771	341	659	500
Other service	3,493	5,047	357	314
Precision Production	*11,075*	*1,088*	*628*	*445*
Mechanics and repairs	4,024	203	649	627
Construction trades	4,341	88	599	475
Other	2,709	796	651	414
Operators, fabricators and laborers	*11,837*	*3,574*	*487*	*351*
Machine operators, assemblers, inspectors	4,240	2,396	495	355
Transportation and material moving	4,221	366	558	407
Handlers, equipment cleaners, helpers and laborers	3,376	812	394	320
Farming, forestry and fishing	*1,374*	*242*	*347*	*294*

Source: United States Bureau of Labor Statistics, Bulletin 2307, 2001.

No one can deny the influence of women entrepreneurs in the overall field of entrepreneurship. Statistics on business ownership in the United States indicated that men continued to dominate the category at 55% (United States Census Bureau, 2000). However, women's dollar contributions were also significant at 26% (United States Bureau of Statistics, 2000).

Table 1.3 shows the number of women-owned firms in the United States by industry. It shows that women business owners are concentrated in industries such as services and retail trade that offer types of businesses such as hairdressing, fitness instruction, massage therapy (for the service industry) and clothing, home centers, window treatments and floor coverings (for the retail trade industry). These businesses are and were seen as extensions of women's roles as wives, homemakers and mothers and represent a viable source of income for them as

Table 1.3   Total Number of Women-owned Firms in the United States by Industry

Type of Industry	Number of Women-owned Firms	Percentages by Industry
Other (Industries Not Classified)	1,351,756	12.71
Agriculture	215,477	2.02
Mining	33,297	0.31
Construction	652,807	6.14
Manufacturing	261,904	2.46
Transportation, Communications and Public Utilities (TCPU)	403,926	3.79
Wholesale Trade	298,721	2.81
Retail Trade	1,781,172	16.76
Finance, Insurance and Real Estate	966,662	9.09
Services	4,876,991	45.87
Total		100.00

Source: The Center for Women's Business Research, 2004a.

business owners as they service other female customers (Oliver, 1996; Levine, 1996; Himelstein and Anderson, 1997; Leibow, 1991). Other industries such as mining, agriculture and manufacturing have extremely low concentrations of women business owners. These low figures are due to a number of factors.

Girls and young women are not often socialized or educated in subject and occupational areas that are traditionally male-dominated (Horst and Merino, 1982; Etzkowitz et al., 1992). Socialization begins at an early age, for example girls are not encouraged to play with trucks and teenage girls are not encouraged to take courses that are traditionally dominated by their male peers (Horst and Merino, 1982). This early process results in fewer women found in male-dominated occupational areas in the labor market. Ultimately, they do not have the experience to transfer into business ownership. Like women in the mainstream labor market, women in the field of entrepreneurship are said to be 'gendered' into industries and roles that are traditionally dominated by women (Smith-Hunter, 2003).

Studies have also shown that women entrepreneurs have previously shied away from pursuing opportunities in non-traditional areas because of the high risks (Scott, 1983); the amount of start-up capital needed (Gregg, 1985; Ayres-Williams and Brotherton, 1999); and the high level of technical expertise needed

Table 1.4 Minority Women Business Ownership in the United States

Race or Ethnicity	Number of Women-owned Firms (2002)	Percentage Growth 1997 to 2002
African American	365,110	16.7
Hispanic	470,344	39.3
Asian and Pacific Islander	358,503	44.6
Native American and Alaska Native	77,483	44.6

Source: The Center for Women's Business Research, 2004a.

in certain industries (Tang, 1995; Robinson and McIlwee, 1991; Etzkowitz et al., 1992).

While white, non-Hispanic women represent approximately 80% of the women business owners in the United States (see Table 1.4), minority women as a group also hold a commanding presence, one that has increased significantly in the past decade. A major source of this increase is attributable to Hispanic American women who stand at a little over 4% and to African American and Asian American women who each currently stand at 4% of the total number of women entrepreneurs. African American women as entrepreneurs date back to the 1800s when they were forced to cater to members of their own race, because of the social distance that was created by segregation practices that prevented white business owners from providing Blacks with certain services (Boyd, 1996). These services included businesses such as dressmaking, hairdressing and laundering – that are of a personal nature (Boyd, 1996). This historical embeddedness of African American women in the services industry is partially responsible for their current concentration in such industries (Smith-Hunter, 2003).

MOTIVATORS FOR WOMEN ENTREPRENEURS

The alarming exodus of women from corporate America towards business ownership has been a result of a number of factors. Studies have repeatedly shown that one of the key motivators for women embracing entrepreneurship is the freedom such choices provided in juggling family issues while at the same time earning an income (Loscocco and Smith-Hunter, 2004; Mills et al., 2000; Kroll, 1998; Goffee and Scase, 1983a; Scott, 1983; Chaganti and Parasuraman, 1996). These work–family conflict issues are said to be partially resolved if women who are wives and mothers can exploit the time, freedom and flexibility afforded from business ownership to pursue both roles.

Work–family conflict issues (Ahrentzen, 1990; Becker and Moen, 1999) as a motivator for women becoming entrepreneurs can be seen as a factor pushing women away from the mainstream labor market and the rigidity of a nine-to-five workday, five days a week, into the possibility of a more flexible work schedule. Studies have shown that the added level of family responsibilities is one of the key factors motivating women to embrace entrepreneurship, regardless of their background or their race (Maysami and Goby, 1999; Inman, 2000; Moore and Buttner, 1997; Nelton, 1997).

Another key variable influencing women to embrace entrepreneurship is the discrimination they experience at their place of employment (Firestone, 1994). This discrimination has a number of dimensions related to it. This stagnation results in a glass ceiling effect, a term originally used to describe women's exclusion from higher level management positions in the labor market (Jones and George, 2003; Lewis, 1995; Kay and Hagan, 1995; Hemenway, 1995). This barrier acts as a deterrent for women to advance in organizations professionally and has resulted in successful and creative women leaving organizations for opportunities not available in massively bureaucratic and mainly male-domi-nated systems (Buzzanell, 1995; DiPrete and Sourle, 1988). It is also important to note that e-Bay and Avon are the only Fortune 500 companies in the United States that currently have female CEOs (chief executive officers). Women may pursue entrepreneurship as a means of assuming leadership roles at earlier stages in their career than is available in a larger firm environment (Daily et al., 1999; Chung and Gibbons, 1997).

A second dimension related to the unfair treatment of women in the main-stream labor market is the wage discrimination they experience. The literature indicates that on average women earn approximately 72–76 cents in the dollar compared to what their male counterparts earn for the same skills-level jobs (Jones and George, 2003; Coughlin and Thomas, 2002; Wright et al., 1995; Boden, 1999b; England et al., 1999). This pay inequity undermines women's wage earning potential, and serves as a factor that pushes them away from cor-porate confinement to an alternative that allows them to fulfill their income earning potential. The alternative is seen as entrepreneurship, where their earn-ings are more likely to be based on their personal conviction, contributions and work.

Other factors that have propelled women into the field of entrepreneurship in-clude wanting to make a contribution to society by delivering a better product or service than current business owners (Smith-Hunter, 2003; Coughlin and Thomas, 2002; Moore and Buttner, 1997) and to fill a void for services that were not being provided in their community (Inman, 2000). Women also launched businesses in order to achieve independence, personal development and job freedom (Scheinberg and Macmillan, 1988; Shane et al., 1991; Godfrey, 1995; Gundry et al., 2002). Changing attitudes towards women as viable income earners over the last half-century has definitely impacted the growing number of women entering entrepreneurship (Goffee and Scase, 1985; Gregg, 1985; Griffiths, 1996).

CHALLENGES FOR WOMEN ENTREPRENEURS

The preceding section focused on the factors that are responsible for propelling women from the mainstream labor market into the sphere of entrepreneurship. The section spoke primarily of the challenges women experienced in the former sphere which caused them to embrace the newer times. It should be noted, however, that the entrepreneurship world does have its share of challenges for women entrepreneurs. The existing literature and studies on women entrepreneurs belie the lack of significant financial start-up capital and access to continuous credit that women entrepreneurs experience. Many of the studies have focused on the difficulties women experience when trying to start a business with limited financial resources (Priesnitz, 1989) and on the difficulties experienced when trying to obtain funding to continue operating the business (Brush and Hisrich, 1986; Inman, 2000; Coughlin and Thomas, 2002; Moore and Buttner, 1997). Financial resources and continuous access to them remain at the heart of any study on entrepreneurship, since this particular resource determines the viability and long-term existence of a business and is the resource that will ultimately determine if a business continues or discontinues its operation (Greenfield, 1979, 1989; Goldenberg and Kline, 1999).

Other challenges facing women included a lack of access to adequate business networks (Aldrich et al., 1989; Bowen and Hisrich, 1986; Aldrich and Sakano, 1995). Researchers have pointed out that women in organizations have often been excluded from the formal network structures afforded their male counterparts (Bilmoria, 1994; Haberfeld, 1992; Ohlott et al., 1994). The inadequate network structures that women entrepreneurs experienced were said to be related to the lack of referrals/contacts they were able to establish while in the mainstream labor market as well as their lack of membership in influential organizations (Moore and Buttner, 1997).

Another challenge facing women entrepreneurs is their level of business ownership experience. This limited experience has primarily been attributable to the lack of exposure afforded them in certain jobs while they were employed in the mainstream labor market. These limitations, as previously mentioned, have been cited as a lack of managerial and supervisory roles being afforded women workers through the glass ceiling effect (Moore and Buttner, 1997). These structural factors, which constrain women from engaging in managerial and influential roles that should provide experience, have a chain reaction effect that is carried over when they transfer from the mainstream labor market to business ownership.

Table 1.5   Selected Occupational Groups and Subgroups by Sex for the United States, 2000

Occupational groups and subgroups	Total Number	Total Percent	Men Number	Men Percent	Women Number	Women Percent
Total population	**281,421,906**	**–**	**137,916,186**	**–**	**143,505,720**	**–**
Employed civilian population 16 years and over	129,721,512	100.0	69,091,443	100.0	60,630,069	100.0
Management, professional, and related occupations	**43,646,731**	**33.6**	**21,708,758**	**31.4**	**21,937,973**	**36.2**
Management, business, and financial operations occupations	17,448,038	13.5	10,131,223	14.7	7,316,815	12.1
Management occupations, except farmers and farm managers	11,115,046	8.6	6,910,883	10.0	4,204,163	6.9
Farmers and farm managers	773,218	0.6	661,288	1.0	111,930	0.2
Business and financial operations occupations	5,559,774	4.3	2,559,052	3.7	3,000,722	4.9
Business operations specialists	2,718,121	2.1	1,248,755	1.8	1,469,366	2.4
Financial specialists	2,841,653	2.2	1,310,297	1.9	1,531,356	2.5
Professional and related occupations	26,198,693	20.2	11,577,535	16.8	14,621,158	24.1
Computer and mathematical occupations	3,168,447	2.4	2,218,400	3.2	950,047	1.6
Architecture and engineering occupations	2,659,298	2.1	2,301,953	3.3	357,345	0.6
Architects, surveyors, cartographers, and engineers	1,926,689	1.5	1,702,234	2.5	224,455	0.4
Drafters, engineering, and mapping technicians	732,609	0.6	599,719	0.9	132,890	0.2
Life, physical, and social services occupations	1,203,443	0.9	709,392	1.0	494,051	0.8
Community and social services occupations	1,953,184	1.5	787,587	1.1	1,165,597	1.9
Legal occupations	1,412,737	1.1	747,170	1.1	665,597	1.1
Education, training, and library occupations	7,337,276	5.7	1,930,948	2.8	5,406,328	8.9
Arts, design, entertainment, sports, and media occupations	2,484,201	1.9	1,302,419	1.9	1,181,782	1.9
Healthcare practitioners and technical occupations	5,980,107	4.6	1,579,666	2.3	4,400,441	7.3
Health diagnosing and treating practitioners and technical occupations	4,144,065	3.2	1,210,571	1.8	2,933,494	4.8
Health technologists and technicians	1,836,042	1.4	369,095	0.5	1,466,947	2.4
Service occupations	**19,276,947**	**14.9**	**8,346,408**	**12.1**	**10,930,539**	**18.0**
Healthcare support occupations	2,592,815	2.0	305,247	0.4	2,287,568	3.8

Protective service occupations	2,549,906	2.0	2,041,698	3.0	508,208	0.8
Fire fighting, prevention, and law enforcement workers, including supervisors	1,536,287	1.2	1,300,671	1.9	235,616	0.4
Other protective service workers, including supervisors	1,013,619	0.8	741,027	1.1	272,592	0.4
Food preparation and serving related occupations	6,251,618	4.8	2,663,418	3.9	3,588,200	5.9
Building and grounds cleaning and maintenance occupations	4,254,365	3.3	2,565,933	3.7	1,688,432	2.8
Personal care and service occupations	3,628,243	2.8	770,112	1.1	2,858,131	4.7
Sales and office occupations	**34,621,390**	**26.7**	**12,341,968**	**17.9**	**22,279,422**	**36.7**
Sales and related occupations	14,592,699	11.2	7,364,006	10.7	7,228,693	11.9
Office and administrative support occupations	20,028,691	15.4	4,977,962	7.2	15,050,729	24.8
Farming, fishing, and forestry occupations	**951,810**	**0.7**	**750,915**	**1.1**	**200,895**	**0.3**
Construction, extraction, and material moving occupations	**12,256,138**	**9.4**	**11,802,699**	**17.1**	**453,439**	**0.7**
Construction and extraction occupations	7,149,269	5.5	6,937,857	10.0	211,412	0.3
Supervisors, construction and extraction workers	911,013	0.7	886,001	1.3	25,012	0.0
Construction trades workers	6,116,087	4.7	5,933,117	8.6	182,970	0.3
Extraction workers	122,169	0.1	118,739	0.2	3,430	0.0
Installation, maintenance, and repair occupations	5,106,869	3.9	4,864,842	7.0	242,027	0.4
Production, transportation, and material moving occupations	**18,968,496**	**14.6**	**14,140,695**	**20.5**	**4,827,801**	**8.0**
Production occupations	11,008,625	8.5	7,437,071	10.8	3,571,554	5.9
Transportation and material moving occupations	7,959,871	6.1	6,703,624	9.7	1,256,247	2.1
Supervisors, transportation and material moving workers	237,902	0.2	193,527	0.3	44,375	0.1
Aircraft and traffic control occupations	158,481	0.1	147,143	0.2	11,338	0.0
Motor vehicle operators	3,852,820	3.0	3,394,798	4.9	458,022	0.8
Rail, water and other transportation occupations	400,826	0.3	352,303	0.5	48,523	0.1
Material moving workers	3,309,842	2.6	2,615,853	3.8	693,989	1.1

Notes: Data based on a sample. For information of confidentiality protection, sampling error, nonsampling error, and definitions see www.census.gov/prod/cen2000/doc/sf3.pdf.

13

The industries and types of businesses that women entrepreneurs operate is another challenge to women entrepreneurs carried over from the mainstream labor market. The current research literature repeatedly laments the fate of women entrepreneurs and their concentration in less lucrative industries, such as personal services and the retail trades which provide lower returns to their operators. This concentration in personal services and the retail trades was common for all groups of women entrepreneurs, occurring across racial lines and across international boundaries whether the enterprise was located inside or outside the home (Boyd, 1996; Maysami and Goby, 1999; Priesnitz, 1989; Olson, 1997).

Women were said to gravitate towards these industries for a number of reasons. First, the investment capital needed for such enterprises was proportionately smaller than what was needed for other industries, such as construction, mining and engineering (Smith-Hunter, 2003). Therefore, women were drawn to industries where the initial capital outlay was probably smaller. Second, studies have also shown that women entrepreneurs were more likely to operate familiar enterprises or businesses that are extensions of their hobbies, often providing

Table 1.6   The Wage Gap, by Gender and Race

Year	White men	Black men	Hispanic men	White women	Black women	Hispanic women
1970	100%	69.0	n.a.	58.7	48.2	n.a.
1975	100	74.3	72.1	57.5	55.4	49.3
1980	100	70.7	70.8	58.9	55.7	50.5
1985	100	69.7	68.0	63.0	57.1	52.1
1990	100	73.1	66.3	69.4	62.5	54.3
1992	100	72.6	63.3	70.0	64.0	55.4
1994	100	75.1	64.3	71.6	63.0	55.6
1995	100	75.9	63.3	71.2	64.2	53.4
1996	100	80.0	63.9	73.3	65.1	56.6
1997	100	75.1	61.4	71.9	62.6	53.9
1998	100	74.9	61.6	72.6	62.6	53.1
1999	100	80.6	61.6	71.6	65.0	52.1
2000	100	78.2	63.4	72.2	64.6	52.8
2003	100	78.2	63.3	75.6	65.4	54.3

Note: Median annual earnings of black men and women, Hispanic men and women, and white women as a percentage of white men's median annual earnings.

Source: National Committee on Pay Equity.

Table 1.7   The Ten Occupations* Employing the Most Women for the United States, 2000

Occupations	Number	Percent
Employed civilian females 16 years and over	**60,630,069**	**100.0**
Secretaries and administrative assistants	3,597,535	5.9
Elementary and middle school teachers	2,442,104	4.0
Registered nurses	2,065,238	3.4
Cashiers	2,030,805	3.3
Retail salespersons	1,775,889	2.9
Bookkeeping, accounting, and auditing clerks	1,526,803	2.5
Nursing, psychiatric, and home health aides	1,469,736	2.4
Customer service representatives	1,396,105	2.3
Child care workers	1,253,306	2.1
Waiters and waitressses	1,228,977	2.0

Notes:
Data based on a sample. For information on confidentiality protection, sampling error, nonsampling error, and definitions, see www.census.gov/prod/cen2000/doc/sf3.pdf
* Based on the most detailed level of occupations available in Census 2000 – 509 occupations.
Confidence intervals are not displayed because they round to the percentages shown in the table.

Source: US Census Bureau, Census 2000, Sample Edited Detail File.

services needed by, and thus catering to, other women (Ayres-Williams and Brotherton, 1999; Bailyn, 1989; Biggart, 1989; Brodie and Stanworth, 1998). In addition, women in the mainstream labor market are concentrated in the services and retail industries (see Tables 1.5, 1.6 and 1.7). Thus, transferring into the same sectors of business ownership from the mainstream labor market sector seems like an obvious transition.

FEMALE ENTREPRENEURSHIP ON A NATIONAL LEVEL

The inroads and exponential impact that women entrepreneurs are having on the national economy were recently documented by the Center for Women's Business Research, who provided the following facts (The Center, 2004a):

- As of 2004, there are an estimated 10.6 million privately held, 50% or more women-owned businesses in the United States, accounting for 47.7% of all privately held firms. These firms are generating $2.46 trillion in sales and employing 19.1 million workers.

- From 1997 to 2004, the number of 50% or more women-owned firms in the United States grew at twice the rate of all United States firms (17.4% versus 9.0%), employment grew at more than twice the rate (24.2% versus 11.6%), and sales rose at a similar rate.
- Between 1997–2000, the number of 100+ employee women-owned firms grew by 44% and $1million-plus women-owned firms increased in number by 32%, both nearly twice the rate of all company-sized firms.
- Women-owned firms continue to diversify into all industries. Construction, agricultural services and transportation have seen the largest recent increases in the number of women-owned firms, although services and retail still make up the largest share.
- As of 2002, there are an estimated 1.2 million firms owned by a woman or women of color – amounting to one in five women-owned firms (20% in the United States).
- Nearly 72% of women business owners have investments in stocks, bonds or mutual funds, compared to 58% of working women.
- At least 86% of women entrepreneurs said that they use the same products and services at home as they sell in their businesses, for familiarity and convenience.
- Women-owned businesses are just as financially strong and creditworthy as the average United States firm, with similar performance on bill payments and levels of credit risk.
- There have been significant improvements in access to capital for women business owners. From 1992 to 1998 their use of credit cards dropped from 52% to 36%, and their use of business earnings to finance growth nearly doubled to 65%. Over half of women (52%) and men (59%) business owners had bank credit as of 1998.
- Fast-growing firms owned by both women and men use a wider variety of sources of capital, and are more likely to use bank credit than other firms. Yet only 39% of fast-growth women owners have a commercial bank loan compared to 52% of fast-growth firms owned by men.
- Women are becoming more active in the equity capital markets, but in a survey conducted in late 1999, just 9% of the institutional investment deals and 2.3% of dollars among the investors interviewed went to women-owned firms.
- The workforce of women-owned firms shows more gender equity. Women business owners, overall, employ a roughly gender-balanced workforce (52% women and 48% men), while men business owners employ on average 38% women and 62% men.
- Most women- and men-owned firms are engaged in e-commerce, but are likely to purchase goods and services for their business (75% of women,

74% of men) and to sell their products or services online (62% and 51% respectively).

- A new generation of women has emerged – women who have started their businesses within the past 10 years and have more managerial experience, more education and the same overall business revenue and employment profiles as women who have been in business for 20 years or more. They are similar to their male cohorts in these respects, and are also more work-oriented than women who have been in business longer.

A closer look at the above phenomena also shows the following as it relates to minority women entrepreneurs (The Center, 2004b):

- Overall, the number of minority women-owned firms increased by 32% between 1997 and 2002 – four times faster than all United States firms and twice the rate of all women-owned firms.
- Latina entrepreneurs are also an integral and growing part of the women business owner population. They are in a wide variety of industries, and have owned their firms for an average of 12 years. Two-thirds were born in the United States and those who are first-generation have lived in the United States for an average of 30 years.
- Access to financial capital is more problematic for women of color. As of 1998, fully 60% of Caucasian women business owners had bank credit, compared to 50% of Hispanic, 45% of Asian, 42% of Native American and 38% of African American women owners.

FEMALE ENTREPRENEURSHIP ON A GLOBAL LEVEL

Recent research has chronicled women entrepreneurs' rise in the global marketplace and the impact they are having on the global economy. While specific figures have remained illusive, it was noted that in the coming century women entrepreneurs, women business owners and women who are self-employed will be a critical issue (Lerner and Almor, 2002). Estimates placed the number of women-owned firms between one-fourth and one-third of all businesses owned in the world (Moore, 2000b).

Historically, women have worked as unpaid employees in their spouses' enterprises, particularly in an international context where available employment alternatives are limited (Dhaliwal, 1998). However, the tide shifted and women-owned businesses began to increase in numbers on a global level (Dhaliwal, 1998; Radhakishun, 2000; Mazumdar et al., 2000; Mueller and Thomas, 2001). The United Nations conducted a study indicating that women entrepreneurs in Africa experience similar problems as those experienced by women entrepre-

Table 1.8 Percentages of Self-Employed Women from Selected Countries Worldwide

Women self-employed Non-agricultural Sector (%)	1990	1991	1992	1993	1994	1995	1996	1997	1998	1999	2000
Argentina	–	36.6	37.8	38.9	38.1	39.9	39.6	39.6	40.9	42.1	42.6
Bolivia	–	–	–	36.8	35.3	35.9	36.9	–	–	–	–
Botswana	–	–	–	–	–	46.6	–	–	46.8	–	–
Brazil	–	–	42.8	43.0	–	44.1	44.3	44.3	44.4	45.4	–
Canada	46.9	47.8	48.0	48.1	47.8	47.8	47.9	47.7	48.1	48.4	48.4
Colombia	–	–	44.4	44.6	43.6	44.9	44.7	46.1	47.1	47.8	48.8
Costa Rica	37.2	37.4	37.8	36.3	36.5	36.7	37.2	37.5	38.8	–	39.3
Croatia	–	–	–	–	–	–	46.7	46.9	47.6	47.7	47.0
Cyprus	–	–	–	–	–	–	–	–	–	43.2	44.4
Czech Rep.	–	–	–	46.1	46.5	46.4	46.3	45.2	46.1	46.6	46.5
Denmark	–	–	–	–	47.7	46.5	47.3	47.6	48.7	–	48.5
Egypt, Arab Rep.	20.5	18.7	17.8	18.8	18.9	18.9	–	18.9	20.0	20.9	–
Estonia	52.3	51.8	51.3	51.2	50.8	50.5	50.8	50.4	50.8	50.9	50.9
Finland	50.6	51.4	52.2	52.1	51.9	51.1	50.6	50.3	49.8	50.3	50.3
Germany	–	–	–	–	–	43.0	43.7	44.0	44.2	44.8	45.1
Greece	–	–	–	36.3	36.4	37.6	37.7	38.8	38.5	39.5	39.8
Iceland	–	52.6	52.2	52.8	53.6	54.0	52.7	51.9	52.5	52.6	52.2
Ireland	41.7	41.4	42.8	43.4	44.0	44.4	44.7	45.2	45.7	46.1	–
Israel	–	–	–	–	–	45.5	46.1	46.6	47.5	48.0	48.3

Italy	38.0	–	–	36.0	36.4	37.0	37.7	38.0	38.5	39.1	39.8
Japan	–	38.4	38.6	38.7	38.9	38.9	39.2	39.5	39.6	39.7	40.0
Korea, Rep.	–	–	37.8	37.6	38.0	38.0	38.5	39.1	38.3	39.3	40.0
Latvia	–	–	–	–	–	49.6	50.7	50.7	49.3	49.8	51.2
Lithuania	–	–	–	–	–	–	–	51.0	52.2	52.9	53.1
Macao, China	42.7	42.8	44.0	43.6	45.0	45.3	46.2	46.3	47.1	49.4	50.1
Mexico	–	36.5	–	34.9	–	35.9	36.1	36.3	36.4	36.3	37.3
Netherlands	–	–	–	–	–	41.7	42.1	42.7	43.0	–	43.9
New Zealand	–	–	–	–	–	–	–	49.2	49.5	49.9	49.8
Norway	–	–	–	–	–	–	47.8	48.0	48.1	48.3	48.2
Panama	–	–	43.4	42.9	42.3	42.7	42.5	43.5	41.7	42.2	–
Peru	–	–	–	–	–	–	31.4	32.5	33.5	35.5	33.3
Philippines	–	40.4	40.3	40.3	40.1	40.0	39.2	39.7	40.5	41.3	41.1
Poland	–	–	–	–	–	47.3	47.1	46.6	46.8	47.1	46.9
Portugal	–	–	44.5	44.7	45.1	45.9	45.8	45.7	45.4	45.9	45.8
Romania	–	–	–	–	43.0	42.0	43.0	43.5	44.0	44.7	45.5
Singapore	–	42.5	42.9	43.3	43.0	41.0	44.7	43.7	44.7	45.4	–
Slovenia	–	–	–	48.8	48.7	48.0	49.0	46.5	48.0	47.9	–
Spain	–	–	–	35.0	35.8	36.1	36.8	37.3	37.5	38.5	39.4
Sweden	50.5	50.7	51.5	52.0	51.6	51.3	51.1	50.9	50.5	50.5	50.6
Trinidad & Tobago	35.6	36.3	38.3	38.5	38.8	39.2	39.7	38.8	39.4	39.9	–

Source: World Bank Group (2004).

19

neurs in the United States. Problems include lack of access to financial capital, inadequate programs offered by government agencies and low education and skill levels, especially skills specifically related to operating a business (de Groot, 2000; Radhakishun, 2000). Another study conducted by Dhaliwal (1998) in England indicates that Asian women entrepreneurs are becoming a prominent feature of the business population and indicates that policy makers are being reminded to appreciate the needs of ethnic minorities in business (Dhaliwal, 1998). Similar studies in Europe, Canada, Australia and Pakistan herald the contributions of women entrepreneurs to their countries' economy.

Globalization has introduced challenges for people, enterprises and governments by altering the relationships between world markets, production, capital and labor. The feminization of poverty (Kottak and Kozaitis, 1999; Herring et al., 1993) has led to entrepreneurship being seen as a viable income earning alternative for women across the world. Small and micro enterprises are some of the largest providers of employment opportunities worldwide, especially for women (Acs and Audretsch, 1990; Aronson, 1991; Bannock, 1981, 1986; Beesley and Wilson, 1984a, 1984b). Table 1.8 shows the number of self-employed women as a percentage of the total number of self-employed persons in selected countries worldwide. Currently, Chinese women entrepreneurs make up 20% of all the entrepreneurs in China, with 41% of them working in the private sector.

DEFINITIONS AND CLARIFICATIONS

The businesses analyzed in this research study were women-owned businesses. In order to define a woman business owner, one can borrow from two definitions of the small business owner since in both instances the owner is heavily involved in the day-to-day operation of the business. The Small Business Act states that a small business concern shall be deemed to be one which is independently owned and operated and which is not dominant in its operation (United States Small Business Administration, 1978). A small business owner is thus the person who owns such a business entity. A business owner can also be defined as an individual who has a financial capital investment in a business that is greater than $0 and annual sales/revenue of at least $1,000 (Bates, 1995a; Devine, 1994a, 1994b).

Carland et al. (1984) alternatively defined a small business owner as an individual who establishes and manages a business for the principal purpose of furthering personal goals. The business must be the primary source of income and will consume the majority of one's time and resources. The owner perceives the business as an extension of his or her personality, intricately bound with family needs and desires. In a similar vein, an entrepreneur could be defined as an individual who perceives an opportunity and partakes in the necessary functions, activities and actions associated with the creation of an organization to pursue that opportunity (Bygrave and Hofer, 1991; Gartner, 1989; Sexton and Smilor, 1986). In the context of this book, all the women who participated satisfy dually the definitions of business owner and entrepreneurs since they owned and were at least one of the parties to form or create a business.

Additional definitions and clarifications in this book are related to issues of race and to what have been referred to in this context as minority women entrepreneurs. Whites: individuals not of Hispanic origin, whose ancestry and roots are related to any of the original peoples of Europe, North Africa or the Middle East. Blacks: persons having origins in any of the black racial groups of Africa, Caribbean or West Indian countries who currently reside in the United States. Hispanic/Latino: persons of Mexican, Puerto Rican, Cuban, Central or South American or other Spanish culture or origin. Asian or Pacific Islander: persons having origins in any of the original peoples of the Far East, Southeast Asia, the Indian subcontinent, or the Pacific Islands. It also includes: China, Japan, Korea, India, Pakistan, Nepal, the Philippine Islands, Samoa and Polynesia. Native American or Alaska Native: persons who maintain cultural identification through tribal affiliation or community recognition with the original people of North America. It should be noted that the preceding definitions have been cited on the United States Census Bureau website and are also the definitions used by the current sample's source, Dun and Bradstreet, to classify the data. Minority women entrepreneurs in this study refer to women who are not classified as Whites, that is, women in the following categories: Blacks, Hispanics, Asians and Native Americans.

ORGANIZATION OF BOOK

Despite the tremendous increases in the number of women-owned enterprises across racial lines, and their ever-increasing impact on the various societal and economic factors, there are few studies that assess women entrepreneurs across racial lines. Most studies have taken a monolithic focus, assuming that all women share similar characteristics and circumstances. Exceptions to the previous statement include Inman (2000) and Smith-Hunter (2003). The current book seeks to increase the number of studies that focus on the issues of women entrepreneurs across racial lines, identifying their differences and similarities. The current book also strives to identify the factors that account for these differences. The organization of the remaining chapters in this book is as follows.

Chapter 2 – The State of Women's Entrepreneurship

This chapter continues with an introduction to the field of entrepreneurship in general and women's minority entrepreneurship in particular. It also provides a brief review of the current literature on women entrepreneurs, specifically addressing what has been done, what has not been done and how the current study addresses some of the previous shortcomings. The chapter looks in-depth at the current state of the woman entrepreneur and why this book and the accompanying study is of such paramount importance at the dawn of the twenty-first century. It also looks briefly at the evolution of women as employees in the labor market. The chapter begins, however, with a look at the changing face of entrepreneurship.

Chapter 3 – Research Study

The research methods that will be applied in the collection and analysis of the study's data are included in this chapter. There is research information about the following: the sample, research design, and measures of the variables and the type of data analyses used in the sample. The three measurement categories to be looked at in this study are human capital, financial capital and network structures. Additional factors, such as the data collection methods, response rates, categorizing and coding of the data, are included in this chapter.

Chapter 4 – Overview of Results

This chapter provides an overview of the results. It includes analyses related to: motivation for becoming an entrepreneur, main start-up problems and problems during the operation of a business, the location, miscellaneous business characteristics and demographic profiles of the women entrepreneurs.

Chapter 5 – Human Capital

This chapter examines white and minority women entrepreneurs, including educational levels, previous work experience, previous supervisory/management experience, age, marital status and number of children. Chapter 5 also looks at the issues of human capital and determines which of these issues are related to the success of the entrepreneurial ventures operated by the women. The human capital of each group is examined separately and comparatively to determine if the same factors are relevant for the success of both groups or if they differ. The differences and/or similarities between the two groups is explored and related to white and minority women employees in the mainstream labor market. Specifically, the chapter explores whether the human capital factors provide similar rates of returns for the women entrepreneurs as they do in the mainstream labor market.

Chapter 6 – Network Structure

The network structure measures for white and minority women entrepreneurs included: membership in professional organizations, assistance from professional organizations, government agencies or informal groups, assistance from family or friends, mentors and other business owners. Chapter 6 looks at the issues of network structures and determines which of these issues are related to the success of the entrepreneurial ventures operated by the women. The network structures of each group are viewed separately and comparatively to determine if the same factors are relevant for the success of both groups or if they differ. It is important to note that data from the study results and from the literature are used to explain why network structures are so critical for women entrepreneurs. The chapter examines why the lack of such structures can thwart the financial success of their businesses.

Chapter 7 – Financial Capital

The financial capital analyses used for the white and minority women entrepreneurs include: source, amount and difficulty in obtaining start-up capital, difficulty in obtaining bank loans at the start-up and during the operation of the business and the issues of profitability (gross income, net profit and personal income). Chapter 7 also looks at the issues of financial capital to determine which of these issues are related to the success of the entrepreneurial ventures operated by the women. The financial capital of each group is looked at separately and comparatively to determine if the same factors are relevant to the success of both groups and if they differ.

This chapter also looks at the overall issues that determine success for white versus minority women entrepreneurs. Thus, the chapter combines results from this study and others on women entrepreneurs or business owners, to determine issues that need to be taken into consideration to obtain successful ventures for white and minority women entrepreneurs. The chapter will also look at why the issues of economic success differ for the two groups, specifically connecting factors from the mainstream labor market that have been carried over and affect minority women versus white women entrepreneurs, regardless of their previous occupational status.

Chapter 8 – Women Entrepreneurs on the National Level

This chapter looks at the most current data developed on the number of women entrepreneurs in the United States. Other issues addressed include the sources for obtaining business assistance and financial capital, reports from government-sponsored agencies as well as the private sector on the place of women entrepreneurs in the national sphere and what women entrepreneurs can do on a personal level to improve their success.

One primary focus of this chapter will be to look at traditional sources of funding and determine how access or barriers to financial capital has impeded the financial success of the businesses for the women entrepreneurs in general. The chapter will also look at government funding and determine the feasibility for women, especially minority women, of obtaining funding from these sources.

Chapter 9 – Women's Entrepreneurial Status in the Global Marketplace

This chapter looks at the current state of women entrepreneurs worldwide, moving beyond the United States. It uses the latest international reports and statistical data to depict where women entrepreneurs stand on an international level. Examples of the type of statistical data presented include location and industry breakdowns and are collected from a number of sources including private and government agencies. The data viewed specifically answers questions of industry involvement important to the individual, national economy and problems faced. The data also looked at what the respective sectors might do to help them counteract their difficulties. The chapter includes a look at the motivations for why women have embraced entrepreneurship as a viable income earning venture and continues with a look at the challenges and opportunities they face. It also looks at the resources that are available to them as their businesses grow and at the various network structures and at other factors that impact their economic success.

Chapter 10 – Conclusion

This concluding chapter begins with discussions based on the study's results, applying theoretical perspectives to the findings of the two samples and assessing the implications of these results. The chapter continues by looking at the critical issues encountered by women entrepreneurs, providing recommendations to promote a new agenda for this often ignored sample group. The chapter ends by making recommendations for future research and provides a final conclusion on how this study's findings relate to broader areas of research.

2. Review of literature on women entrepreneurs

INTRODUCTION

The literature on women entrepreneurship, while not as vast as that on male entrepreneurship, does provide a varied picture of women entrepreneurs' differing critical dimensions. The contributions in the past decade on the latter group have, however, been significant, providing us with a look into an area of entrepreneurship that is said to be explosive and significant to the well-being of any modern society. Significant, because most women entrepreneurs are concentrated in the small business sector and this sector is often seen by economists as important to the survival and continuous cyclical patterns of a country's economy (Watkins and Watkins, 1986; Maysami and Goby, 1999). With this backdrop in mind, this chapter looks at what has been covered and investigated in the literature on women entrepreneurship. It can be seen as being divided into two distinct sections. The first section covers areas such as: (i) the ever-increasing numbers of women entrepreneurs in today's marketplace; (ii) their motivation for entering entrepreneurship, their viability and the obstacles they face; and (iii) participation rates in franchising and in traditional (industries such as services and retail trade) and non-traditional (construction, mining and wholesale trade) industries. Women entrepreneurs are also looked at in terms of their participation in home-based businesses, with a brief look at women on the international front.

The second section of this chapter is threefold and takes a look at the issues most pertinent to the current study, under the headings of human capital, financial capital and network structures. The chapter ends by taking a step back from the literature and focuses on the interrelationships of the various literature review components from a graphical perspective, striving to understand their impact on the model of women's entrepreneurial success.

INCREASING NUMBERS

The past several decades have seen increases in the number of women entrepreneurs, a trend that is expected to continue and has been well documented by various sources in the literature (Warbington, 2000; Pope, 2002; Browne, 2001; Clark and James, 1992). Clark and James (1992) lamented the fact that businesses operated by women were mainly small, undercapitalized and affording their employees primarily part-time work. The authors conceded that these limitations were primarily attributable to their low levels of start-up capital and the fact that their motivation for operating their own businesses was not primarily financial. This argument could be extended to explain what has often been described as a 'double bottom line' for women entrepreneurs – not being unilaterally focused on economic gains, but on other factors used to define success, such as independence and autonomy in the decision-making process of their work (ibid.).

The literature on the increase in the number of women business owners shows that this increase is across industries and racial lines (Dhaliwal, 1998; Kessler, 2001). It is a fact that is not shocking and was well documented in Chapter 1 of this book. The illumination is also important for some types of women entrepreneurs, such as Asians – who often occupied a 'hidden role' in their spouse's business ventures (Dhaliwal, 1998). A few studies have looked at the growing female entrepreneur segment of the population (Brush and Hisrich, 1991; Hisrich and Brush, 1992; Haynes and Helms, 2000), urging banks and other financial agencies to embrace these groups of entrepreneurs as being vital to the financial entities they operate, not only in gaining, but also in maintaining a competitive advantage. The authors go further in pointing out that the relationship between women entrepreneurs and financial institutions is a two-way relationship, concluding that the women entrepreneurs who relied on bank funding for initial capital performed better than their counterparts who chose to forgo the bank funds, and that banks who supplied initial funding to these women entrepreneurs also benefited when compared to their competitors (Hisrich and Brush, 1992; Haynes and Helms, 2000).

The importance of banks to women entrepreneurs and alternatively the importance of women entrepreneurs to the banks was echoed in an article by Kessler (2001), who focused on what banks were doing to target women entrepreneurs – a segment of the economy that they view as a vital link to the future profitability of financial institutions.

VIABILITY AND OBSTACLES

The viability and type of obstacles faced by women entrepreneurs while operating a business venture have also been adequately explored by a number of authors. More specifically, Orser et al. (2000) looked at the types of problems small business owners and managers confronted at different times during their businesses' development. Using a sample of 1,004 small and medium-sized

Canadian enterprises and assessing the female enterprises that represented approximately 14% of the total sample (n = 142), the authors came to a number of conclusions. They concluded that the female-owned enterprises were smaller in terms of size, had fewer employees and produced lower levels of revenue when compared to the rest of the sample (Orser et al., 2000).

A further investigation of various independent variables that had an impact on the dependent variable of revenue, was also assessed. The authors found that growth firms tended to be those which relied on a business plan, were younger and larger, were incorporated and were in the manufacturing, rather than service sector (Orser et al., 2000). Overall, women entrepreneurs in the study were primarily concerned with the lack of access to financial capital. However, when the authors compared the nature of the firm and the management experience of the male-owned versus female-owned firms, the women entrepreneurs' perception did not reflect reality. A pertinent conclusion made by the authors was that the intensity of problems and concerns differed by sector, gender, size and legal structure of the business, as well as the age of the firm (Orser et al., 2000).

The lack of access to financial capital that was emphasized by Orser et al. (2000) has been in large measure agreed to by others (Mason and Harrison, 1995; Burr and Strickland, 1992; Goffee and Scase, 1983b). One explanation for this lack of access to financial capital has been attributable to the difficulty in assessing the future of women entrepreneurs' human capital potential (Smart, 1999). Based on this uncertainty, banks, lending institutions and others tend to rely exclusively on the past experiences and behavior of the entrepreneurs seeking the funding and since women are less likely to have a substantial financial past, they are also less likely to be successful in obtaining financial capital (Smart, 1999).

An alternative explanation is that women who enter self-employment are more likely to obtain lower base-year wage earnings (Boden, 1999b). This could be interpreted to mean that these women entering business ownership have less accumulated wealth and are thus less favorable prospects to attract additional sources of financial capital. This argument has been further extended by Cliff (1998), who found that, compared to their male counterparts, women entrepreneurs were more likely to want their businesses to remain below a certain threshold and not become too large. This was so that they could continue to balance their work and family life, among other factors (Cliff, 1998). This often-cited small size of the women entrepreneurship entities and its impact on their development and profitability has a circular effect. It occurs because women entrepreneurs are more likely to have started small businesses, are less likely to obtain a loan to expand because of the size of the business and thus stay small because they are less likely to be able to obtain a loan to expand.

Other obstacles women entrepreneurs face in the start-up and operation of their businesses include a lack of adequate training (Cook et al., 2001; Dumas, 2001) as well as being taken seriously as business owners, work–family conflict issues and a lack of adequate entrepreneurial education (Brush, 1997).

MOTIVATION FACTORS

The reasons why women have exited the mainstream labor market to enter the field of entrepreneurship have been explored by a number of researchers. Push factors such as insufficient family income, dissatisfaction with salaried jobs, difficulty in finding work and the need for a flexible work schedule because of family responsibilities have all been identified as key exit reasons for women in the mainstream labor market (Orhan and Scott, 2001). The authors also cited entry or pull factors to include: the need for independence, self-fulfillment and the desire for wealth, social status and power. They utilized 25 in-depth interviews with women entrepreneurs in France, Paris and Lyon (larger economic areas in France) to determine their motivation for leaving the mainstream labor market. The reason women most often gave for becoming entrepreneurs was that they had family members who were entrepreneurs, resulting in a natural succession into this type of income earning area.

Another prominent reason for the embracing of entrepreneurship by women is the glass ceiling – which has been defined as an invisible barrier preventing women from advancing into upper management positions in organizations (Lewis, 1995; Jones and George, 2003). This argument has been supported by studies from Belcourt (1990) and Moore and Buttner (1997) and Cromie and Hayes (1988). Entrepreneurship's attraction in allowing women to manage their own business and giving them a chance to earn income while addressing family issues have also been cited as motivating reasons to exit the mainstream labor market and embrace entrepreneurship (Loscocco, 1997; Orhan and Scott, 2001; Clain, 2000).

PARTICIPATION RATES IN INDUSTRIES

One of the strongest and most consistent points that has been made over the last two decades concerns the concentration of women entrepreneurs in the retail and the services industry. A historical look back as far as 1977 reveals an unusually high concentration of women entrepreneurs in the retail and services industries (Clark and James, 1992; Humphreys and McClung, 1981). There are three main reasons for this concentration. First, it is felt that these industries require less start-up capital and are thus attractive pull industries for women and even minorities who are more likely to have less start-up capital for their business ventures (Kirby, 2001; Keefe, 2002; Clark and James, 1992; Humphreys and McClung, 1981). Second, it is felt that women's occupations in the mainstream labor market are also primarily rooted in the retail and the services industry, thus serving as a push factor and a carryover for women who enter such industries because of their familiarity through previous exposure (Anna et al., 1999). Third, women entrepreneurs often enter industries that are extensions of their roles as women, wives and mothers, as well as industries that cater to other women and their personal needs – in other words, industries such as retail and services (Ehlers and Main, 1998).

Although their numbers in the non-traditional industries such as construction and mining have increased significantly in terms of aggregate numeric quantities in the last decade (The Center, 2004a), a look at a number of studies and statistics indicates that women are still concentrated in the traditional areas of services and retail industries (Smith-Hunter, 2000; Devine, 1994a; Smith et al., 1992).

CHARACTERISTICS

In one of the most comprehensive studies to look at self-employed women, Devine (1994b) employed data from the United States 1990 Current Population Survey to study the characteristics of self-employed women. The author viewed factors such as age, marital status, education level and earnings of women. Devine's in-depth analysis indicated that on average, the women tended to be older, married, had more years of education or had completed college, and were characterized as obtaining lower earnings than their wage and salary counterparts.

Similar findings are offered regarding entrepreneurial women in a study by Hisrich (1986). Like Devine (1994b), the author also looked at Census Data, but provided a comparison of entrepreneurial women with entrepreneurial men. Hisrich (1986) also concluded that, on average, entrepreneurial women were older, married and more likely to be college educated, when compared to their male counterparts. The author also indicated that women entrepreneurs had lower earnings when compared to their male counterparts.

Moore and Buttner's (1997) study on women entrepreneurs showed that, on average, the women entrepreneurs were in their mid-forties, college educated, and married with at least one child. In addition, this same study found women's earnings to be comparable with, or more than, what they received in their previous employment in the mainstream labor market. The authors also concluded that the women entrepreneurs worked an average of 52 hours per week, and had been in business for an average of 7.4 years.

In one of the rare studies to look at a comparison of minority and non-minority female entrepreneurs, DeCarlo and Lyons (1979) assessed the characteristics of the two groups. The authors randomly selected participants from directories of women business owners and directories of minority-owned firms. The results indicated that minority female entrepreneurs were older than their non-minority counterparts. Minority female entrepreneurs were also less educated, with non-minority females more likely to have graduated from college. However, the authors found that non-minority females were less likely to be married, and more likely to have started a business with a partner.

More recent studies to look at the personal characteristics of women entrepreneurs across racial lines include Inman (2000) and Smith-Hunter (2003). Inman (2000) looked at 65 women entrepreneurs from rural, urban and small city areas and found that the women were mainly involved in the services industry, regardless of their race. In addition, minority business owners were slightly older at 43 years, compared to their white counterparts, who were 40.6 years old on average. This difference in age between the two groups of women was echoed in Smith-Hunter's (2003) study, which looked at 30 minority and 30 white women entrepreneurs and found that the minority women business owners were also slightly older than their white counterparts, with average ages of 46.6 years and 45.7 years respectively.

The 65 women entrepreneurs in Inman's study had been in business for 6.22 years on average, with the white women entrepreneurs having a longer tenure in owning their own business at 6.6 years, compared to the minority women entrepreneurs who had a tenure of 5.87 years on average. While Inman (2000) did not look at educational levels and number of children, the Smith-Hunter (2003) study did, and found that white women entrepreneurs were more educated, had fewer children and were more likely to have formal business training, when compared to their minority counterparts.

OTHER

Other research areas that have garnered attention as they relate to female entrepreneurs are: participation rates in franchising, management style and choice of business location – home or commercial site. More specifically, Dant et al. (1996) found that women's concentration in franchises is extremely low and may partly be explained by the large initial infusion of cash that is needed to partake of a franchise investment. On another note, Buttner (2001) found that women entrepreneurs' management style was more participative and democratic in manner: a style that is nurturing to subordinates and akin to the issues highlighted when the management literature speaks of transformational leadership (Jones and George, 2003).

Home-based businesses for women entrepreneurs have received some support, albeit limited, with much of the focus occurring in the last 17 years. Priesnitz (1989) and Trent (2000) found that these businesses have allowed women to occupy dual roles as wives/mothers and income earners. Priesnitz (1989) also indicated that locating in the home was mainly due to lack of access to significant amounts of start-up capital to rent or lease a commercial space. Home-based businesses were generally small, but expansion usually resulted in a move to commercial space.

HUMAN CAPITAL LITERATURE

Based on the definition of entrepreneurship (previously defined in this book), it is obvious that the individual, as a focus, is the core of and thus the very essence of what an entrepreneur is. With that focus in mind, a look at entrepreneurship, absent a specific type of entrepreneurial venture with such factors as gender, race and geographic location of business – requires a look at the individual as a critical focus of any research in this area (Shaver and Scott, 1991; Stearns and Hill, 1996; Gartner, 1985). An integral part of the individualistic focus is to look at the definitions and dimensions of the term 'human capital'. Human capital has been defined as the propensity of a person or group to perform behavior that is valued from an income earning perspective by an organization or a society. The term was originally used by Nobel Prize economist Gary Becker to refer to the stored value of knowledge or skills of members of the workforce (Smart, 1999). The consensus among scholars is that human capital is critical to the formation and performance of entrepreneurial ventures (ibid.).

Human capital also refers to the knowledge, skills, competencies and attributes embodied in individuals that facilitate the creation of personal, social and economic well-being. This definition of human capital extends beyond those capital assets linked directly to productivity, to encompass factors that reflect the broader values associated with a well-educated population (Becker, 1993). The term 'human capital' has traditionally been applied to educational attainment and includes the knowledge and skills that the labor force accumulates through formal instruction, training and experience (ibid.).

It has also been referred to in terms of the time, experience, knowledge and abilities of an individual household or a generation, which can be used in the production process. (Heckman, 2000). This definition relates to the income earning potential of individuals as workers in the mainstream labor market or the field of entrepreneurship.

A myriad of studies have taken a varied look at the dimensions that encompass the growth of an individual's human capital potential. They range from educational attainment and work experience (Beggs, 1995; Raymo and Xie, 2000; Gimeno et al., 1997; Godoy et al., 2000; Gartner and Bhat, 2000) to include issues such as knowledge of the dominant language in the geographic region (Sanders and Nee, 1996; Pendakur and Pendakur, 2002) to the impact of parents' educational levels and background (Farkas et al., 1997; Bates, 1990; Hendricks, 2001; Guaitoli, 2000). The dimensions also extend to additional sources of learning that are obtained from contact with friends and associates (Heckman, 2000; Boucekkine et al., 2002). In specific reference to entrepreneurs, it is felt by some authors that having parents who were themselves entrepreneurs increases your human capital measure and also increases your chances of becoming an entrepreneur (Cooper and Dunkelberg, 1987).

Consistently the research studies indicate that an increase in the percentage of human capital that one possesses has a positive impact and thus denotes a positive relationship with one's income earning potential (Evans and Leighton, 1989; Greller and Stroh, 2002; Godoy et al., 2000) and that human capital differences are a key factor that results in labor market inequalities for various groups (Beggs, 1995). Others see human capital as an intangible asset, whose skills, such as educational levels, knowledge and experience, can be used for economic gains (Moses, 1998; Christou, 2001; Cianni and Romberger, 1995). Boyd's (1996) article points out that the undervaluing of disadvantaged groups' human capital potential, in particular minorities, has led to their income earning potential being given lower rewards, compared to their more advantageous counterparts. This argument has been echoed by Kazemipur and Halli (2001) who looked at immigrants in Canada through the use of Census Data and found that human capital factors were less rewarding for immigrants than for natives.

Bowser's (1972) study of 83 minority entrepreneurs found that education is needed in order to improve the economic success of a business Using a convenience sample of 83 minority entrepreneurs in Wisconsin, the author, after conducting personal interviews, concluded that the entrepreneurs' personal abilities (i.e., their human capital measures) were a key determinant of their business success. Bates's (1995a) article, which also looked at the same factors, concurred with Bowser's (1972) findings. The authors also added that financial capital inputs will provide higher returns to minority entrepreneurs, but only if linked to higher human capital inputs (Bates, 1995a).

Bates (1990) looked at a nationwide sample of male entrepreneurs and found that human capital (measured in the study as age, educational level, managerial experience and family background), especially the educational component, had an important impact on the entrepreneurs' access to financial capital. The author also found that an owner's education (a key component of human capital) and financial capital consistently explained a firm's longevity (Bates, 1990).

In a related article, Gimeno et al. (1997) found that organizational survival was not strictly a function of economic performance, but depended on the owner's threshold (expectations/standards) of the firm's specific performance. This threshold was found by the authors to be heavily dependent on the entrepreneur's human capital characteristics. They defined the human capital dimensions as consisting of: educational levels, prior work experience, prior work experience of a management or supervisory kind, prior work experience that is similar in occupation to the current entrepreneurial experience and finally prior entrepreneurial experience.

Specific studies on the human capital potential of and other issues related to the occurrence of women entrepreneurship are limited, but they do exist. Sanders and Nee (1996), who used the 1980 Census Data for New York and Los Angeles, looked at self-employment among Asian and Hispanic immigrants. The authors found that the odds of self-employment are 50% greater for women with a high school or college degree than for those without, for each group. They also extolled the importance of human capital, even for immigrants, whose education and experiences occurred mainly in their homeland, saying that it might not be as valued as that gained in their host country.

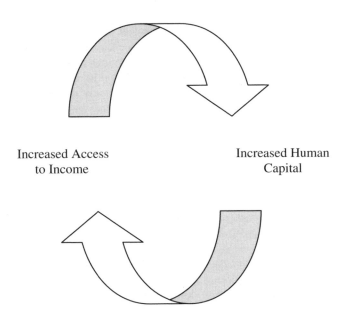

Increased Access   Increased Human
to Income   Capital

Figure 2.1   The Reciprocal Relationship Between Increased Access to Income and Increased Human Capital

In direct relation to the focus of this book, Glover et al. (2000) found that women were consistently rewarded less than their male counterparts for the same human capital levels and qualifications. Another compelling area of knowledge regarding human capital is the circular relationship it shares with income (see Figure 2.1). As depicted in the diagram and echoed in several studies, more access to income leads to greater human capital gains, and greater human capital gains lead to higher income (Christou, 2001; Bates, 1995a; Evans and Leighton, 1989).

Brush (1992) looked at the human capital impact of women entrepreneurs on their income earning potential and compared the results to that of their male counterparts. Her findings indicated that women's entrepreneurial income may differ from men's because of the variation in the type of human capital that each group possessed. Specifically, she found that women entrepreneurs were more likely to have experience in administrative and secretarial areas, while their male counterparts were more likely to have management and supervisory experiences. In addition, the author found that while both groups had approximately the same percentage of members with college degrees, the women were more likely to have liberal arts degrees, while the men were more likely to hold degrees in mathematics or engineering (Brush, 1992). It can also be said that greater values are applied and higher returns are earned, in the latter subject areas (Reskin and Roos, 1990).

Loscocco and Robinson (1991) also looked at the impact of human capital measures on the income of male versus female entrepreneurs using the US Census Data. In addition to finding that women are segregated into lower paying entrepreneurial sectors, the authors also found that business and managerial skills developed in employment contexts are extremely important to eventual success and that women carry their labor market disadvantage with them to the small business sphere.

The previous findings were repeated in a follow-up study by Loscocco et al. (1991), who looked at 540 small businesses in the New England area. The authors again looked at female versus male entrepreneurs in small businesses, concluding that while both groups used the same process to generate income and sales, women were more likely to be disadvantaged by the human capital dimensions of lack of managerial experience. These findings are coupled with a concentration in less profitable industries, leading to less income generation for their businesses.

One of the most recent studies to perform a comparative analysis of women entrepreneurs across racial lines was done by Inman (2000) who looked at white versus minority women and their comparative economic success. The author found that the types and levels of human capital the women entrepreneurs accumulated depended on the motives and circumstances surrounding the business start-up. The women who planned to own businesses frequently sought formal training through continuous education, trade associations, employment situations and social contacts. Women who did not expect to own a business acquired human capital through on-the-job training, self-taught methods and social contacts. Inman also found that black women business owners who sought occupational training more frequently learned a trade rather than a profession, as compared to their white counterparts (Inman, 2000). Human capital and its level of accumulation had a direct impact on the women's access to financial capital, which represents a form of asset to financial institutions. Such findings echo arguments made previously in this section by Bates (1995a), Christou (2001) and Evans and Leighton (1989).

The current study zeroes in on the more pertinent human capital issues. More specifically, the questionnaire used gathered evidence regarding the women entrepreneurs' human capital potential by looking at such factors as their educational levels, their pre-business ownership experience (such as sales, marketing, accounting experience, seminars, programs attended) and organizational knowledge or experience. The objective was to determine whether these factors differed across racial lines and to assess the kinds of impact, if any, they

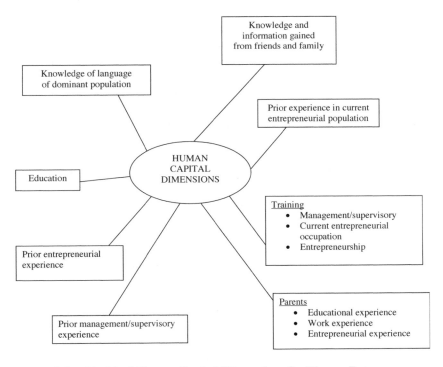

Figure 2.2   Model of Human Capital Dimensions for Women Entrepreneurs

had on the economic successes of the women. Figure 2.2 details all the potential elements of a woman entrepreneur's human capital dimensions. The diagram represents an extensive list of all the possible human capital dimensions of a woman entrepreneur. Much of this has been explored in the current study.

FINANCIAL CAPITAL LITERATURE

There remains a definitive link between one's access to financial capital and the economic success of any business (Finnerty and Krzystofik, 1986). While there are different ways to measure financial success for business owners (Begley and Boyd, 1987), studies have repeatedly shown that access to financial capital at the start-up stage and during the operation of a business is a key determinant to the expansion, sustainability and consistency of its existence (Ong, 1981; Terpstra and Olson, 1993; O'Hare and Suggs, 1986). Possible sources of financial capital include, but are not limited to, the following: liquid assets (checking and saving accounts), credit lines, loans, capital leases (mortgages and motor vehicle loans), financial management services (transaction and cash management), owner loans, credit cards and trade credits (Bitler et al., 2001). This section starts by drawing a general picture of the issues that are of critical financial interest to entrepreneurs. Later in the chapter, there is a specific focus on the financial capital dimensions that have been studied, illuminating such factors as the risks, discriminatory practices and other reasons for women entrepreneurs' predicament in obtaining and having continuous access to financial capital.

As noted previously, financial capital is one of the key ingredients enabling businesses to expand, remain viable and to become sustainable with long-term goals. While this is not necessarily the forum to undertake a comprehensive criticism of all the factors impacting the financial status of all groups of entrepreneurs, it is necessary to invoke a framework in which to understand and evaluate the predicament faced by women entrepreneurs and a related disadvantaged group – minority entrepreneurs.

A number of studies have detailed the disadvantaged position for women entrepreneurs regarding their access to financial capital. This unfavourable position is attributable to the undermining of their human capital potential (Loscocco and Leicht, 1993; Cressey, 1996; White, 1982). This has led to a continuing disadvantaged position both in the start-up stage and the operational stage of the business and it will continue to plague women entrepreneurs who choose to operate businesses. This argument has been extended and applied to the positions occupied by: international entrepreneurs (Chen, 1986; Stevenson, 1986), immigrant entrepreneurs (Wilson and Martin, 1982; Hoffman and Marger, 1991), minority entrepreneurs (Christopher, 1998; Horton and De Jong, 1991;

Light, 1979; Van Auken and Horton, 1994; Scott, 1983; Bates, 1997; Bates, 1991), and black entrepreneurs (Russell, 1981; Bates, 1990, 1995b; Woodson, 1988; Bates and Osborne, 1979).

The lower returns and ultimately the lower financial gains of the previously mentioned disadvantaged groups have been attributable to: limited markets for their businesses, an inability of business owners to collect the debts due to their businesses, low financial returns on investment, low earnings of the business owners' clientele, racial discrimination, unpredictable business cycles, limited access to secured credit, limited demand for products and services and unfavorable commercial bank behavior (Christopher, 1998; Chen,1986; Hoffman and Marger, 1991; Woodson, 1988).

In a similar vein to the difficulties faced by immigrants, minority and small business owners, numerous studies cite lack of access to financial capital as a key factor impacting women entrepreneurs in the operation of their businesses. Articles by Hurtado (1989), Ibarra (1993), Hustedde and Pulver (1992), Nelton (1999), Brotherton (1999), Lerner and Almor (2002) and Hisrich and Brush (1984) among others lament the fate of women entrepreneurs who lack the necessary access to financial capital to adequately sustain and develop their businesses. More specifically, Hisrich and Brush (1984), who looked at 468 women entrepreneurs, found that although the majority (68%) were highly educated, they persistently had problems trying to access financial capital, including being unable to obtain lines of credit and securing loans with an adequate collateral base.

The above findings have been echoed in articles by Collerette and Aubry (1990) in a parallel study in Canada and Lerner and Almor (2002), who looked at 220 Israeli female business owners. The latter articles have attributed lower access to financial capital as being the result of the types of industries that women entrepreneurs predominantly operated in. In industries, such as retail and personal services, the financial returns offered were lower than those of other industries. The service and retail businesses are seen as attractive options for women entrepreneurs, because of the lower investments in start-up capital required to instigate the initial existence of the business (Hisrich and Brush, 1984; Pellegrino and Reece, 1982; Brush and Hisrich, 1991). However, these lower initial capital outlays will more than likely result in smaller enterprises and limited access to capital will also prevent expansion efforts by women entrepreneurs. Hundley (2001) used data from a sample of 659 self-employed men and women to conclude that the major differential between the earnings of the two groups is a result of the differences in the type of industries they were concentrated in. The author went further to state that the lack of access to financial capital is partially explained by the low returns offered by the industries they chose to concentrate in, rather than discriminatory practices, per se, by banks and lending institutions (Hundley, 2001).

An expansion of this argument by Robinson-Jacobs (2002) indicates that it is only by moving into unchartered territories and non-traditional industries where women entrepreneurs have previously been underrepresented that women can make significant advances. The author further states that women entrepreneurs can earn economic returns that increase their borrowing potential for their business operations but that to do so requires taking these non-traditional routes (Robinson-Jacobs, 2002).

Discriminatory practices levied against women entrepreneurs seeking funds to start or continue the operation of their businesses have been documented by several authors (Riding and Swift, 1990; Brush and Hisrich, 1991; Hisrich and Brush, 1984; Charboneau, 1981; Neider, 1987). Charboneau (1981) stated in an article more than two decades ago that one of the biggest obstacles facing women entrepreneurs is the discrimination they suffer from the banking and finance communities. Later, Neider (1987) looked at the demographic characteristics and experiences of 52 female entrepreneurs from the state of Florida, concluding that credit discrimination by banks and major lending agencies was the major barrier for these female entrepreneurs.

Riding and Swift (1990) in a national survey of women entrepreneurs in Canada concluded that they were, in fact, often discriminated against, incurring higher interest rate charges than their male counterparts. The authors also noted that the businesses started by the women were newer and smaller than those of their male counterparts, and that this might, in fact, be the cause of the discriminatory loan practices; the problem was not necessarily due to gender (Riding and Swift, 1990). Loscocco and Leicht (1993) also questioned the unfavorable financial status of women entrepreneurs, pointing as possible reasons for their predicament to their low human capital potential and their less than favorable financial positions, when compared to their male counterparts.

In contrast to the previous findings, Bates (1995a) indicates that women are more likely to be treated favorably as regards access to financial sources by government agencies, because of their protected status. Meanwhile, Buttner and Rosen (1989, 1992) in repeated studies that used a simulation exercise to evaluate possible discriminatory practices against women entrepreneurs who sought operating funds found no such bias against women entrepreneurs. In fact, the authors concluded that, while the financial data of firms were important to the loan officers, the officers indicated that the characteristics attributable to successful entrepreneurs were more commonly ascribed to male, rather than female entrepreneurs.

These results have been echoed by Coleman (2000) in a more recent study, which again looked at lenders' practices towards male and female entrepreneurs. Coleman (2000) used data from the 1993 National Survey of Small Business Finances and concluded that three factors contributed to women having greater difficulty obtaining debt capital. They included: adverse discrimination in the lending process, which includes unfavorably being denied credit or being discouraged from applying for credit; women being more risk averse than men and less likely to take on debt; and less demand for debt capital by women entrepreneurs because of the small size of their businesses. The author further noted that, while lenders did not discriminate on the basis of firm size, women entrepreneurs operated smaller businesses and were less likely to rely on external financing as a source of capital, preferring to rely on their own personal funds. This reliance on personal funds which could stymie the growth potential of these businesses and result in a cyclical pattern, continues to result in women choosing to operate small businesses.

In addition to the issues of financial capital that have been detailed in previous sections, the current study again explores some of these issues, plus additional financial capital issues. It covers such factors as the amount, level of difficulty and the impact of start-up capital on women entrepreneurs' success, as well as

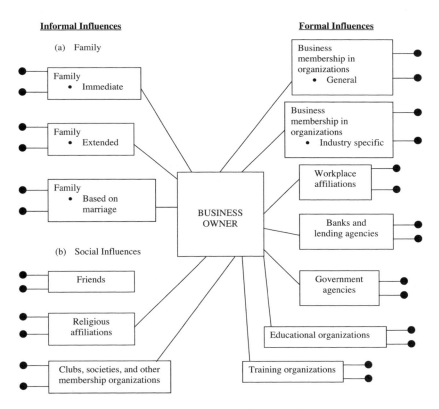

Figure 2.3   Model of Network Structures of Women Entrepreneurs

the significance of cash flow problems to business owners. The current study also takes a look at the indirect links of human capital and network structure issues to women entrepreneurs' access to financial capital and ultimately to the success of the business. Economic success in this book has been classified in three different ways: as sales revenue/gross revenue, as net profit and as personal income. Again, all the analyses were done across racial lines to ascertain if the factors differed when the latter dimension was included.

Figure 2.3 details all the elements that impact a woman entrepreneur's access to financial capital and include: family members, friends, angels, venture capitalists, previous business owners, partners in the business, banks, lending agencies, government sources, financial institutions, other organizations (that may provide grants, etc.), as well as income that can be procured from the entrepreneur's personal resources.

NETWORK STRUCTURES LITERATURE

Putnam (1995) indicates that our social connections and civic engagements pervasively influence our public life as well as our private prospects. These social bonds are said to be essential to a group's success and a substantial stock of social trust is said to make life easier for participants in their community (Putnam, 1995; Henry, 2002). Nowhere is this concept and its resulting implications more critical than in the area of entrepreneurship. A number of studies have highlighted the importance of the connections of entrepreneurs to others who can influence their progress (Wilkinson and Young, 2002; Hyden, 2001; Loscocco et al., 1991; Gassenheimer et al., 1996). With this backdrop in mind, the following section embarks on a discussion of the issue of network structures and its impact on one's income earning potential. The section begins with a comprehensive look at the definition of what is considered a network structure, especially as it applies to entrepreneurs.

Network structures can be defined as the formal and informal connections of overlapping organizational, family and social memberships that account for our level of success, the resources we have available to us to satisfy our needs, obligations and expectations (Hogan, 2001; Easter, 1996; Aldrich et al., 1989; Coughlin and Thomas, 2002). It has been described as the 'hidden hand of influence' that impacts the development of business markets (Hogan, 2001; Choi and Hong, 2002; Chung and Gibbons, 1997). The theory has its roots in the sociological world that speaks of one's social capital, which has been defined as the weaving of interpersonal relationships and values within families and their communities (Hogan, 2001). Information exchange and learning is said to take place in network structures (Chung and Gibbons, 1987). It looks at how someone is related to others in their families and communities as well as the type of relationships that are developed between these family and community members (Fukuyama, 2002; Van Horn and Harvey, 1998). It is also said to depend on people's ability to work together in groups through communication and cooperation and is determined by three key group influences: work, family and social life (Aldrich et al., 1989). Network structure is also said to be of a formal nature (banks, lawyers, business organizations) as well as an informal (family, friends, associates) nature (Bailey and Waldinger, 1991; Low and Macmillan, 1988).

The key factor that makes the entrepreneurs' network structure so critical to their development and success is access to additional network structures. In essence, not only are entrepreneurs connected formally and informally through relationships with other individuals and sectors, but depending on the type of relationship, the potential is there for each of these individuals in the entrepreneur's 'primary' network structure to, in turn, provide access to their own network structures, allowing the entrepreneur access to a 'secondary' network structure. Using Figure 2.4 as an example, friends, workplace affiliations and government agencies would represent the primary network structure, while the dots at the end of the links, which show links to these primary structures, represent individuals or organizations in one's secondary network structure. This can lead to a level of interconnected relationships for entrepreneurs through indirect sources (Lucas et al., 2001). The strength of each network link is said to be dependent on the amount of assistance provided to the entrepreneurs through these links. Therefore, there are strong network links and weak network links, depending on what type of access is available and what resources they are in turn linked to (Lucas et al., 2001; Fratoe, 1986; Low and Macmillan, 1988; Feagin and Imani, 1994).

It is important for individuals to seek groups of individuals through coordinated efforts for their locus of support, instead of operating in a vacuum. The dimension of one's network structure is said to include: family, friends, religious and work affiliations, banks, lending agencies, government agencies and associates. These connections, in turn, are deemed to provide role models, training experiences, advice, financial support, sources of labor, clientele, business advice and contracts for market shares (Fratoe, 1986; Molm et al., 2001). The role of weak or strong tied social networks has been particularly important in understanding how individuals are steered to opportunities and vice versa (Mier and Giloth, 1986).

Some of the important works on entrepreneurship and network structure have focused on immigrant entrepreneurship. Specifically, Marger (2001), Hyden (2001) and Light et al. (1999) have indicated that social capital is a vital resource, enabling immigrant entrepreneurs to find their economic and social niches in the host society. Issues such as securing investment capital, finding labor to help in the business and acquiring information are highlighted as some of the potential benefits (Marger, 2001). These three sources of assistance are said to come mainly from the immigrant entrepreneurs' ethnic and family ties.

The benefits of having a lucrative network structure for immigrants cannot be over-emphasized. Recent studies by Hyden (2001) and Light et al. (1999) have looked at the benefits of networks as a viable source of opportunity for migrants in a host country given their lack of knowledge regarding the new system and for co-ethnics in developing countries where resources are limited (Light et al., 1999). Hyden (2001) and Light et al. (1999) also indicate that a viable network in the host country is able to help in the assimilation of new migrants regarding housing, jobs and business start-ups with lower investments in terms of money, when compared with those who do not use a network structure. And there are three key reasons for the formation of these network structures or more specifically its relative complement, social capital, as provided by Hyden (2001). The author speaks of a class solidarity growing out of a common sense of being exploited. This has historically been viewed as a cause for collective actions. Then, there is the 'moral economy' argument, put forward originally by James Scott, which states that people whose traditional values are being threatened by modernization get together to defend these values. Finally, the cooperation that emanates from the presence of strong communal ties helps foster the development of a para-public realm, often in conflict with the norms underpinning the civic public realm (Hyden, 2001). In essence, individuals who feel threatened and suffer from a sense of vulnerability will form into collective forces to overcome and develop themselves beyond their vulnerabilities.

In the labor market, women and minorities, like immigrants and other disadvantaged groups, share an emphatic relationship that would result in the former two groups also benefiting from a network structure. Employees in organizations are promoted based on their access to individuals in high level positions. Such access is said to be limited for disadvantaged groups, such as women and minorities (Monk-Turner, 1992; Bates, 1973, 1986, 1991, 1994; Cox, 1994). The limitations are said to be caused by the fact that different groups are embedded in various types of network structure that offer different levels of opportunities, values and benefits (Molm et al., 2001). Thus, benefits obtained by various groups affect and are affected by opportunities, and the different access to power and resources presented by and to them. The relationships created by the network links are thus of a collaborative nature (Fukuyama, 2002) and are as vital as links to economic successes and outcomes. This is especially true for women entrepreneurs, whose mainstream labor market links might not have been as strong as their male or non-minority counterparts. This status is said to carry over when they enter the entrepreneurial world.

While a few studies have downplayed the importance of network structures and emphasized the importance of human and financial capital in entrepreneurial success (Bates, 1986, 1987, 1994), the vast majority emphasize the positive aspects of network structures and their resulting network links (Beech, 1997; Gassenheimer et al., 1996; Chung and Gibbons, 1997; Low and Macmillan, 1988). Entrepreneurs are also said to be able to use their network structures to obtain financial capital through the transfer of credit and financial wealth from one entrepreneurial offspring to another entrepreneurial offspring (Dunn and Holtz-Eakin, 2000; Steinmetz and Wright, 1989). In fact, as previously stated, having kin or a parent that is an entrepreneur is said to increase the likelihood of someone entering into an entrepreneurial venture (Scherer et al., 1989; Boyd, 1991; Covin and Slevin, 1994).

A few studies have shown that the network structures of men and women are different, while others have shown that the network structures for majority groups are more adequate and productive than those for minority groups. Specifically, Renzulli et al. (2000) used a sample of Research Triangle area business owners and potential owners to conclude that heterogeneous rather then homogeneous structures were advantageous. The authors also found that these differences were not significant enough to explain the differences between the male and the female entrepreneurs' success. Instead, the authors found that women's entrepreneurial networks consisted of a higher level of kin and that this factor was the key reason for their disadvantaged position (Renzulli et al., 2000). A previous study by Aldrich et al. (1989) using the same data source found that male and female entrepreneurs did indeed have different network structures, with women having mainly men in their network structures, whereas men had very few or no women in their network structures. This disadvantageous position of women's network structures compared to that of their male counterparts is akin to the disadvantageous position of the minority women entrepreneurs when compared to their non-minority counterparts. The disadvantageous position of minority entrepreneurial networks was confirmed in studies by Bates (1994), Fratoe (1986, 1988) and Feagin and Imani (1994).

Authors who took a comprehensive look at the issues of network structures for women were: Moore and Buttner (1997), Inman (2000) and Coughlin and Thomas (2002). Moore and Buttner (1997) assessed how women entrepreneurs developed and sustained networks as they moved from corporate environments to entrepreneurial ventures. They borrowed from ideas proposed by others to define and assess the network structures of women entrepreneurs, identifying them as follows:

(i)   the propensity to network (to connect with others);
(ii)   network activity (number of people connected to and the time spent making contacts);
(iii) network density (degree to which an entrepreneur reaches beyond immediate friends and the actual size of their network);

(iv)   network intensity (number of years a member has known other members of their network and the frequency of their interaction).

The authors grounded their research assumptions based on two perspectives: that contact with others is important to the start-up and development of a business (Aldrich et al., 1987, as cited in Moore and Buttner, 1997); and that the growth of a business is significantly related to time spent developing contacts with the stakeholders in a business (Ostgaard and Birley, 1996, as cited in Moore and Buttner, 1997). Moore and Buttner (1997) concluded that an adequate network structure is essential for the profitability and economic success of business. They go further to state that network membership is expensive in terms of investment value in time, energy and resources if an effective system for women entrepreneurs is to identify subgroups of network links in larger organizations that can ultimately comprise one's network structure.

Inman's (2000) study, one of the few to look at women entrepreneurs across racial lines, also focused on network structures as a part of its analysis. The author looked at both strong network ties (such as family, friendship and community contacts), as well as weak network structures (such as affiliates of friends or families and institutions or organizations that provided little contact) and concluded that both sets of ties were critical to the information gathering and knowledge creating process that women used to start their businesses (Inman, 2000). The author also observed that owners of small-scale businesses relied primarily on kin and friendship ties to help with business tasks, while larger and more professional owners hired full-time employees and larger service providers to assist them. The author also noted that African American women use their ties to learn occupational skills, while the European American (whites) women were more likely to use their network ties to learn business skills.

The current study looked at a variety of network structure factors that were also identified in the preceding sections of this chapter. Issues such as the assistance obtained from family, friends, organizations and acquaintances were specifically analyzed. This assistance was viewed from two perspectives – at the start-up stage and during the operation of the business. Factors such as type and level of assistance obtained from these sources were also addressed.

The current study also looked at the relationship between human capital, network structures and financial capital issues and the impact they had on the economic success of the women entrepreneurs. These relationships were looked at primarily from the perspectives of the white and then the minority women entrepreneurs respectively. An additional purpose was to determine if these relationships differed across the two groups, what they were and what factors accounted for them. The study went deeper than previous studies by addressing the interrelationships between the human capital, network structures and financial capital issues and by assessing the differences in these interrelationships across racial lines. The main purpose and thus objective of this book was to determine the differences between the three key areas (human capital, financial capital and network structures), to determine the interrelationship of these three areas and to determine the impact they have on the economic success of the businesses in the respective groups. Figure 2.4 depicts all the network structure dimensions that have been identified in reviewing previous literature on network structures. While the dimensions illustrated are exhaustive, the depiction captures all the pertinent factors.

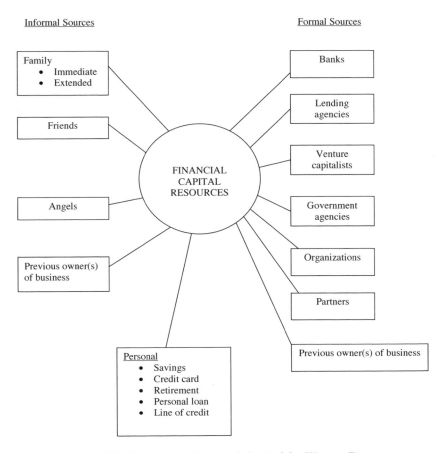

Figure 2.4   Model of Access to Financial Capital for Women Entrepreneurs

CONCLUSION

The literature reviewed in the preceding sections details a number of strong findings in some key critical areas. Women entrepreneurs were found to be highly educated and more likely to have children. In addition, they primarily operated small businesses in the retail and service industries that limited their abilities to expand and/or to obtain additional financial gains. They were also less likely to have strong human capital potential, based primarily on their lack of experience in management, the industry of the business or from an entrepreneurial perspective. They were also likely to have weaker network structures when compared to their male counterparts, thus limiting their access to financial capital, as well as their economic success as it related to business. The relationships between network structures, human and financial capital, along with economic success are presented in Figure 2.5. The diagram is based on the review of the current literature, which states that the dimensions of network structure, human and financial capital impact on women entrepreneurs' economic success.

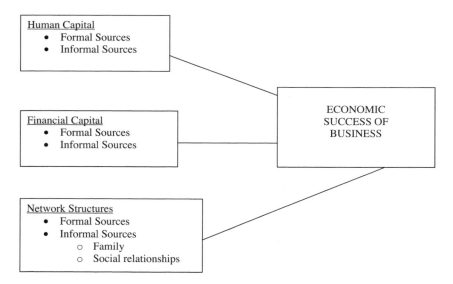

Figure 2.5   Model of Entrepreneurial Success

3. Research design and methods

This study provides a comparative analysis of women business owners across racial lines. The primary focus centers on the human capital, network structures and access to financial capital that women entrepreneurs display. The study also looks at how three factors converge and impact these two groups of women entrepreneurs and culminates in an analysis that looks at the impact on the women's economic successes. This chapter reviews the research design and methodology that was employed in the study, providing insight into women entrepreneurs' position in today's society and their impact in the current marketplace.

STUDY FOCUS

The original intent of this book was to use quantitative data only to look at women entrepreneurs across racial lines. This would be done through mailing a questionnaire, with a cover letter explaining its purpose and soliciting the participation of the women entrepreneurs based on a nationwide listing source. As the completed questionnaires were received and reviewed, there was a sense that a more qualitative perspective was also needed to supplement and clarify some of the quantitative responses. Thus, the decision was made to contact some of the participants, with the idea of having them answer follow-up questions that would allow for clarification, in-depth explanations and additional insight into women's true experiences in the entrepreneurial world.

DATA COLLECTION

Data collection was conducted by seeking a broad range of information from a number of women entrepreneurs in different industries over a wide geographic area in a relatively short span of time. This was accomplished by a mass mailing of 1,000 questionnaires to potential participants, followed by telephone interviews with a sample of the original respondents. Study participants were white women and minority women, defined here as Blacks, Hispanics, Native Americans and Asians.

A pilot study was not done, since the questions in this study have been used and rigorously tested in other research studies (see Loscocco and Cozzens, 2000 and Smith-Hunter, 2003). The survey questionnaire included questions on business ownership, business, financing, employees, network structures, human capital, key problem areas and key motivational factors. The interview questionnaire included questions that expanded on the previously mentioned areas by delving into clarifications and explanations, as well as providing an explanation of how certain factors impacted others. Three key questions on the interview questionnaire also looked at how women saw themselves as business owners; how they felt they were viewed by wider society as business owners; and if they had regrets about embarking on their entrepreneurial journey.

SAMPLING

Dun and Bradstreet, who are internationally known for providing sample frames on businesses provided the original sample frame for this study. The company stratifies (Babbie, 1998; Agresti and Finlay, 1986) businesses by: geographic region, gender, industry, sales volume and number of employees. They also break down industry listings into various types of businesses in each industry category. It should be noted that the type of industry breakdown obtained from Dun and Bradstreet is the same as that of the Standard Industry Code (SIC).

Dun and Bradstreet is a nationally recognized database firm. The company sells information on businesses nationwide to interested parties, including: individuals, private and public organizations, government agencies and institutions. They obtain the information from the businesses, who contact, or are contacted by, Dun and Bradstreet in order to be listed with this database firm. The firm of Dun and Bradstreet was instructed on the number of women entrepreneurs needed in each racial stratum for this study. The racial minority categories were over-sampled, to ensure that an adequate response rate was obtained for this sector of business owners. This latter practice has been employed in other studies (Inman, 2000; Bates, 1995a).

The women entrepreneurs who responded to the call to complete the questionnaires represent a biased sample and the results have to be viewed with this in mind. Notwithstanding this fact, however, the selected groups that responded represented approximately 32% of the participants originally contacted (with correct addresses), with 124 minority women entrepreneurs completing the questionnaire and 139 white women entrepreneurs completing the questionnaire. A total of 1,000 potential participants were originally contacted; 18% of the questionnaires were returned as undeliverable. A few of the questionnaires that were returned had missing information and follow-up calls were made to complete the questionnaires. The sample frame was obtained in January 2003; the questionnaires were sent out in early February 2003. The returned questionnaires were collected up to June 2003 and the follow-up in-depth phone interviews were conducted from October 2003 to February 2004.

SELECTING PARTICIPANTS

When reporting the qualitative data, all the locations, types of businesses operated and racial information is accurate because altering these factors would compromise the findings. However, in order to protect the privacy of the participants in this study, fictitious names have been used. The sample information obtained included women of various ages, industries, states and lengths of time involved in business ownership. No conscious attempt to obtain a certain number of women entrepreneurs in any one of the previously mentioned categories was undertaken and the responses are as they appear, without over-sampling in the preceding mentioned categories or over-emphasis on any particular area.

The original intent was to obtain 100 women entrepreneurs in the white and minority racial categories in each area for the quantitative analysis. The length of time needed to conduct the phone interviews for the qualitative questions was hampered by busy schedules, with many of the women requesting callbacks in order to complete the questionnaire. In addition, no effort was made to get women entrepreneurs who were operating sole proprietorships, partnerships or corporations. However, one factor deserves special emphasis: the women entrepreneurs in this study are all primary owners and operators of their businesses. This original goal was surpassed, with 124 minority women business owners and 139 white women business owners completing the survey.

CONTACTING PARTICIPANTS AND RESPONSE RATE

Using the names and addresses selected by Dun and Bradstreet, potential participants were sent information and surveys by mail. A percentage (18%) of the surveys were returned because of incorrect or incomplete information or because the businesses had relocated without leaving forwarding addresses. Follow-up letters were sent three weeks after the initial mailing, reminding participants to complete and return the survey if they were willing to participate in the study. A few respondents called to request clarification on the study before completing the questionnaire. A few individuals also faxed the completed questionnaires. Based on the original number of 1000 questionnaires, 43.44% (139 out of 320) of the white women entrepreneurs returned the questionnaires, while 24.90% (124 out of 498) of the minority women entrepreneurs returned their questionnaires. It should be noted that these percentages do not take into account the undeliverable surveys (18% of the 1000).

An equal percentage of white and minority women entrepreneurs were selected for the follow-up interviews. Potential participants were randomly contacted from the list of respondents who originally returned the quantitative questionnaires. They were then asked questions from the list of questions on the in-depth qualitative questionnaires.

STUDY DESIGN

To better understand the differences in human capital, network structures and financial capital issues impacting women entrepreneurs across racial lines, a quantitative as well as qualitative approach was used to garner information. In order to obtain a broader perspective and a more complete picture, the decision was made to sample women entrepreneurs from various industries and geographic regions to obtain a broader perspective and obtain a more complete picture. Part of this initiative included sampling minority women entrepreneurs from different racial origins including: Native Americans, Blacks, Hispanics and Asians. The following states were selected for the study: California, Florida, Illinois, Michigan, New York, North Carolina, Ohio, Texas, Washington and Pennsylvania. According to the United States Census Bureau, these states have the greatest populations of women entrepreneurs. The industry categories sampled included: agriculture, mining, construction, manufacturing, transportation-communications-public utilities (TCPU), wholesale, retail, fire-insurance-real estate (FIRE) and services.

The decision to use a quantitative and qualitative focus was important to the type of information that was obtained. The quantitative measures were used to provide objective measures and to allow constructive comparisons. Qualitative analyses were used to complement, clarify and explore the quantitative measures.

QUANTITATIVE MEASURES

The quantitative measures cover three key areas: human capital, financial capital and network structures. Additionally, there are some other focus areas in this section.

Human Capital

Many of the quantitative measures have previously been used in other studies on women entrepreneurs. In particular, the human capital measures are taken from a study by Loscocco and Cozzens (2000), but were also used in Smith-

Hunter (2003). The human capital measures included a look at the business owners' experiences, their occupational experiences, educational levels, and family members, friends and organizations that assisted the women entrepreneurs with their businesses and also encompassed their network structures.

Financial Capital

The measures for financial capital came from questions which looked at the difficulties women entrepreneurs experienced when starting a business. Further questions looked specifically at the profitability of the businesses and their financial standing: sales/gross revenue, net profit and the personal income of the business owners.

Network Structures

Again, the quantitative measures regarding network structures are taken from Loscocco's study, which have been repeated in studies by other authors regarding women entrepreneurs, namely Moore and Buttner (1997) and Smith-Hunter (2003). The network structures measured included a look at business owners' assistance from other organizations, friends and family members. This study borrows from that literature and looks at the assistance the women entrepreneurs obtained from family members. In addition, the assistance women entrepreneurs obtained from friends was investigated. Finally, the assistance women entrepreneurs obtained from others, including membership organizations, was examined.

Other

Other measures included the demographic characteristics of the business owner, such as race, marital status, number of children and age. The questionnaires viewed problems experienced while operating the businesses, and motivating factors for starting the business. The characteristics of the businesses were also analyzed, including the age, the type, location and male/female employee ratio breakdown.

QUALITATIVE METHODS

The qualitative questions raised focus on the three key areas: human capital, network structures and financial capital. Of these, the most important aspect was the human capital factor. Additional questions focused on the owners' previous business ownership experience, why they entered this specific type of business or industry and what they would have done differently, if anything, in terms of their training or experience, before starting their businesses.

In terms of the network structures, additional qualitative questions, included the percentage of immediate acquaintances, friends and family members that are business owners. How much assistance respondents received from individuals in their circle, whether they knew someone who helped them in the business who had significant experience in the business owners' field, and how long on average they had known these individuals, were also investigated.

The area of financial capital focused on why the women entrepreneurs felt that women often had a difficult time obtaining financial capital. Additional questions looked at how the business owners defined success. The qualitative questions also focused on what factors could improve the business owners' financial position.

Other qualitative areas focused on the business owners' hopes for the long-term progress of their business, and what changes they would make. In addition, questions focused on what societal, governmental issues would need to be addressed to assist women entrepreneurs in the United States. They were also asked, what level of assistance was obtained from organizations, whether membership in any organization or women's was helpful, what advice they would give to other women entrepreneurs and how being a female had impacted their entrepreneurial position.

Overall, the questions in the qualitative portion of the study provided expansion, exploration and clarification of the quantitative questions and helped to explore how far the quantitative questions reflected the women entrepreneurs' true feelings.

Qualitative questions and the answers to them allowed the women space to describe their business experiences. Qualitative answers also provided the how, why and who of what was asked. Qualitative answers also aided in the understanding of the dichotomous stories that were told as between the white and the minority women entrepreneurs. Another benefit of qualitative research is that it aided in the examination of how women entrepreneurs' human capital potential interacts and intersects to impact their network structures and the key issues related to accessing financial capital and ultimately economic success.

CONDUCTING THE INTERVIEWS AND INTERVIEW FORMAT

At the beginning of the phone interview, the women were reminded that they had already completed the quantitative portion of this survey by mail and that we were asking for their permission to augment the original questionnaire and obtain additional information. If they agreed, they were asked a series of questions and they were told that their responses would be recorded by the interviewer in writing.

Each woman entrepreneur provided a unique contribution to the study and was thoughtful and extremely generous with her time. While not all of the responses are detailed in this book, the quotes that accompany and explain the quantitative data are representative of the overall tone of the arguments made in a particular area. Some of the phone interviews were done over the course of two or more calls. However, every effort was made to make sure that the call-back time between interviews was as short as possible.

DATA ANALYSIS

Several statistical analytical techniques were used in the evaluation of the quantitative data. These techniques included an analysis of the mean groups and t-tests of the values that evaluated their statistical significance. Correlation analyses were also performed to ascertain the relationships between particular variables.

The qualitative data was evaluated by using analytical strategies outlined by Strauss and Corbin (1990) and Frost and Stablein (1992) and supplemented with lessons garnered from Stanfield (1993) and Stanfield and Dennis (1993). The data for each section (such as human capital, network structures and financial capital) were coded under the corresponding question areas and emerging themes were identified. The themes were used to supplement reporting of the quantitative data.

LIMITATIONS OF STUDY

The sample had approximately the same number of white and minority women entrepreneurs, 124 and 139 respectively, allowing an equal number in each category. The sample size of each group also allowed for statistically significant analyses to be obtained. The sample used in this study cannot be said to be a representative sample of women entrepreneurs in the United States, since the names were not randomly selected from all women entrepreneurs in the United States. The question or criteria of generalizability to a wider sample would require repetition and analysis of a larger randomly selected sample.

4. Overview of results

Before addressing the issues of human capital, network structures and financial capital and the findings from the current study that are related to these overall areas, it is pertinent to take a look at an overview of the sample and the results related to the sample. The outcome of the current study was impacted by the racial component and percentages of the women entrepreneurs in each category. Also important are the types of business operated by the women entrepreneurs, specifically by industry, with race as an additional component of this breakdown and an analysis of the sample by state, again with race as a by-product of the breakdown. In addition, the size of organization, as well as differences in demographic characteristics across the two samples are also addressed.

SAMPLE DESCRIPTION BY RACE, STATE AND INDUSTRY

The chapter begins with a look at the race of the women entrepreneurs (see Table 4.1). The table shows that approximately half of the women entrepreneurs who participated in this study were white (52.85%). The minority women entrepreneurs participating in the study represented the remaining 47.15%, this latter group being from four major races. In order of dominant participation in the overall sample, the percentages of the minority women entrepreneurs were as

Table 4.1   Race of Women Entrepreneurs in Sample

Race of Women Entrepreneurs	Number of Women Entrepreneurs	Percentages (%)
Whites	139	52.85
Blacks	52	19.77
Hispanics	35	13.31
Asians	25	9.50
Native Americans	12	4.56
Total	**263**	**100.00**

Table 4.2   Differentiation of Minority Women Entrepreneurs in Sample

Race of Minority Women Entrepreneurs	Numbers	Percentages
Blacks	52	41.94
Hispanics	35	28.22
Asians	25	20.16
Native Americans	12	9.67
Total	**124**	**100.00**

follows: Blacks (19.77%); Hispanics (13.31%); Asians (9.50 %) and Native Americans (4.56%). Minority women entrepreneurs' participation level, as a percentage of the total minority sample, is depicted in Table 4.2 and displays values as follows: Blacks (41.94%); Hispanics (28.22%); Asians (20.16 %) and Native Americans (9.67%).

Most of the women entrepreneurs in this study (see Table 4.3) were from California (25.85%), New York (15.21%) and then Michigan (9.51%). Table 4.3 also indicates that most of the white women entrepreneurs were from California (34.53%), Washington (11.51%) and Michigan (10.79%). As for the minority women entrepreneurs, most were from New York (21.77%), California (16.13%) and North Carolina (13.71%).

Table 4.4 provides a detailed breakdown of the number and percentages of participation rates for women entrepreneurs in this study by industry and race. Overall, most of the women entrepreneurs were concentrated in the services industry (44.48%), followed by the retail industry (16.73%) and then FIRE (fire, insurance and real estate) (12.55%). By race, the top three industries for each racial stratum of women entrepreneurs were as follows:

- white women (services – 44.60%, retail trade – 17.27%, and FIRE and manufacturing at 11.51% each);
- black women (services – 44.23%, FIRE – 19.23% and retail trade – 17.31%);
- Hispanic women (services – 54.29%, retail trade – 20.00% and construction and FIRE at 8.57% each);
- Asian women (services – 40.00%, manufacturing, wholesale trade and FIRE, all tied at second place with 16.00% each and retail trade at 8.00%);
- Native American women (manufacturing – 58.33%, services – 25.00% and retail trade – 16.67%).

Table 4.3   Women Entrepreneurs by State and Race

State	Minority Women Entrepreneurs	White Women Entrepreneurs	Total
California	20 (16.13%)	48 (34.53%)	68 (25.85%)
Florida	13 (10.48%)	7 (5.03%)	20 (7.60%)
Illinois	8 (6.45%)	14 (10.07%)	22 (8.37%)
Michigan	10 (8.06%)	15 (10.79%)	25 (9.51%)
New York	27 (21.77%)	13 (9.35%)	40 (15.21%)
North Carolina	17 (13.71%)	6 (4.32%)	23 (8.75%)
Ohio	14 (11.29%)	9 (6.47%)	23 (8.75%)
Texas	12 (9.68%)	7 (5.03%)	19 (7.22%)
Washington	2 (1.61%)	16 (11.51%)	18 (6.84%)
Pennsylvania	1 (0.81%)	4 (2.88%)	5 (1.90%)
Total	**124 (100.0%)**	**139 (100.0%)**	**263 (100.0%)**

The concentration of women entrepreneurs in the services industry and re-tail trade has been repeatedly documented by others, including Humphreys and McClung (1981), Hisrich and Brush (1985), Pellegrino and Reece (1982), Birley (1989), Belcourt (1990), Loscocco and Robinson (1991), Loscocco et al. (1991), Devine (1994a), Chaganti and Parasuraman (1996), Lerner and Almor (2002) and Watkins and Watkins (1986). These longstanding findings indicate that, despite making strides overall in the field of entrepreneurship during the last few decades, women entrepreneurs remain largely embedded in lower paying industries (Loscocco and Robinson, 1991; Smith-Hunter, 2003).

A number of reasons have been advanced for this concentration by women entrepreneurs in the services and retail trade industries. They include the fact that these industries require less start-up capital on average, when compared to others such as construction, and mining and engineering, thus affording entre-preneurs with limited financial resources easy access. A second explanation advanced for the concentration of women entrepreneurs in the services and retail industry is that the type of businesses that encompass such industries are seen as extensions of women's roles as wives, mothers and homemakers. The con-centration of the women entrepreneurs in the services and retail sector, even across racial lines, reinforces the claims made by Loscocco and Robinson (1991), Collerette and Aubry (1990), Devine (1994b) and Hisrich and Brush (1984) that women entrepreneurs tend to concentrate in female-dominated in-dustries. This concentration has been attributable to the lower costs of entering these businesses (Horton and DeJong, 1991).

Table 4.4 Type of Industry and Race

Industry	Blacks	Hispanics	Native Americans	Asians	Whites	Total
Agriculture	1 (1.92%)	0	0	0	2 (1.44%)	3 (1.14%)
Mining	0	0	0	0	1 (0.72%)	1 (0.38%)
Construction	2 (3.85%)	3 (8.57%)	0	0	4 (2.88%)	9 (3.42%)
Manufacturing	3 (5.77%)	1 (2.86%)	7 (58.33%)	4 (16.00%)	16 (11.51%)	31 (11.79%)
TCPU	2 (3.85%)	0	0	1 (4.00%)	11 (7.91%)	14 (5.32%)
Wholesale	2 (3.85%)	2 (5.71%)	0	4 (16.00%)	3 (2.16%)	11 (4.18%)
Retail	9 (17.31%)	7 (20.0%)	2 (16.67%)	2 (8.00%)	24 (17.27%)	44 (16.73%)
FIRE	10 (19.23%)	3 (8.57%)	0	4 (16.00%)	16 (11.51%)	33 (12.55%)
Services	23 (44.23%)	19 (54.29%)	3 (25.00%)	10 (40.00%)	62 (44.60%)	117 (44.48%)
Total	52 (100.00%)	35 (100.00%)	12 (100.00%)	25 (100.00%)	139 (100.00%)	263 (100.00%)

Notes:
TCPU – Transportation, Communications and Public Utilities
FIRE – Finance, Insurance and Real Estate

The study by Loscocco and Robinson (1991) used United States Treasury Data for their sampling, while the Loscocco et al. (1991) study used a sample data source of 540 small businesses in the New England area of the United States. The study by Hisrich and Brush (1984) used mailing lists from government publications and state offices to contact the women entrepreneurs in the study. Regardless of the sample source, all of the preceding studies unanimously agree that the services and retail industries are heavily populated by women entrepreneurs. Rampant racial discrimination against minorities in some more lucrative industrial sectors, such as construction, have prevented them from entering such industries (Feagin and Imani, 1994). The problems that come with being a woman in a male-dominated industry were best documented by a statement made by Karen, an Asian woman entrepreneur in Auburn, Washington:

> As a woman owning a business you have to be passionate about your work, especially in my field. This is definitely a man's world. Men think women are not capable of operating in this field and that we are too emotional or stupid. So you find yourself defending or almost apologizing, for being female in this business, which should not be happening.

BUSINESS START-UP

A look at the origins of the current study's businesses by the business owners' start-up procedure is presented in Table 4.5. Overall, the women business owners in this study started their business from scratch, either by themselves or with someone else, making them entrepreneurs as defined in Chapter 1 of this book, when the definitions and clarifications as between business owners, self-employed individuals and entrepreneurs were discussed. The results show that the white women entrepreneurs were more likely to start the business themselves (82.73%) when compared to their minority counterparts (75.00%).

The fact that minority women business owners in this study were more likely to start their businesses with someone else may be an indication that they had difficulties deriving resources to start the business by themselves. In a similar

Table 4.5   Origins of Women's Businesses

Origins of Business	Minority Women Entrepreneurs	White Women Entrepreneurs
Start Business Themselves	93 (75.00%)	115 (82.73%)
Start Business with Someone Else	31 (25.00%)	24 (17.27%)
Total	**124 (100.00%)**	**139 (100.00%)**

vein, previous studies have pointed out that minority firms faced difficulties in the start-up phase of their business, and indicated that such difficulties persisted during the operational stage of the business (Van Auken and Horton, 1994). The initial difficulties experienced by some minority women entrepreneurs may best be expressed by Celia, who lives in Georgia and owns a used merchandise store:

> When I first started, finances were tight, but I got a partner. We started small and ex-
> panded a little at a time. We didn't do anything too big or too fast. We just kept the
> business within certain boundaries and continued to expand, first with additional
> products and then with the square footage.

FORMS/TYPES OF BUSINESSES

Table 4.6 details the form of business enterprise the women entrepreneurs operated. Most of the minority women entrepreneurs operated sole proprietorships
(75.81%), followed by partnerships (12.90%) and corporations (11.29%). In a
similar vein, most white women entrepreneurs operated sole proprietorships
(63.31%). However, in contrast to their minority counterparts, the white women
entrepreneurs' next largest form of business was corporations (28.78%), followed by partnerships (7.91%). Minority women entrepreneurs were more likely
to operate a sole proprietorship and a partnership than their white counterparts
and the latter group of women entrepreneurs were more likely to operate a corporation. Of the 27 women entrepreneurs who operated partnerships – 16
minorities and 11 Whites, the breakdown of female versus male partnership
ratios differed significantly (see Table 4.7). The white women entrepreneurs
were more likely to have a male as a partner (45.45%) compared with the minority women entrepreneurs (12.50%).

The responses of the women entrepreneurs in the current study indicate that
most operated businesses as sole proprietors, which was particularly true for the
minority women entrepreneurs. Studies by Riding and Swift (1990) and Clark

Table 4.6   Type of Businesses

Type of Business	Minority Women Entrepreneurs	White Women Entrepreneurs
Sole Proprietorship	94 (75.81%)	88 (63.31%)
Partnership	16 (12.90%)	11 (7.91%)
Corporation	14 (11.29%)	40 (28.78%)
Total	**124 (100.00%)**	**139 (100.00%)**

Table 4.7   Partnership Distribution by Gender

Gender	Minority Women Entrepreneurs	White Women Entrepreneurs
Male	2 (12.50%)	5 (45.45%)
Female	14 (87.50%)	6 (54.54%)
Total	**16 (100.00%)**	**11 (100.00%)**

and James (1992) confirmed the tendency of women entrepreneurs to operate sole proprietorships. Earlier studies that run counter to the above-mentioned findings include Moore and Buttner (1997), whose sample of exceptionally successful women entrepreneurs showed that most operated corporations. These results were confirmed by Hisrich and Brush (1984) who used a trade association to survey 468 women business owners in Canada and also found them to be mainly incorporated. Along similar lines, Aldrich et al. (1989) in a comparative analysis of women entrepreneurs in the United States and Italy found that the women entrepreneurs doing business in the former country were more likely to be incorporated, while those in the latter were more likely to operate partnerships.

Inman's (2000) study of women entrepreneurs across racial lines (African American versus European American) from the southern United States reported that most were indeed involved in sole proprietorships, with the minority women being more likely to be so. It should be noted that Inman's sample consisted of only 65 women entrepreneurs in total, while the present study's sample consisted of 263 women enetrepreneurs. Bates (1995b) looked at entrepreneurs across racial lines (not necessarily women entrepreneurs) and also found support for Inman's (2000) results, which mainly indicated that minorities are less likely to have partners or form a corporation in the conduct of their business when compared to their non-minority counterparts.

The reasons for the reduced numbers of minority women entrepreneurs in partnerships and corporations are several and can be summarized by stating that the network structures of minorities are less likely to contain network links that have access to entrepreneurial resources to open and operate a business with a partner (Bates, 1995a; Inman, 2000; Smith-Hunter, 2003). In addition, a lack of knowledge of the ramifications including benefits of operating a corporation could deter minorities from entering into such ventures (Light and Rosenstein, 1995). Coupled with this reasoning, a lack of knowledge regarding the process necessary to incorporate a business could also prevent such a form of business from being seen as viable by minority business owners, that is, they may not realize what exactly are the benefits of operating a corporation versus a sole proprietorship.

SIZE OF BUSINESSES AND NUMBER OF EMPLOYEES

In terms of the number of employees of business owners in this study, we see numbers ranging from a low of zero to a high of 189 employees. White women entrepreneurs were more likely (91.50%) to have employees when compared to their minority counterparts (67.50%). Number of employees by women entrepreneurs are displayed in Tables 4.8 and 4.9. Table 4.8 depicts the range of the number of employees and the corresponding average number of employees for the two groups of women entrepreneurs. Overall, the white women entrepreneurs (Table 4.9) had more male employees (45.09%) when compared to their minority counterparts (36.49%). In terms of the aggregate, 139 white women entrepreneurs had a total of 445 male employees and 542 female employees. For the 124 minority women entrepreneurs, the number of male and female employees were 135 and 235 respectively.

The current study's findings indicate that overall the women businesses are small (Table 4.8 and 4.9), with minority women entrepreneurs having smaller enterprises with fewer employees on average (2.98) when compared to their white counterparts (7.10). This smaller size can be attributed to the lack of resources to expand characteristic of members of the former group. The small size of women's enterprises has been documented by Loscocco et al. (1991), Loscocco and Robinson (1991) and Inman (2000) among others (Clark and James, 1992; Burr and Strickland, 1992; Brush, 1997). The small size of the

Table 4.8   Number of Employees

Number of Employees	Minority Women Entrepreneurs	White Women Entrepreneurs	Total
0–20	122	130	252
21–40	1	4	5
41–60	1	1	2
61–80	0	2	2
81–100	0	0	0
101–120	0	1	1
121–140	0	0	0
141–160	0	0	0
161–180	0	0	0
181–200	0	1	1
Total	**124**	**139**	**263**
Average Number of Employees	**2.98**	**7.10**	**5.16**

Table 4.9   Number and Gender of Employees

Gender of Employees	Minority Women Entrepreneurs	White Women Entrepreneurs	Total
Male	135 (36.49%)	445 (45.09%)	580 (42.74%)
Female	235 (63.51%)	542 (54.91%)	777 (57.26%)
Total Number of Employees	**370 (100.00%)**	**987 (100.00%)**	**1357 (100.00%)**
Average Number of Employees	**2.98**	**7.10**	**5.16**

business was also found to have an impact on women entrepreneurs by lowering their potential earnings and their ability to obtain financial capital (Loscocco and Robinson, 1991; Smith-Hunter, 2003).

The average number of employees found in this study is consistent with the findings of studies conducted by DeCarlo and Lyons (1979), Birley et al. (1987), Burr and Strickland (1992), Riding and Swift (1990), Fischer et al. (1993), Chaganti and Parasuraman (1996) and Brush (1997). The studies indicated that women entrepreneurs had, on average, 10 employees or less. For example Burr and Strickland's 1992 database of 669 women business owners in Wisconsin (USA) produced ten as the average number of employees. These results were supported by Chaganti and Parasuraman (1996), who used Dun and Bradstreet data samples to assess economic success for 372 women business owners. Brush's (1997) exploratory study of eight women business owners who were involved in the White House Conference Research Project showed that all had five or fewer employees. The latter results were confirmed by Birley et al. (1987), who analyzed 47 women business owners enrolled in an entrepreneurial program in London, England, also finding that the businesses employed five people on average. The small size of women-owned firms makes them vulnerable to personal economic setbacks, environmental economic changes, individual customers and subcontracting work they receive from larger corporations (Clark and James, 1992).

While most support the notion that women entrepreneurs tend to operate relatively small businesses, a few studies using targeted samples have found conflicting evidence. For example, Belcourt (1990), through a sample of Canada's most successful women entrepreneurs, found that, out of 36 businesses, the number of employees ranged from 11–20 employees. It should be noted that the author specifically focused on female entrepreneurs operating businesses with higher than average sales (Belcourt, 1990). Another study to find larger numbers of employees (26 employees) was done by Smith et al. (1992), who analyzed 56 woman-owned businesses in fields that were traditionally male-dominated, such as construction, manufacturing and wholesale distribution.

MARITAL STATUS AND NUMBER OF CHILDREN

When compared to their minority counterparts, white women entrepreneurs in this study were more likely to be married (Table 4.10), less likely to be separated/divorced, approximately equally likely to be widowed and less likely to be single/never married. In the current study, the finding that most of the women entrepreneurs in the sample were married echoes results from Danhauser (1999), Olson (1997), Furry and Lino (1992), Moore and Buttner (1997). The finding from this current study on women entrepreneurs' marital status is said to be one of the most consistent factors marking women entrepreneurs' demographic profiles. Danhauser (1999) relied on a national survey sample, while Olson (1997) used the same nine-state research project sample as Furry and Lino (1992) and Moore and Buttner (1997), who used a convenience sample of women entrepreneurs from major national organizations that catered to women business owners. Caputo and Dolinsky (1998) also found the women entrepreneurs in their study were more likely to be married, but their status did not influence their choice of self-employment or have an impact on their economic success. The National Longitudinal Study of Labor and Market Experience (NLSLME) was used in the previously mentioned study.

The results from the current study also show that marital status is higher among white versus minority women entrepreneurs. These results echo an ear-

Table 4.10   Marital Status of Women Entrepreneurs

Marital Status	Minority Women Entrepreneurs	White Women Entrepreneurs	Total
Married	59 (47.58%)	99 (71.22%)	158 (60.07%)
Separated/ Divorced	39 (31.45%)	22 (15.83%)	61 (23.19%)
Widowed	5 (4.03%)	5 (3.60%)	10 (3.80%)
Single, Never Married	21 (16.94%)	13 (9.35%)	34 (12.93%)
Total	124 (100.00%)	139 (100.00%)	263 (100.00%)

lier study by Smith-Hunter (2003), who also looked at a comparative group of white and minority women entrepreneurs. In contrast, to some previous findings, Aldrich et al. (1989) conducted one of the few studies that showed women entrepreneurs as less likely to be married, while DeCarlo and Lyons (1979) and Schwartz (1976) found minority women entrepreneurs were more likely than their white counterparts to be married.

Table 4.11   Women Entrepreneurs who have children

Have Children	Minority Women Entrepreneurs	White Women Entrepreneurs	Total
Yes	93 (75.00%)	105 (75.54%)	198 (75.29%)
No	31 (25.00%)	34 (24.46%)	65 (24.71%)
Total	124 (100.00%)	139 (100.00%)	263 (100.00%)

Table 4.12   Number of Children

Number of Children	Minority Women Entrepreneurs	White Women Entrepreneurs	Total
0	31 (25.00%)	34 (24.46%)	65 (24.72%)
1	25 (20.16%)	26 (18.71%)	51 (19.39%)
2	39 (31.45%)	55 (39.57%)	94 (35.74%)
3	18 (14.52%)	18 (12.95%)	36 (13.69%)
4	9 (7.26%)	4 (2.88%)	13 (4.94%)
5	0 (0.00%)	2 (1.44%)	2 (0.76%)
6	1 (0.80%)	0 (0.00%)	1 (0.38%)
10	1 (0.80%)	0 (0.00%)	1 (0.38%)
Total	124 (100.00%)	139 (100.00%)	263 (100.00%
Average Number of Children	1.68	1.54	

Both groups of women entrepreneurs were equally likely to say 'yes' to the question of having children, 75.00% and 75.40% (Table 4.11). The number of children for the two groups ranged from one to ten (Table 4.12). In addition, there was almost no disparity between the average number of children. The 139 white women entrepreneurs in the study averaged 1.54 children, while the minority women entrepreneurs averaged 1.68 children.

Most of the women entrepreneurs in the current sample said they had children, which supported findings from previous studies by Danhauser (1999), Olson (1997), Furry and Radhakrishna (1992) and Brush and Hisrich (1991). Women entrepreneurs' status as mothers is portrayed as another consistent factor marking women entrepreneurs' demographic profile. Collerette and Aubry (1990) embarked on a longitudinal study in Quebec, Canada, while Brush and Hisrich (1991), also through the use of a longitudinal study of 344 women entrepreneurs, determined that, not only did women entrepreneurs have children, but on average they had two children (Brush and Hisrich, 1991).

ALTERNATIVES IN ENTREPRENEURSHIP

What has been referred to in other studies as 'survivalist entrepreneurs' (Boyd, 1998) or accidental versus intentional entrepreneurs in previous literature (Orhan and Scott, 2001) was again tested in the current study by asking the women entrepreneurs if they saw going into business as their only alternative at the time of the inception of the business. The results in Table 4.13 show that minority women were more likely to choose entrepreneurship as their only alternative by a margin of 44.35% compared to 26.62 % for white women entrepreneurs. Chi-square values for these results showed a value of 6.819 with a p value of 0.009, which was significant.

The results from this section which highlighted that minority women entrepreneurs were more likely to see going into business as their only alternative support Boyd's (1998) theory of minority women entrepreneurs, whose study's results concluded that this group, when compared to their white counterparts, were more likely to be 'survivalist entrepreneurs'. However, in assessing the overall results from the current study, the majority of the women entrepreneurs did not see going into business as their only alternative. These findings have been echoed by Inman (2000), Moore and Buttner (1997), Dolinsky et al. (1993) and Clark and James (1992).

Table 4.13 Alternative For Going Into Business

Response	Minority Women Entrepreneurs	White Women Entrepreneurs
Yes	55 (44.35%)	37 (26.62%)
No	69 (55.64%)	102 (73.38%)
Total	124 (100.00%)	139 (100.00%)

Notes: Chi-Square = 6.819, p = 0.009.

Dolinsky et al. (1993) looked at the link between educational levels and entrance into entrepreneurship in light of the liquidity constraint theory which states that less educated individuals are less likely to have accumulated assets, and thus more likely to face liquidity constraints that make it relatively difficult to pursue entrepreneurship (Evans and Jovanovic, 1989). The study concluded that more education provides individuals with more alternatives to secure income (Dolinsky et al., 1993). The latter point appears logical, in light of the information in the next chapter that shows, overall, that women entrepreneurs in this study were highly educated (see also Table 5.1). Clark and James (1992) used the 1987 Business Census figures to assess 617 women business owners and found similar results. However, these findings are in contrast to the disadvantage theory that posits that individuals who possess limited wage labor skills (or face discrimination) are more apt to earn higher incomes being self-employed than working for wages (Light, 1972, 1979; Min, 1988; Evans and Leighton, 1987, as cited in Dolinsky et al., 1993).

All the studies above summarize their findings by concluding that many of the women seeking their own business felt as if they had no alternative. In addition to higher levels of education, more sources and access to income and more incidents of accumulated wealth, all these factors are likely to place the white women entrepreneurs in better stead to procure other sources of income and not necessarily to see entry into the field of entrepreneurship as their only alternative.

Inman (2000) looked at a comparative analysis of white and minority women entrepreneurs and indicated that, while minority women entrepreneurs were more likely than Whites to see going into business as their only alternative at the time of inception, the overall sample of women business owners felt they had a choice. Moore and Buttner (1997) and Dolinsky et al. (1993) looked at general samples of women entrepreneurs (without a comparison between races), and showed that the majority of the women in the sample felt they had no other alternatives at the time they entered business ownership. The current findings regarding a lack of alternative on the part of minority women entrepreneurs at the businesses' inception is best relayed by the following statement from Lorraine, a minority woman business owner:

> A combination of things influenced my starting this business. It had become obvious to me that I had reached the highest level in terms of working with my old company, and to tell the truth I wasn't sure it would be any better working for another company. Then, my mother needed to come live with us. I realized I couldn't keep working as hard as I was and be able to take care of my husband, my kids and now my mother. At that point, the decision was easy. It gets tough sometimes, but I have never regretted my decision.

The point made in the quote above can be further extended to a related finding by Fairlie (1999), who performed a comparative analysis of white and African

American businesses to assess the discrepancy in their survival rates. The author indicated that the discrepancy is caused by the lower transition rates into and higher departure rates out of self-employment by Blacks versus their white counterparts (Fairlie, 1999). The author also noted that lower levels of assets and lower probabilities of having a self-employed father provide important contributions to the lower average probability of entering self-employment. The findings seem to indicate that minority business ownership is precarious and operates in a survivalist mode almost from the beginning.

LOCATION OF BUSINESSES

One of the final percentage analyses in this overview chapter looks at the physical location of the businesses (Table 4.14). The results indicate that for minority women entrepreneurs, their place of business operation was primarily in the home (53.23%), while for the white women entrepreneurs, it was primarily at a commercial office site (55.40%). However, the results did not show a significant value from the chi-square analysis.

Table 4.14   Physical Location of Women Businesses

Location of Business	Minority Women Entrepreneurs	White Women Entrepreneurs	Total
Home	66 (53.23%)	62 (44.60%)	128 (48.67%)
Office Space	58 (46.77%)	77 (55.40%)	135 (51.33%)
Total	**124 (100.00%)**	**139 (100.00%)**	**263 (100.00%)**

Notes: Chi-Square = 1.514, p = 0.219.

Previous studies have detailed the benefits that support the reasons women entrepreneurs have used for locating their businesses in their home, including the opportunity to combine work and family roles (Furry and Lino, 1992; Priesnitz, 1989; Jurik, 1998), and that it is an obvious inexpensive investment alternative (Olson, 1997; Edwards and Field-Hendrey, 1996). This latter factor is particularly critical for those women entrepreneurs with limited financial capital. The final factor is the inexpensive and convenient assistance in labor afforded by other family members, whether on a paid or non-paid basis (Edwards and Field-Hendrey, 1996).

Two of the few non-home-based studies to report the physical location of businesses by women entrepreneurs were done by Cuba et al. (1983) and Lerner and Almor (2002). Using the telephone book, 58 women business owners were ultimately selected to take part in a lengthy 75-item questionnaire by Cuba et al. (1983). While a cross-comparative racial analysis was not done, the study found that women entrepreneurs were less likely to locate their businesses in the home (Cuba et al., 1983). These were supported by another non-home-based study conducted by Lerner and Almor (2002). Their assessment of 220 Israeli women business owners found that only 40% of the sample chose to locate their businesses in the home (Lerner and Almor, 2002). Both of these studies reinforce the findings in the current study, demonstrating that overall women entrepreneurs are less likely to locate their business in the home (48.67% of sample).

REASONS FOR BECOMING AN ENTREPRENEUR

In Table 4.15, the top reasons for minorities becoming entrepreneurs were: the need to make more money (2.516), needing/wanting a job (2.403) and being dissatisfied with their work situation (2.355). For white women entrepreneurs, the top three reasons for becoming entrepreneurs were: being their own boss (2.359), family responsibilities (2.353) and the need to make more money (1.871). All the values of mean differences between the two groups had significant values at p = 0.01, except for 'thought I could do a better job than others', which was significant at p = 0.05. Not significant at p = 0.05 or p = 0.01 were

Table 4.15   Mean Ratings of Reason for Becoming a Business Owner

Reasons	Mean Ratings (Minorities)	Mean Ratings (Whites)	t-test	p value
To be my own boss	1.742	2.359	−5.494	0.000*
To make more money	2.516	1.871	6.438	0.000*
Always wanted	1.887	1.576	3.049	0.002*
Opportunity presented self	1.306	1.324	−0.227	0.825
Family	1.452	2.353	−9.348	0.000*
Needed/wanted a job	2.403	1.065	18.895	0.000*
Hit glass ceiling/dead end	1.919	1.446	4.799	0.000*
Dissatisfied with work	2.355	1.647	7.680	0.000*
Inherited business	1.088	1.014	−0.488	0.625
Someone else got me in	1.032	1.259	−4.872	0.000*
Wanted to contribute	1.258	1.691	−5.454	0.000*
Thought I could do better	1.661	1.863	−1.994	0.047**

Notes: ** p = 0.05, * p = 0.01.

the responses: 'the opportunity presenting itself' and 'inherited the business'. The idea of owning their own business was stressed in a statement by Karen, a white woman entrepreneur who lives in California:

> My husband had the idea and I had the skills. He saw the long hours I was working for someone else and thought I could do better by opening my own business. I guess the urge started there.

While Karen was propelled into owning her own business because of her unsatisfactory work situation, Diane, another white woman entrepreneur who owns a travel agency in the state of Washington, felt that she needed to explore new territories:

> I would never do anything else, I love the idea of owning my own business. There is a tremendous amount of fulfillment in knowing that what I am doing is for my total benefit, instead of doing my job and waiting for a manager to give me a raise.

A study by Shane et al. (1991) concluded that the three main motivating factors impacting female entrepreneurs' decision to start a business were: to have greater impact on their work, to control their time, and to have greater flexibility for work and family life. A related article by Boden (1999a), indicated that women are more likely than men to cite flexibility to schedule and family-related reasons for becoming self-employed. Data came from a supplement of the 1995 Current Population Survey. The study also found that women with no children were more likely to have been employed for a longer period.

Moore and Buttner's (1997) study analyzed the perceptions of 129 women entrepreneurs, former executives and professionals, who, in general, left the corporate world because of a lack of career advancement and discrimination in the workplace. The authors also noted that the women entrepreneurs wanted to balance family and work responsibilities. These three previously mentioned factors have been reinforced in other studies, which have shown that work–family conflict issues (Ahrentzen, 1990; Becker and Moen, 1999); workplace discrimination (Firestone, 1994, Lewis, 1995; Kay and Hagan, 1995; Hemenway, 1995; Boden, 1999b; England et al., 1999); or lack of challenging experiences (Scheinberg and MacMillan, 1988; Shane et al., 1991) have propelled women into business ownership. Other factors that have propelled women into business ownership included the need to fill a void for a service that was not being provided in their community (Inman, 2000), as well as wanting to make a contribution to society by delivering a better product or service (Coughlin and Thomas, 2002; Moore and Buttner, 1997).

PROBLEMS FOR WOMEN ENTREPRENEURS

Table 4.16 displays the mean values of problems faced by the women entrepreneurs. The top three mean values for the minority women entrepreneurs are: cash flow problems (2.419), too many factors out of their control (2.177) and not enough time for business/personal life (1.839). The top three mean values for the white women are as follows: not enough time for business/personal life (2.209), cash flow problems (2.014) and the rising cost of business (1.942). The t-tests for all values were all significant at p = 0.01, except for the values for 'too much competition', 'too much paperwork', 'state and federal regulations' and 'finding good employees'.

Table 4.16   Mean Values of Problems Faced by Business Owners

Variables	Mean Ratings (Minorities)	Mean Ratings (Whites)	t-test	p value
Too much competition	1.387	1.503	−1.366	0.173
Too much paperwork	1.532	1.424	1.210	0.227
State and federal regulations	1.629	1.719	−0.933	0.351
Not enough time for business/personal life	1.839	2.209	−3.345	0.000*
Not enough business knowledge	1.290	1.539	−3.036	0.002*
Cash flow problems	2.419	2.014	4.312	0.000*
Too many factors out of my control	2.177	1.468	7.589	0.000*
Having others take you seriously as a business person	1.452	1.209	2.930	0.004*
Finding good employees	1.669	1.568	1.027	0.305
Keeping customers happy	1.040	1.331	−5.316	0.000*
Rising costs of business	1.637	1.942	−3.032	0.003*

Notes: ** p = 0.05, * p = 0.01.

A key factor in addressing the needs of women entrepreneurs lies in the identification of the major problems they face in the operation of their businesses. The lack of business and management skills, as well as a lack of access to financial capital, government contracts and adequate network structures have been documented in earlier studies (Loscocco and Robinson, 1991; Loscocco et al., 1991) as well as more recent research (Henry, 2002; Weiler and Bernasek, 2001). Of particular concern to women entrepreneurs has been the issue of access to financial capital (Finnerty and Krzystofik, 1986; Neider, 1987; Brush and Hisrich, 1991; Charboneau, 1981) even across racial lines (Mason-Draffen, 2001; Inman, 2000).

In a study by Bitler et al. (2001) that looked extensively at the types of financial capital and more specifically credit accessed by women entrepreneurs, the authors found that in addition to financial capital, the women entrepreneurs' other major problems included labor issues (finding good employees) and competition (Bitler et al, 2001). Maysami and Goby (1999) found that internationally the issues were: obtaining credit (cash flow problems), work–home conflicts (not enough time for business/personal life) and competition.

RESULTS FOR CORRELATION FACTORS

Correlation coefficient values measure the rate of correlation between two variables and indicate the level at which a change in one variable impacts another variable (Bailey, 1994; Kerlinger, 1986). The value of a correlation coefficient can range from -1 to $+1$ and is seen as either a negative value (indicating that a change in one value is likely to result in the opposite change in the other related variable) or a positive value (indicating that a change in one value results in a similar change in the other related variable). In the latter case, both changes can be positive or negative (Bailey, 1994). The following overview results look at the general correlation coefficients between variables that were presented in the questionnaire sent to women entrepreneurs. The results are presented in a comparative format across the two groups of women.

Business Ownership as the Sole Alternative

A set of correlation coefficient values looked at the relationship between seeing the entrance to business ownership as the only alternative for the women entrepreneurs and having a number of children (Table 4.17). For the minority women entrepreneurs, there was a significant and positive relationship between having children and the women being 'survivalist entrepreneurs', defined previously as those who see going into business as their only alternative to obtain income or earn a living (Boyd, 1998). In contrast, it is only by having more children that the white women entrepreneurs show a significant correlation coefficient value. This can be interpreted to mean that an increase in the number of children for the white women entrepreneurs is related to an increase in seeing business as the only way to obtain income or vice versa.

Table 4.17   Correlation Coefficients for Number of Children and Business as Only Alternative

	Correlation Coefficients for Minorities	Correlation Coefficients for Whites
Having children and business as only alternative	0.185*	0.039
Number of children and business as only alternative	0.063	0.210*

Notes: ** p = 0.05, * p = 0.01.

One of the few studies to look at the relationship between having children and entry into entrepreneurship was undertaken by Taniguchi (2002). The author used the National Longitudinal Survey of Youth (NLSY79), specifically looking at white, African American and Hispanic American women born during the period from January 1, 1957 to December 31, 1964, to assess the factors that contributed to their entry into self-employment. The author concluded that young children had no effect on entry into self-employment among white and African American women (Taniguchi, 2002). By contrast, young children slowed down the rate of entry into self-employment for Latinas (Taniguchi, 2002). The author also found that the number of children had a positive (but not significant) effect on rates of entry into self-employment for white women (Taniguchi, 2002).

Table 4.18   Correlation Coefficients for Type of Business and Business as Only Alternative

	Correlation Coefficients for Minorities	Correlation Coefficients for Whites
Type of business and business as only alternative (sole proprietorship)	−0.098	0.126
Type of business and business as only alternative (partnership/corporation)	0.146	−0.210***

Notes: *** p = 0.10, ** p = 0.05, * p = 0.01.

Table 4.18 looks at the relationships between type of business and going into business, as the only alternative, and depicts only one significant correlation coefficient value in this case. This occurred for white women entrepreneurs, and was related to the relationship between operating a partnership/corporation and seeing going into business as an only alternative. It resulted in a negative value of −0.210, indicating that the more likely the white women entrepreneurs were to operate a partnership/corporation, the less likely they were to be 'survivalist entrepreneurs'.

CONCLUSION

The overall dimensions and characteristics of the two groups of women entrepreneurs were analyzed in this chapter. Differences between the minority and white women were viewed under the umbrella of location of the business, both physical and by geographic region. Form and type of business were examined, in addition to looking at a detailed breakdown of business owners by race. The demographic characteristics of the businesses and business owners were also looked at. Much of the information presented in this chapter does not fall into the areas of human capital, network structures or financial capital. These areas are addressed in Chapters 5, 6 and 7.

The results reporting business start-up characteristics indicated that white women entrepreneurs were more likely to start the business themselves when compared to their minority counterparts, who were more likely to start the business with someone else. The need for minority women entrepreneurs to partner with someone at the start of their business may be the result of a lack of resources. So collaboration is a benefit. Such an argument is consistent with the findings of Boyd (1998), Bates (1995b), Fratoe (1988) and Feagin and Imani (1994) regarding the lack of resources minority entrepreneurs are apt to experience at the start-up stage of their ventures.

In a similar vein, the white women entrepreneurs were more likely to operate corporations when compared to their minority counterparts, who were apt to operate partnerships and sole proprietorships. This may have occurred because minority women were unaware of differences between corporations versus partnerships or sole proprietorships. The minority women might also not be as familiar with incorporation procedures.

The size of the women business ventures in the current study are in congruence with other studies (Birley et al., 1987; Burr and Strickland, 1992; Loscocco and Robinson, 1991). The relatively small size of the minority women ventures when compared to the ventures of the white women were confirmed in earlier studies by DeCarlo and Lyons (1979), Inman (2000), Boyd (1998) and Smith-Hunter (2003), who looked exclusively at women business owners across racial lines, and Bates (1987, 1989, 1997) and Christopher (1998), who looked in general at business owners, with no emphasis on gender. The small size of the women ventures and the even smaller size overall of the minority enterprises have been attributed to a lack of resources on the part of the women to expand into larger enterprises and the cautionary nature of not wanting to expand over a certain (maybe unmanageable) size.

Business entry as sole alternative was one of the main points in this chapter, thus placing the women entrepreneurs in the category of 'accidental' (similar to survivalist entrepreneurs), rather than 'intentional' entrepreneurs. The former group is seen as falling into entrepreneurship as a means of obtaining income, without a plan or previous intent. The minority women entrepreneurs could be classified as 'survivalist entrepreneurs' (Boyd, 1998), indicating that they saw entrepreneurship as their sole alternative in obtaining a source of income.

Minority women entrepreneurs were seen as more likely to locate their business in the home. This might again be due to a lack of resources, especially financial resources to find a commercial site to operate the business, as well as an opportunity for the woman to combine work and family roles (Furry and Lino, 1992; Priestnitz, 1989; Olson, 1997; Edwards and Field-Hendrey, 1996).

The literature repeatedly shows that women entrepreneurs are concentrated in the services and retail industry, regardless of race (Loscocco and Robinson, 1991; Brush, 1990; Smith-Hunter, 2003: Devine, 1994a, 1994b). This was again confirmed in the current study, which reported that, regardless of the race of the sample, women entrepreneurs remained concentrated in gendered industries. A number of reasons have been advanced for this concentration, including the fact that: these industries require lower initial capital investments compared to others (such as construction, manufacturing and wholesale trade), they require fewer technical skills, and women in the mainstream labor market are also concentrated in the retail and services industries, therefore it seems natural that this same concentration would extend to the entrepreneurial sector. Finally, the fact that the types of businesses in these industries are often closely aligned with the roles of women as wives and/or mothers.

5.   Human capital issues

In Chapter 2, human capital and its related dimensions were described as being at the heart of what was critical to entrepreneurial success. This elevated status results from an understanding that the person – the entrepreneur – and what that individual possesses in terms of skills and abilities, is critical to the ultimate impact those skills and abilities have on the business. The human capital derived throughout a person's life journey is instrumental to their potential entrepreneurial journey (Carter et al., 1997). This is said to be even more potent if the human capital derived is more specific to business – albeit experiences such as entrepreneurial, management, work and educational experiences (Carter et al., 1997; Carland et al., 1984).

When one thinks of an entrepreneur who owns a business, the different roles they play in the labor market process are important and must be considered. First, the entrepreneur is an investor of financial capital. Second, he/she is an owner of the production factors and third, the entrepreneur is an employee and an employer (see Table 5.1). With this multidimensional perspective in mind, it is easy to see why the entrepreneur's skills and abilities are critical elements in the success of the business. This chapter looks at the dimensions of human capital possessed by the women entrepreneurs across racial lines. The dimensions looked at include: educational levels, pre-business ownership experience, prior entrepreneurial venture experience, similar industry experience and management/supervisory experience, accounting experience and knowledge and experience gained from family, friends and organizations regarding the operation of the women's entrepreneurial ventures.

EDUCATIONAL EXPERIENCES

Table 5.2 details the level of educational experiences of all the women entrepreneurs in the sample. The results show that the overall majority completed four years of college (42.21%). The next largest percentage completed graduate school (26.62%), followed closely by high school (25.09%), with a small number having only completed elementary school (4.56%) and a minuscule amount never completing any level of school (1.52%). A closer look at the numbers across racial lines indicated that the white women entrepreneurs had

Table 5.1   The Various Dimensions of the Small Business Owner

Dimensions of Small Business Owner	Aspects of Each Dimension

Manager	(1) Operation of business
	(2) Strategic decisions
	   (i) Manage someone else's business
	   (ii) Manage Own Business

Entrepreneur	(1) Risk (2) Creation of new venture (3) Investment of income
Self-employed	(1) Working for oneself
Employee	(1) Wage earner
Small Business Owner	(1) Often manager, responsible for daily operations (2) Risk from investment (3) Start new venture, take over existing venture (4) Work for oneself (5) Wage earner (6) Investment of income

higher levels of education when compared to their minority counterparts. These higher levels were seen at both the four-year college level (46.76% vs. 37.10%), as well as the graduate school level (33.09 vs. 19.35%) respectively. Minority women entrepreneurs had higher percentages at the high and elementary school level (33.87% vs. 17.27%) when compared to their white counterparts and also at the elementary school level (7.26% vs. 2.16%).

Sanders and Nee (1996) showed that higher educational levels increased one's chances of self-employment. The high educational levels of women business owners have been trumpeted in the literature and reconfirmed in the last two decades of study (Aldrich et al., 1989; Hisrich and Brush, 1984; Boden, 1999b; Clain, 2000; Fischer et al., 1993; Lerner and Almor, 2002; Cuba et al., 1983). Cuba et al. (1983) looked at 58 business owners in Atlanta, Baltimore and Richmond; Brush and Hisrich (1991) and Hisrich and Brush (1984) looked at nationwide samples; Boden (1999b) analyzed the Current Population Survey

Table 5.2   School Education

Level of School Completed	Minority Women Entrepreneurs	White Women Entrepreneurs	Total
None	3 (2.42%)	1 (0.72%)	4 (1.52%)
Elementary School	9 (7.26%)	3 (2.16%)	12 (4.56%)
High School/ Vocational School	42 (33.87%)	24 (17.27%)	66 (25.09%)
College	46 (37.10%)	65 (46.76%)	111 (42.21%)
Graduate School	24 (19.35%)	46 (33.09%)	70 (26.62%)
Total	**124 (100.00%)**	**139 (100.00%)**	**263 (100.00%)**

and Clain (2000) used data from the Public Use Microdata Sample (PUMS) of 1990. Research done on an international level by Aldrich et al. (1989), who looked at Italian women entrepreneurs, and Lerner and Almor (2002), who looked at Israeli women entrepreneurs, reconfirmed the high educational levels of this sector of women income earners. These results were not surprising in that they reinforced the conclusions drawn from Brush (1997), Moore and Buttner (1997), Loscocco et al. (1991) and Loscocco and Robinson (1991), which stated that women entrepreneurs are a highly educated group. The results from this study also show that the minority women entrepreneurs had less education than their white counterparts, reinforcing findings by others (Smith-Hunter, 2003; Hurtado, 1989; Boyd, 1996).

The higher educational levels of the white versus the minority women entrepreneurs in this study were also found by DeCarlo and Lyons (1979) who sampled 122 women entrepreneurs from several mid-Atlantic states in the United States. Studies that documented low educational levels among women entrepreneurs have focused on micro-enterprise programs, which provide training and assistance to low income women pursuing entrepreneurship (Ehlers and Main, 1998; Dumas, 2001).

PREVIOUS SELF-EMPLOYMENT EXPERIENCES

It is said that pre-business ownership experiences is a critical link to the development of future entrepreneurial ventures, in addition to being linked to the

Table 5.3   Previous Self-Employment Experience

Response	Minority Women Entrepreneurs	White Women Entrepreneurs	Total
Yes	43 (34.68%)	68 (48.92%)	111 (42.21%)
No	81 (65.32%)	71 (51.08%)	152 (57.79%)
Total	124 (100.00%)	139 (100.00%)	263 (100.00%)

viability of these ventures. In the current study, most (see Table 5.3) of the women entrepreneurs lacked previous entrepreneurial experiences (57.79%). However, the white women entrepreneurs were more likely to have been previously self-employed in the past and to have been involved in entrepreneurial ventures (48.92%) when compared to their minority counterparts (34.68%).

In this study, white women entrepreneurs were more likely to have self-employment experience when compared to their minority counterparts (see Table 5.4). Table 5.5 confirms findings by Smith-Hunter (2003) and Inman (2000), who looked at comparative analyses across racial lines and found that white women entrepreneurs did indeed have more previous business ownership experiences when compared to their minority counterparts. These results are in contrast, however, to DeCarlo and Lyons (1979), who also looked at a comparative analysis of women entrepreneurs across racial lines. They found that minority women entrepreneurs were twice as likely to have previous entrepreneurial experience when compared to their white counterparts.

The lower rate of self-employment for minorities was said to result from the lack of access to start-up capital and lower viability levels of minority businesses highlighted by Christopher (1988), who felt that, overall, African American and Hispanic American businesses experienced lower formation and higher dissolution rates when compared to their minority counterparts. However, Christopher's study (1998) did not focus exclusively on women entrepreneurs, but looked aggregately at entrepreneurs across racial lines.

In a similar way to previous studies, the current study looked at the dimensions of human capital, such as education, age, previous business, entrepreneurial and industrial experience, in addition to knowledge gained from family, friends and associates (Raymo and Xie, 2000; Bates, 1990; Cooper and Dunkelberg, 1987; Beggs, 1995; Guaitoli, 2000; Gimeno et al., 1997).

The lower prior self-employment levels of the minority women entrepreneurs support Horton's (1988) finding which showed that African American women entrepreneurs were less likely to be self-employed when compared to their non-African American counterparts. Horton (1988) employed Public Use Microdata Samples (PUMS) for his study, which crossed gender lines. Fratoe (1988) also

Table 5.4   Pre-Business Ownership Experience

Pre-Business Ownership Experience	Minority Women Entrepreneurs	White Women Entrepreneurs	Total
Job in the Same Field as Business			
– A Lot	46 (37.10%)	79 (56.83%)	125 (47.53%)
– Some	33 (26.61%)	51 (36.69%)	84 (31.94%)
– None at all	45 (36.29%)	9 (6.47%)	54 (20.53%)
Total	124 (100.00%)	139 (100.00%)	263 (100.00%)
School Education Directly Related to Business			
– A Lot	44 (35.48%)	65 (46.76%)	109 (41.44%)
– Some	39 (31.45%)	52 (37.41%)	91 (34.60%)
– None at all	41 (33.06%)	22 (15.83%)	63 (23.95%)
Total	124 (100.00%)	139 (100.00%)	263 (100.00%)
Seminars, Programs Relevant to Business			
– A Lot	29 (23.39%)	58 (41.73%)	87 (33.08%)
– Some	51 (41.13%)	52 (37.41%)	103 (39.16%)
– None at all	44 (35.48%)	29 (20.86%)	73 (27.76%)
Total	124 (100.00%)	139 (100.00%)	263 (100.00%)
Hobby, Personal Experience in Same Field as Business			
– A Lot	39 (31.45%)	67 (48.20%)	106 (40.30%)
– Some	37 (29.84%)	49 (35.25%)	86 (32.70%)
– None at all	48 (38.71%)	23 (16.55%)	71 (26.99%)
Total	124 (100.00%)	139 (100.00%)	263 (100.00%)
Supervisory/Management Experience			
– A Lot	29 (23.39%)	48 (34.53%)	77 (29.28%)
– Some	26 (20.97%)	42 (30.22%)	68 (25.86%)
– None at all	69 (55.65%)	49 (35.25%)	118 (44.87%)
Total	124 (100.00%)	139 (100.00%)	263 (100.00%)
Accounting Experience			
– A Lot	17 (13.71%)	37 (26.62%)	54 (20.53%)
– Some	34 (27.42%)	49 (35.25%)	83 (31.56%)
– None at all	73 (58.87%)	53 (38.13%)	126 (47.91%)
Total	124 (100.00%)	139 (100.00%)	263 (100.00%)
Sales/Marketing Experience			
– A Lot	35 (28.23%)	41 (29.50%)	76 (28.90%)
– Some	35 (28.23%)	43 (30.93%)	78 (29.66%)
– None at all	54 (43.55%)	55 (39.57%)	109 (41.44%)
Total	124 (100.00%)	139 (100.00%)	263 (100.00%)

Table 5.5   Pre-Business Ownership Experiences

Variables	Mean Values (Minorities)	Mean Values (Whites)	t-test	p value
Job in the same field as business	1.008	1.503	−5.307	0.000*
School education directly related to business	1.024	1.310	−2.939	0.001*
Seminars, programs relevant to business	0.879	1.208	−3.496	0.000*
Hobby, personal experiences in the same field as business	0.927	1.316	−3.965	0.000*
General supervisory/ management experience	0.677	0.992	−3.058	0.002*
General accounting	0.548	0.884	−3.579	0.002*
General sales/marketing experience	0.814	0.899	0.827	0.204

Note: * $p = 0.01$.

found lower self-employment rates among minorities when compared to their white counterparts.

PRE-BUSINESS OWNERSHIP EXPERIENCES

The human capital dimensions looked at in this study specifically related to pre-business ownership for the women entrepreneurs were: experience in previous employment, jobs in the same field, education directly related to the business, attendance at seminars and exposure to programs relevant to the business and hobbies or personal experience. The study also looked at supervisory/ management, accounting and sales/marketing experience (see Table 5.4).

Overall, most of the women entrepreneurs indicated that they had experience with jobs in the same field as the business (47.53%). However, the white women entrepreneurs tended to have more pre-business ownership experience with jobs in the same field as the business when compared to their minority counterparts (56.83% versus 37.10%). Both groups of women entrepreneurs had high percentages of their samples having 'some' or a 'lot' of pre-business ownership experiences with a job in the same field as the business.

In terms of school education directly related to the business, the majority of the women entrepreneurs in this study indicated that overall they had 'a lot' of education. This breakdown across racial lines remained consistent with previous areas of domination, with white women entrepreneurs more likely to have acquired school education directly related to the business (46.76%) as compared to their minority counterparts (35.48%). The dominance stayed consistent but was minuscule when looking at 'some' experience in the same category for both groups (Whites = 37.41%; minorities = 31.45%). Overall, the values in this category from a totality perspective indicated that most (76.04%) of the women entrepreneurs said they had 'some' educational experience directly related to the business ('a lot' = 41.44%; 'some' = 34.60%).

Seminars or programs relevant to the operation of the business were attended by some (39.16%) and a lot (33.08%) of the time by most of the women entrepreneurs, with the minority women entrepreneurs being less likely to attend at least 'some' of the time ('some' = 41.13% and 'a lot' = 23.39%) versus their white counterparts ('some' = 37.41% and 'a lot' = 41.73%).

Having at least some hobby or personal experience in the same field as the business was true for most of the women entrepreneurs ('some' = 32.70% and 'a lot' = 40.30%). The figures across racial lines indicate that white women entrepreneurs were more likely to have experience on the two levels when compared to their minority counterparts. With results on the 'some' (Whites = 35.25%; minorities = 29.84%) and 'a lot' category (Whites = 48.20%; Minorities = 31.45%) being consistently more for the former group of women.

Overall, most of the women entrepreneurs had 'some' or 'a lot' of supervisory/management experience, with a total percentage of 55.14% versus 44.87% having no experience ('none at all'). The minority women entrepreneurs were also less likely to have supervisory/management experience as a group. They showed less experience when compared to their white counterparts in both the 'some' (minorities = 20.97%; Whites = 30.22%) and 'a lot' categories (minorities = 23.39%; Whites = 34.53%).

A look at the level of accounting experiences showed slightly worse values than the level of supervisory/management experience reported by the group of women entrepreneurs, with 52.09% of the overall number of women entrepreneurs having 'some' or 'a lot' of experience. Across racial lines, the results showed that the white women entrepreneurs were more likely to have accounting experience, both in the 'a lot' categories (26.62% versus 13.71%) and the 'some' (35.25% versus 27.42%) categories as compared to their minority counterparts.

The picture was somewhat brighter for the sales/marketing experience for the group of women entrepreneurs overall, with 58.56% having 'some' or 'a lot' of sales/marketing experience. This can be compared to the 52.09% for the accounting experience and 55.14% for the supervisory/management experiences.

The white and minority women entrepreneurs had approximately the same values for the sales/marketing experiences in the 'a lot' category (whites = 29.50%; minorities = 28.23%) as well as the 'some' category (Whites = 30.93%; minorities = 28.23%).

Table 5.5 displays the mean values of pre-business ownership experiences for the women entrepreneurs. The top three mean values for the minority women entrepreneurs are: school education directly related to the business (1.024), job in the same field as the business (1.008) and a hobby/personal experience (0.927). For the white women entrepreneurs, the top three mean values are as follows: a job in the same field as the business (1.503), hobby/personal experiences (1.316) and school education directly related to the business (1.310). The t-tests for all values were all significant at p = 0.01, except for general sales/marketing experience, which was not statistically significant.

In terms of the pre-business ownership experiences, white women entrepreneurs in this study dominated all categories (namely: job in the same field as the business; hobby or personal experience, sales/marketing experience, supervisory/management experience and accounting experience) when compared to their minority counterparts. These results were echoed in the Inman (2000) study, Fratoe (1988) study and Bates (1995a) studies. All three indicated that minorities were less likely to have pre-business ownership experiences when compared to their white counterparts. The latter two studies (Fratoe, 1988 and Bates, 1995a) looked at minority groups as a whole, not necessarily distinguishing men from women in the sample. Inman (2000), however, looked at women business owners across racial lines.

The entrepreneurs in this study seemed to have at least some experience in the related field of their business, as well as school education and seminars and programs directly related to the business, although they lacked large amounts of supervisory, sales/marketing and accounting experiences. This latter finding was especially poignant for the minority women entrepreneurs, who showed no majority holding in any of the categories. Other studies that report on the previous entrepreneurial experiences of women entrepreneurs provide mixed results. Brush and Hisrich (1991) indicated that the women entrepreneurs in their sample included primarily first generation entrepreneurs, with little previous entrepreneurial experience. The results are confirmed by Barrett (1996), who contends that women business owners have less relevant experience as it relates to business ownership when compared to their male counterparts, while a previous study by Hisrich and Brush (1984) found that most (64%) of the sample did indeed have previous entrepreneurial experience (Hisrich and Brush, 1984).

In addition, in terms of the previous work experience of women entrepreneurs, a number of studies indicate that women entrepreneurs have some level of experience that is relevant to their business ventures but there are some deficiencies

(Hisrich and Brush, 1984; Brush and Hisrich, 1991; Neider, 1987). These experiences range from general work experiences to specific managerial or supervisory experiences. The lack of previous entrepreneurial experience was identified as one of the top problems by 52 women entrepreneurs interviewed from the state of Florida in a study by Neider (1987). In another vein, Stevenson (1986) found that women entrepreneurs lacked sufficient experience in the industry in which they operated their business, a deficiency which had a direct impact on the businesses' low economic returns, which was seen as a top problem for the business owners (Stevenson, 1986). Other studies to detail the limited work experience of women entrepreneurs include Bowen and Hisrich (1986), Fischer et al. (1993), Loscocco and Robinson (1991) and Schwartz (1976). The latter article reported that a majority of the women entrepreneurs in the sample had some managerial experience, but it was two years or less in duration (Schwartz, 1976). An article from Chaganti and Parasuraman (1996) came to a different conclusion, using a Dun and Bradstreet sample which showed that women entrepreneurs had on average 14 or more years of previous work experience.

Three key problems were identified by minority and women business owners in the start-up and operation of their businesses, including: lack of training, access to financial capital and management experience (Hisrich and Brush, 1984). This indicates that pre-business ownership experience of women entrepreneurs is a key ingredient needed by women entrepreneurs, but that it is severely lacking at times and can result in problems. While the overall results show that most of the women business owners in this study indicated that they had at least 'some' experience in the various pre-business ownership areas, it must be remembered that the questionnaire was primarily a self-reporting tool and might not accurately reflect their actual experiences. In addition, the issue of previous business ownership experience was a concern expressed by a number of the women entrepreneurs in the study. When interviewed, a woman entrepreneur who operates a travel agency in Washington heralded the point made by many studies that one key area of deficiency for women business owners is their level of pre-business ownership experience:

> I would definitely tell women to get more experience before starting a business. Once you start a business, it is all on you. Make a list of all the things you have to do, like getting and selling the product, obtaining a line of credit, networking with customers and making business contacts. Although you don't necessarily have to do your own books, you have to at least have a basic level of accounting knowledge. It makes a difference.

AGE OF BUSINESSES AND BUSINESS OWNERS

Another dimension of human capital was identified as the business owner's age and indirectly, the age of the business. The latter is included, because it is felt that the number of years one operates a business could impact the human capital potential through experience. In terms of the business owner's age, the overall age of the women entrepreneurs was 44.24 years (see Table 5.6), with minorities in the study being slightly older at 46.37 years, compared to the white women entrepreneurs whose average age was 43.11 years. The minority women entrepreneurs ranged in age from 26 to 87 years old, while the white women entrepreneurs ranged from 27 to 81 years.

Table 5.6   Age of Women Entrepreneurs

Age Ranges (Birth Years)	Minority Women Entrepreneurs	White Women Entrepreneurs	Total
1907–18	1 (0.80%)	0	**1 (0.38%)**
1919–30	3 (2.42%)	3 (2.16%)	**6 (2.28%)**
1931–42	12 (9.68%)	8 (5.76%)	**20 (7.60%)**
1943–54	45 (36.29%)	57 (41.01%)	**102 (38.78%)**
1955–66	43 (34.68%)	51 (36.69%)	**94 (35.74%)**
1967–79	20 (16.13%)	20 (14.39%)	**40 (15.21%)**
Total	124 (100.00%)	139 (100.00%)	**263 (100.00%)**
Average	**46.37 years**	**43.11 years**	**44.24 years**

A review of the literature shows that the average age of women entrepreneurs, regardless of racial categories overall, was in the forties. More specifically, the average age findings were echoed by Moore and Buttner (1997), Dannhauser (1999), Olson (1997) and Furry and Lino (1992). Dannhauser (1999) relied on a national survey for her sample, while Olson (1997) used data from the same nine-state research project as Furry and Lino's (1992) sample source of 899 randomly selected home-based owners. Devine (1994a) also found similar estimates using the 1990 Census Data, while Moore and Buttner's (1997) 129 convenience sampling of women entrepreneurs nationwide yielded similar results. These results regarding the age of women entrepreneurs remained fairly consistent over a number of studies (Neider, 1987; Buttner, 2001; Smith et al., 1992; Loscocco, 1997; Brush, 1997; Clain, 2000; Anna et al., 1999). As an extension of the previous information, the current study found that minority women entrepreneurs were slightly older than their white counterparts. These results were consistent with Devine (1994a and 1994b), Smith-Hunter (2003),

Inman (2000) and DeCarlo and Lyons (1979), who also found minority women entrepreneurs to be slightly older than their white women entrepreneurs.

Studies whose results conflicted with the previously detailed findings include Birley et al. (1987), whose small sample of participants (11 women entrepreneurs) in an entrepreneurial developmental program placed their average age at 32.7 years and Aldrich et al. (1989), whose comparative sample of United States and Italian women entrepreneurs found the former to be older than the latter (39 versus 29 years). In addition, Dumas (2001) used data from a Community Enterprise Program to assess the overall characteristics of the program and its participants. The author found that the women entrepreneurs in the sample were on average 38 years old, which is younger than found by most other studies. Another study finding women entrepreneurs to be younger (37 years old), was conducted by Collerette and Aubry (1990). They performed a five-year longitudinal study of female entrepreneurs in Canada.

In terms of the number of years in business, the findings are approximately similar, with Whites being in business longer at 12.3 years and minorities not far behind at 11.24 years, leading to an overall average of 11.77 years for the whole group of women entrepreneurs (see Table 5.7). Results have been mixed regarding the number of years women-owned enterprises have been operating. Bitler et al. (2001) looked at a sample from the survey of Small Business Finances for 1998, which included a sample of women-owned businesses, and found that, on average, the businesses had operated for 13.3 years. Buttner and Rosen (1992) found that the businesses in their sample (which comprised male and female entrepreneurs on the East Coast of the United States) showed spe-

Table 5.7   Number of Years in Business

Year Started Business	Minority Women Entrepreneurs	White Women Entrepreneurs
1932–42	1	0
1943–53	1	2
1954–64	1	0
1965–75	5	1
1976–86	14	25
1987–97	62	63
1998–2003	40	48
Total Number of Women Entrepreneurs	**124**	**139**
Average Number of Women Entrepreneurs	**11.24 years**	**12.30 years**

Table 5.8   Age When Started Business

Age Started Business	Minority Women Entrepreneurs	White Women Entrepreneurs	Total
16–26	12	11	**23**
27–37	58	59	**117**
38–48	35	53	**88**
49–59	18	16	**34**
60–67	1	0	**1**
Total	124	139	**263**
Average Age	**35.13 years**	**30.81 years**	**32.57 years**

cifically that the female enterprises had operated for an average of 7 years. These results are echoed for the most part by Moore and Buttner (1997), Loscocco and Smith-Hunter (2004) and Smith-Hunter (2003). Smith-Hunter (2003) looked exclusively at women entrepreneurs and found that women entrepreneurs had been in business for an average of 7–10 years. Meanwhile Bowser's (1972) study looked at a minority sample of business owners which included women and found that they had operated their enterprises for an average of 5 years.

Table 5.8 shows the ranges of ages at which women entrepreneurs started their business, both as totals and across racial lines. The table shows that minority women entrepreneurs started at an older age (35.13 years) compared with their white counterparts (30.81 years). One of the few studies to focus on average start-up age was undertaken by Moore and Buttner (1997), who found that on average the 129 women entrepreneurs in their sample had started their business at 37 years old (Moore and Buttner, 1997).

ASSISTANCE FROM FAMILY AND FRIENDS

Among the secondary variables impacting an entrepreneur's human capital potential is the knowledge they gain from family, friends, organizations and other social and business contacts. Overall, 45.25% (see Table 5.9) of the women entrepreneurs indicated receiving start-up assistance from family, while 33.08% indicated receiving start-up assistance from friends (see Table 5.10). In an assessment of the in-depth interviews conducted with women entrepreneurs, they explained that this start-up assistance ranged from help with writing a business plan, to being introduced to others who could provide additional knowledge to the women entrepreneurs regarding factors related to business ownership, to actual assistance regarding help on how to actually operate a business. Vera, an

Table 5.9   Assistance from Family at Business Start-Up

Response	Minority Women Entrepreneurs	White Women Entrepreneurs	Total
Yes	73 (58.87%)	46 (33.09%)	**119 (45.25%)**
No	51 (41.13%)	93 (66.91%)	**144 (54.75%)**
Total	**124 (100.00%)**	**139 (100.00%)**	**263 (100.00%)**

Notes: Chi-Square = 16.676, p = 0.000.

Table 5.10   Assistance from Friends at Business Start-Up

Response	Minority Women Entrepreneurs	White Women Entrepreneurs	Total
Yes	56 (45.16%)	31 (22.30%)	**87 (33.08%)**
No	68 (54.84%)	108 (77.70%)	**176 (66.92%)**
Total	**124 (100.00%)**	**139 (100.00%)**	**263 (100.00%)**

Notes: Chi-Square = 16.597, p = 0.000.

African-American woman entrepreneur who owns a novelty store, explained this assistance:

> My family has always been supportive. When I first started I was sometimes unsure if I had made the right decision, but whenever I needed a reminder that I had done the right thing, all I would do is call a family member and they would be willing to help me in any way they could. They provided contacts to customers, fellow business owners, loan officers and anyone else that could help me with the business. They provided their expertise and knowledge in areas that I was lacking. They always assured me things would work out and that I had made the right decision. All of that was so important when you are starting to build a business.

The results from this study also showed that the minority women entrepreneurs were more likely than their white counterparts to have received assistance from family at the start-up stage (58.87% versus 33.09%). The former group of women entrepreneurs were also more likely to receive assistance from friends (45.16%) when compared to the latter group (22.30%). The obvious follow-up question of whether or not the women entrepreneurs continued to receive assistance from family and friends during the operation of the business carried results in the same vein. Minority women entrepreneurs indicated that they received assistance from family (see Table 5.11) during the operation of the

Table 5.11   Assistance from Family during Business Operation

Response	Minority Women Entrepreneurs	White Women Entrepreneurs	Total
Yes	75 (60.48%)	46 (33.09%)	**121 (46.01%)**
No	49 (39.52%)	93 (66.91%)	**142 (53.99%)**
Total	**124 (100.00%)**	**139 (100.00%)**	**263 (100.00%)**

Notes: Chi-Square = 19.859, p = 0.000.

Table 5.12   Assistance from Friends during Business Operation

Response	Minority Women Entrepreneurs	White Women Entrepreneurs	Total
Yes	46 (37.10%)	29 (20.86%)	**75 (28.52%)**
No	78 (62.90%)	110 (79.14%)	**188 (71.48%)**
Total	**124 (100.00%)**	**139 (100.00%)**	**263 (100.00%)**

Notes: Chi-Square = 10.489, p = 0.001.

business (60.48%) at almost twice the rate of their white counterparts (33.09%). Assistance from friends during the operation of the business (see Table 5.12) was again also almost twice the rate for minority women entrepreneurs (37.10%) compared with white women entrepreneurs (20.86%). What was interesting from the preceding results, however, was that while 46.01% of women entrepreneurs overall indicated receiving assistance from family during the operation of the business, overall only 28.52% of the women entrepreneurs, indicated receiving assistance from friends during the operation of the business.

Overall, start-up assistance from other sources, such as churches, women's organizations and affiliated institutions, at the start-up of the business (see Table 5.13) occurred for only 14.07% of the group of women entrepreneurs, with the numbers remaining approximately equal across racial lines, with Whites (15.11%) being more likely to receive assistance from other sources, but only by a slight margin compared to their minority counterparts (12.90%). A closer look at the listing of the type of sources providing assistance indicated that minority women entrepreneurs obtained assistance from less formal sources (e.g., churches) when compared to their white counterparts, who received assistance from more formal sources (e.g., membership organizations) in the start-up stage of their businesses. Assistance from other sources during the operation of the business (see Table 5.14) was also experienced by a minimal number of women

Table 5.13   Assistance from Other Sources at Business Start-Up

Response	Minority Women Entrepreneurs	White Women Entrepreneurs	Total
Yes	16 (12.90%)	21 (15.11%)	**37 (14.07%)**
No	108 (87.10%)	118 (84.89%)	**226 (85.93%)**
Total	**124 (100.00%)**	**139 (100.00%)**	**263 (100.00%)**

Notes: Chi-Square = 1.764, p = 0.414.

Table 5.14   Assistance from Other Sources during Business Operation

Response	Minority Women Entrepreneurs	White Women Entrepreneurs	Total
Yes	29 (23.39%)	28 (20.14%)	**57 (21.67%)**
No	95 (76.61%)	111 (79.86%)	**206 (78.33%)**
Total	**124 (100.00%)**	**139 (100.00%)**	**263 (100.00%)**

Notes: Chi-Square = 0.309, p = 0.578.

Table 5.15   Family Members who are Business Owners

Response	Minority Women Entrepreneurs	White Women Entrepreneurs	Total
Yes	74 (59.68%)	91 (65.47%)	**165 (62.74%)**
No	50 (40.32%)	48 (34.53%)	**98 (37.26%)**
Total	**124 (100.00%)**	**139 (100.00%)**	**263 (100.00%)**

Notes: Chi-Square = 0.955, p = 0.328.

entrepreneurs (21.67%), these results remaining approximately consistent across racial lines (minorities = 23.39%; Whites = 20.14%).

Having family members and friends who are business owners has long been heralded as a major factor in increasing one's human capital potential. White women entrepreneurs were much more likely to have family members who were business owners (see Table 5.15) when compared to their minority counterparts (65.47% versus 59.68%). However, the majority of the minority women entrepreneurs still had family members who were business owners (59.68%). The story was similar when looking at friends who were business owners (see Table

Table 5.16   Friends who are Business Owners

Response	Minority Women Entrepreneurs	White Women Entrepreneurs	Total
Yes	98 (79.03%)	111 (79.86%)	**209 (79.47%)**
No	26 (20.97%)	28 (20.14%)	**54 (20.53%)**
Total	**124 (100.00%)**	**139 (100.00%)**	**263 (100.00%)**

Notes: Chi-Square = 0.024, p = 0.878.

5.16), with most white women entrepreneurs stating that they had friends who were business owners (79.86%) and most minority women entrepreneurs also stating that they had friends who were business owners (79.03%). Overall figures for the number of women who had family and friends who were business owners showed that most did (family = 62.74%; friends = 79.47%).

Regarding assistance from family members and friends, the minority group were more likely to receive such assistance from family and friends when starting and operating a business. In contrast, white women entrepreneurs were more likely to belong to and receive assistance from organizations during the start-up and operation of their business enterprises. Overall, minority women entrepreneurs in this study received more assistance from family and friends compared with their white counterparts, who received more assistance from other sources (such as membership organizations, banks, network groups) at the start-up and during the operational stages of their business. Assistance from family and friends has been covered in a handful of studies (Maysami and Goby, 1999; Renzulli et al., 2000; Caputo and Dolinsky, 1998) and has been viewed as having a primarily negative impact on women's entrepreneurial ventures by two (Renzulli et al., 2000; Caputo and Dolinsky, 1998) of the three studies.

Two studies that looked at assistance received by women entrepreneurs using a racial comparison found that minority women entrepreneurs were indeed more likely to receive assistance from family and friends, while their white counterparts were more likely to receive such assistance from other, mainly formal sources, such as banks and membership organizations (Inman, 2000; Smith-Hunter, 2003). These two studies also confirmed the current study's findings that white women entrepreneurs were more likely than their minority counterparts to belong to membership organizations, which may boost the assistance they receive from other sources (see Tables 5.17 and 5.18 and the following section on Membership in Organizations) (Inman, 2000; Smith-Hunter, 2003).

MEMBERSHIP IN ORGANIZATIONS

In a related aspect to the above section, 44.11% of the women entrepreneurs indicated that they had memberships in organizations, a source from which they could receive assistance. The occurrence was higher for white women entrepreneurs, whose rate of membership in organizations when compared to their minority counterparts stood at 48.92% versus 38.71% (see Table 5.17). A more detailed look (see Table 5.18) at respondents who declared membership in organizations showed that the majority who had memberships belonged to between one and five organizations, even across racial categories, with the majority percentages in the one to two range for the minorities, but in the two to five range for the Whites. This indicates that white women entrepreneurs were

Table 5.17   Membership in Organizations

Response	Minority Women Entrepreneurs	White Women Entrepreneurs	Total
Yes	48 (38.71%)	68 (48.92%)	**116 (44.11%)**
No	76 (61.29%)	71 (51.08%)	**147 (55.89%)**
Total	**124 (100.00%)**	**139 (100.00%)**	**263 (100.00%)**

Notes: Chi-Square = 16.597, p = 0.000.

Table 5.18   Number of Organizations

Number of Organizations	Minority Women Entrepreneurs	White Women Entrepreneurs	Total
0	76 (61.29%)	71 (51.08%)	**147 (55.89%)**
1	22 (17.74%)	5 (3.60%)	**27 (10.27%)**
2	12 (9.68%)	17 (12.23%)	**29 (11.03%)**
3	6 (4.84%)	20 (14.39%)	**26 (9.89%)**
4	5 (4.03%)	14 (10.07%)	**19 (7.22%)**
5	1 (0.80%)	9 (6.47%)	**10 (3.80%)**
6	1 (0.80%)	2 (1.44%)	**3 (1.14%)**
8	1 (0.80%)	1 (0.72%)	**2 (0.76%)**
Total	**124 (100.00%)**	**139 (100.00%)**	**263 (100.00%)**
Average Number of Organizations	**0.83 organizations**	**1.58 organizations**	**1.23 organizations**

more likely to belong to more membership organizations compared with minority women.

The impact of membership organizations was found to be lackluster at best for the 129 women entrepreneurs in Moore and Buttner's (1997) study. The authors found that women entrepreneurs in the study, on average, belonged to four membership organizations. However, many of the benefits derived from forming a more close-knit subset of the larger group of individuals who provided meaningful support.

RELATIONSHIPS FOR HUMAN CAPITAL DIMENSIONS

Human capital variables have been previously defined as the dimensions that impact an individual's knowledge level and ultimately determine how this knowledge is transformed into a viable entity (Becker, 1993). The human capital dimensions include, but are not limited to, formal educational experience, work experience, experiences or knowledge gained from attending seminars and conferences, general life experiences, hobbies and experiences gained from friends, family or through organizations and affiliations (Beggs, 1995; Sanders and Nee, 1996; Farkas et al., 1997; Heckman, 2000; Cooper and Dunkelberg, 1987).

This section begins with an assessment of human capital dimensions and their relationship to the various elements related to the level of difficulty experienced by women entrepreneurs in obtaining financial capital.

Difficulty in Obtaining Financial Capital

Table 5.19 provides the results of the correlation coefficient values of human capital dimensions and the level of difficulty in obtaining financial capital for women entrepreneurs. A first look at minority women entrepreneurs shows nine significant correlation coefficient values. The first significant value shows that an increase in the number of years in business experience decreases the level of difficulty in accessing financial capital (correlation coefficient value of –0.212). A second significant value is previous entrepreneurial experience, which impacts on minority women entrepreneurs by reducing their difficulty to obtain financial capital (correlation coefficient value of –0.262). This indicates that the more previous entrepreneurial experience the minority women entrepreneurs had, the less difficulty they were likely to have in obtaining financial capital. In contrast, for the white women entrepreneurs, it was formal educational levels that favorably impacted their level of difficulty in obtaining financial capital.

To date, no known study has looked specifically at the relationship between years in business and the difficulty in obtaining capital, a relationship that was

Table 5.19   Correlation Coefficients of Human Capital Dimensions and Difficulty in Obtaining Financial Capital

Human Capital Dimensions	Correlations (minorities)	Correlations (whites)
Years in business	−0.212**	0.011
Previous self-employment	−0.262*	0.001
Educational levels	0.022	−0.199**
Age of business owner	−0.152	0.060
Start-up assistance from family	−0.018	−0.155*
Start-up assistance from friends	−0.179***	0.008
Start-up assistance from others	0.134	0.024
Business assistance from family	0.039	0.079
Business assistance from friends	−0.209**	−0.242*
Assistance from other sources	−0.193**	0.064
Friends working in the business (paid/ unpaid)	−0.219**	0.049
Family working in the business (paid/ unpaid)	−0.193**	−0.031
Family members business owners	0.032	0.022
Friends business owners	0.068	−0.051
Membership in organizations	0.102	−0.210**
PBOE: job in same field	−0.023	−0.118
PBOE: school education	−0.032	−0.241*
PBOE: seminars/programs	0.002	−0.056
PBOE: hobby/personal experience	−0.099	0.151
PBOE: supervisory experience	−0.235*	0.009
PBOE: accounting experience	−0.180***	−0.032
PBOE: sales/marketing experience	0.133	−0.197**

Notes:
PBOE = Pre-Business Ownership Experiences
*** $p = 0.10$, ** $p = 0.05$, * $p = 0.01$.

negatively significant for the current study in terms of minority women entre-preneurs. However, through an extrapolation based on a study done by Belcourt (1990), it was shown that the more successful women entrepreneurs, who were able to gain access to financial capital, had been in business for more than the average number of years (more than 10 years).

One compelling factor that is said to impact the continuous operation of women businesses is their level of access to previous entrepreneurial experience

(Bowen and Hisrich, 1986; Orser et al., 2000). Bowen and Hisrich (1986) cited previous work-related experience as being a crucial factor relevant to the process and operation of the business ventures and important to the women entrepreneurs' success. Previous self-employment experience has been recorded as having a positive impact on women's entrepreneurial status (Carter et al., 1997). This finding was repeated in the current study, where a negative and significant relationship was found between previous self-employment experience and difficulty in obtaining financial capital for the minority women entrepreneurs. The fact that this latter issue shows such dominance correlates significantly with the need for a critical observation. The authors have contended that business growth requires continuous and favorable access to financial capital (Orser et al., 2000; Bowen and Hisrich, 1986).

Assistance from friends and family members also had a significant relationship with the level of difficulty of obtaining financial capital in the current study. The results overall, for both groups of women, indicated that the more assistance was received by the women entrepreneurs, the less difficulty they would have in trying to obtain financial capital. These results are in contrast to findings from Renzulli et al. (2000), who found that having a greater proportion of kin in your network structure creates disadvantages. The author used data from the Research Triangle Area of North Carolina and conducted a study through the use of questionnaires and telephone interviews (Renzulli et al, 2000). Highly educated and wealthier minority (specifically Korean immigrant) entrepreneurs were able to secure loans with financial institutions or obtain funds from family members (Bates, 1997). Their less successful colleagues relied on rotating credit associations (RCAs), whereby supportive peer and community subgroups assisted in the creation and operation of firms by providing a lucrative network link in the form of loans (ibid.).

The section that follows provides information regarding the type of assistance received from family, friends and others in the operation of the business. The minority women entrepreneurs had five significant relationships and the white women entrepreneurs had two significant relationships for the assistance received from family and friends, impacting favorably on the level of difficulty of obtaining financial capital for the women entrepreneurs. The results indicated that assistance received from friends, family and other sources decreased the level of difficulty minority women entrepreneurs experienced when trying to access financial capital (correlation coefficient values of –0.179, –0.209, –0.193, –0.219 and –0.193). In a similar vein, assistance received by white women entrepreneurs from family favorably impacted their ability to obtain financial capital, showing a correlation coefficient value of –0.242.

Finally, the results in Table 5.19 show that for minority women entrepreneurs, an increase in supervisory and accounting experience reduced their level of difficulty in obtaining financial capital (correlation coefficient values of –0.235

and –0.180 respectively). In contrast, white women entrepreneurs who had school education directly related to the business (–0.241), membership in organizations (–0.210), increased educational levels (–0.199) and sales/marketing experience (0.197) had a favorable impact on accessing financial capital. Hisrich and Brush (1984), in repeated studies, found that higher educational levels increased one's success level as an entrepreneur. The authors indicated that it did so by providing increased knowledge and by helping the communication factors (Hisrich and Brush, 1984)

One of the few studies to declare that previous work experience did not impact economic success was performed by Collerette and Aubry (1990). The authors looked at 917 women entrepreneurs in Quebec, and drew a general portrait of the women entrepreneurs from the surveys they completed (Collerette and Aubry, 1990). The authors found, after conducting a detailed analysis, that previous work experiences did not impact economic success. What was lacking from the analysis was a breakdown by type and various forms of previous work experience.

Difficulty in Obtaining a Bank Loan

The relationships between possessing certain human capital dimensions and the difficulty of obtaining a bank loan are presented in Table 5.20. The number of years in business as well as the age of the business owner showed significant relationships for the minority and white women entrepreneurs. The results showed correlation coefficient values of –0.236 for minority women entrepreneurs and –0.269 for white women entrepreneurs for the former relationship. This indicates that increased entrepreneurial experience acquired from spending time in the business decreases the difficulty experienced when trying to obtain a bank loan. In addition, there were also correlation coefficient values of –0.255 for minority women entrepreneurs and –0.207 for white women entrepreneurs between age and the difficulty experienced in obtaining a bank loan. The interpretation may be that the older a woman entrepreneur, the less likely she was to experience difficulties in obtaining a bank loan.

There were also two additional correlation coefficient values not shared by both groups of women entrepreneurs. Minority women entrepreneurs who received start-up assistance from friends had less difficulty obtaining a bank loan (correlation coefficient value = –0.239), while white women entrepreneurs, who had school education directly related to the business, had less difficulty obtaining a bank loan (correlation coefficient value = –0.262).

One study that looked at the issue of bank loans and women entrepreneurs assessed the proportions of bank loan officers and the characteristics they attributed to successful women entrepreneurs (Buttner and Rosen, 1989). The study looked at psychological characteristics such as need for achievement rather than demographics or human capital characteristics.

Table 5.20   Correlation Coefficients of Human Capital Dimensions and Difficulty in Obtaining Bank Loan

Human Capital Dimensions	Correlations (minorities)	Correlations (whites)
Years in business	−0.236*	−0.269*
Previous self-employment	0.037	0.043
Educational levels	0.058	−0.004
Age of business owner	−0.255*	−0.207**
Start-up assistance from family	−0.122	−0.075
Start-up assistance from friends	−0.239*	−0.119
Start-up assistance from others	−0.140	−0.054
Business assistance from family	−0.065	−0.103
Business assistance from friends	−0.104	−0.109
Assistance from other sources	−0.176	0.110
Friends working in business (paid/ unpaid)	−0.086	0.116
Family working in business (paid/ unpaid)	−0.017	0.166
Family members business owners	0.125	0.046
Friends business owners	0.154	0.065
Membership in organizations	0.082	0.139
Marital status	0.147	0.154
PBOE: job in same field	0.047	0.013
PBOE: school education	0.058	−0.262*
PBOE: seminars/programs	−0.023	0.153
PBOE: hobby/personal experience	0.055	0.066
PBOE: supervisory experience	−0.026	0.039
PBOE: accounting experience	0.055	0.032
PBOE: sales/marketing experience	−0.071	−0.155

Notes:
PBOE = Pre-Business Ownership Experiences
*** $p = 0.10$, ** $p = 0.05$, * $p = 0.01$.

Start-Up Capital

Table 5.21 details the correlation coefficient values regarding the amount of start-up capital and the human capital dimensions. For minority women entrepreneurs, being older increased significantly the amount of start-up capital of the business owner (correlation coefficient value of 0.257). In addition, the re-

Table 5.21   Correlation Coefficients of Human Capital Dimensions and Amount of Start-Up Capital

Human Capital Dimensions	Correlations (minorities)	Correlations (whites)
Years in business	−0.016	0.062
Previous self-employment	0.059	0.089
Educational levels	0.020	−0.005
Age of business owner	0.257*	0.009
Start-up assistance from family	0.117	0.359*
Start-up assistance from friends	0.081	0.162***
Start-up from other sources	0.252*	0.045
Business assistance from family	0.117	0.005
Business assistance from friends	0.076	0.172***
Assistance from other sources	0.176***	0.057
Family working in the business (paid/ unpaid)	0.105	−0.089
Friends working in the business (paid/ unpaid)	0.065	−0.129
Family members business owners	0.118	0.142
Friends business owners	0.171***	0.220*
Membership in organizations	0.073	0.111
Marital status	0.011	0.276*
PBOE: job in same field	0.031	−0.058
PBOE: school education	0.015	0.129
PBOE: seminars/programs	−0.094	0.021
PBOE: hobby/personal experience	0.153	−0.094
PBOE: supervisory experience	−0.093	−0.077
PBOE: accounting experience	−0.147	−0.018
PBOE: sales/marketing experience	−0.133	−0.120

Notes:
PBOE = Pre-Business Ownership Experiences
*** $p = 0.10$, ** $p = 0.05$, * $p = 0.01$.

sults (see Table 5.21) show that start-up assistance, assistance received from others and having friends who are business owners (significant correlation coefficient values of 0.252, 0.176 and 0.171 respectively) also increased the amount of start-up capital for minority women entrepreneurs. For white women entrepreneurs, the factors impacting on increases in start-up capital were slightly different. Start-up assistance received from family and friends (correlation coef-

Table 5.22   Correlation Coefficients of Human Capital Dimensions and Business Ownership as Only Alternative

Human Capital Dimensions	Correlations (minorities)	Correlations (whites)
Years in business	0.105	0.173**
Previous self-employment	0.104	0.100
Educational levels	−0.305*	0.046
Age of business owner	0.076	0.072
Start-up assistance from family	0.052	−0.033
Start-up assistance from friends	0.116	0.029
Start-up assistance from others	0.002	0.069
Business assistance from family	0.186**	0.054
Business assistance from friends	0.104	0.112
Assistance from other sources	0.121	−0.017
Family working in business (paid/ unpaid)	0.140	−0.041
Friends working in business (paid/ unpaid)	0.253*	−0.101
Family members business owners	−0.049	−0.277*
Friends business owners	0.109	−0.119
Membership in organizations	−0.035	−0.069
Marital status	−0.165***	−0.134
PBOE: job in same field	0.195**	−0.128
PBOE: school education	−0.013	−0.076
PBOE: seminars/programs	0.085	−0.026
PBOE: hobby/personal experience	0.107	−0.074
PBOE: supervisory experience	−0.036	−0.083
PBOE: accounting experience	−0.064	−0.068
PBOE: sales/marketing experience	−0.075	0.011

Notes:
PBOE = Pre-Business Ownership Experiences
*** p = 0.10, ** p = 0.05, * p = 0.01.

ficient values of 0.359 and 0.162 respectively) had a positive impact on their start-up capital. Having friends who were business owners and being married also improved the amount of start-up capital of white women entrepreneurs (correlation coefficient values of 0.220 and 0.276 respectively). Finally, business assistance received from friends also had a positive impact on white women entrepreneurs (correlation coefficient value = 0.172).

Business as Only Alternative

There were a few interesting results for the relationships between human capital dimensions and the business owner who saw going into business as their only alternative (see Table 5.22). For example, minority women entrepreneurs who were better educated were less likely to see going into business as their only alternative (correlation coefficient value of –0.305). In addition, being married was also less likely to result in minority women entrepreneurs seeing going into business as their only alternative (correlation coefficient value = –0.165), while obtaining assistance from family, having friends working in the business and having a job in the same field as the business were more likely to result in minority women entrepreneurs seeing going into business as their only alternative (correlation coefficient values of 0.186, 0.253 and 0.195 respectively).

White women entrepreneurs who were in business for a longer time were more likely to see entrepreneurship as their only alternative (correlation coefficient value = 0.173). Meanwhile, having family members who were business owners was less likely to result in white women entrepreneurs seeing going into business as their only alternative (correlation coefficient value = –0.277).

One study that looked directly at the impact of previous work experience, marital status and a formal education on entry into entrepreneurship was undertaken by Taniguchi (2002). The author used the National Longitudinal Survey of Youth (NLSY79), specifically looking at white, African American and Hispanic American women born during the period from January 1, 1957 to December 31, 1964, to assess the factors that contributed to their entry into self-employment. The author concluded that: cumulative work experiences and marital status significantly increased rates of entry into self-employment for all three groups of women. However, the author also concluded that additional schooling (formal education) did not increase the rates of self-employment for any of the three groups of women.

CONCLUSION

While the data resulting from the current study is important as stand-alone information, it is important to look beyond the data and link it to the findings in the literature. Doing so will provide a substantive base to build a logical argument related to the area of women's entrepreneurship. This chapter looked at the elements of human capital, such as education, pre-business ownership experience, age, membership in organizations, age of the business owner and assistance obtained from family and friends, across the two groups of women entrepreneurs. In addition, correlation coefficient values, which assessed the relationship of the preceding variables with other logical factors were also examined to discern the impact the human capital dimensions had on other relevant areas for the women entrepreneurs. The chapter's analysis ends by looking at different factors behind the reasons for the two groups of women's decision to embrace entrepreneurship.

The results showed that, overall, the white women entrepreneurs occupied a more favorable position when compared to their minority counterparts. The higher educational levels of the former group compared with the latter group have been supported in a previous study by DeCarlo and Lyons (1979), who looked exclusively at women entrepreneurs and by Horton (1988), Bates (1995a) and Boyd (1996), who looked at entrepreneurs overall, without distinguishing by gender. The high educational level of women entrepreneurs overall has been documented in a number of studies (Moore and Buttner, 1997; Loscocco and Robinson, 1991; Loscocco and Smith-Hunter, 2004). However, high educational level does not always transfer into lucrative enterprises for women entrepreneurs (Loscocco and Robinson, 1991; Loscocco et al., 1991). Therefore the women entrepreneurs have not been fairly compensated in the entrepreneurial world for their formal educational levels. Instead, other factors have played a part in their compensation.

In the current study, results on previous work experience showed that, on average, the two groups of women entrepreneurs had at least 'some' experiences in the fields analyzed. The white women entrepreneurs in the current study were more likely to indicate that they had pre-business ownership experiences in all areas, including supervisory, accounting and marketing experiences. Studies on minority women entrepreneurs have shown that they tend to lack relevant pre-entrepreneurial experiences when compared to their counterparts (Fratoe, 1986, 1988; Feagin and Imani, 1994; Bates, 1986). This deficit can be attributed to the lack of mentorship and exposure that minorities experience in the mainstream labor market (Cox, 1994). In addition, minority women are discouraged from participating in key areas when they operate in the mainstream labor market, instead, operating in areas that do not necessarily prepare them for the entrepreneurial world (Tang, 1995; Coughlin and Thomas, 2000).

Overall, most of the women entrepreneurs in this study had 'some' or 'a lot' of pre-business ownership experience. Previous studies have indicated that this self-perception by women entrepreneurs was not shared by others and that such experience does not necessarily translate well into the entrepreneurial world (Smith-Hunter, 2003; Devine, 1994b; Loscocco and Robinson, 1991).

The average age of the business owners and the age of the business for the two groups of women were approximately the same, indicating that both groups had, on average, embraced entrepreneurship after working for a number of years in the mainstream labor market. One could further extrapolate that the women entrepreneurs had tried working in the mainstream labor market, but for whatever reason had chosen to embrace entrepreneurship after approximately 10 years in the mainstream labor market.

White women entrepreneurs were more likely to have previous self-employment experience and more likely to have family members and friends who were business owners. The argument could be made that this link to business ownership allowed the white women entrepreneurs more access to learning about and gaining self-employment experience. Overall, the literature on women entrepreneurs supports the advantageous position of white women entrepreneurs, as well as their overall favorable acquisition of entrepreneurial, self-employment or business ownership experience when compared to their minority counterparts.

The results from this study further pointed out that minority women entrepreneurs were more likely to get assistance from family and friends during the start-up and operation stage of the business and that the assistance they obtained from other sources was more likely of an informal nature such as from churches and community groups, as opposed to their white counterparts, whose assistance came from more formal sources such as membership organizations and banks. Reliance on informal sources of assistance by minority women entrepreneurs might be the result of a lack of resources, thus requiring them to accept assistance from sources that do not require financial commitments.

The minority women entrepreneurs who had more assistance from family had less difficulty obtaining financial capital and/or bank loans. The white women entrepreneurs had less difficulty in obtaining financial capital and or bank loans. This was attributed to their higher educational levels and their higher levels of pre-business ownership experience. In addition, for both groups of women entrepreneurs, age, assistance from other sources and friends who were business owners tended to increase the amount of their start-up capital. An argument could be made that women entrepreneurs waited longer to start their business in order to obtain more start-up capital for their businesses and that the assistance received from others, including friends, allowed the entrepreneurs to increase their start-up capital amounts. In addition, marital status also increased the amount of start-up capital for white women entrepreneurs. This finding is in line with the findings of other studies which show that having a spouse increases the assistance given to women entrepreneurs in the form of financial assistance.

Finally, minority women entrepreneurs with higher educational levels were less likely to be 'survivalist' (Boyd, 1998) entrepreneurs (seeing business as their only alternative), while assistance from others and having a job in the same field as the business were likely to result in women entrepreneurs seeing business as an only alternative. In addition, those with family members who were business owners were less likely to be survivalist entrepreneurs, as were those with more years in business (being a business owner). This can be attributed to the fact that these women entrepreneurs were more likely to have experience in the area of business ownership through family members and were more likely to have planned their entry into entrepreneurship.

6. Network structure issues

INTRODUCTION

The profile of an entrepreneur's network structure has been exalted and vilified as the key component that serves to heighten their human capital potential and to positively impact their entrepreneurial success. Network structure, or social capital as it has been termed in the sociology literature, is often portrayed as the 'hidden hand' (Hogan, 2001) impacting an entrepreneur's access to resources, whether financial or otherwise, and serves as a positive influence in the sphere of business ownership (Easter, 1996; Aldrich et al., 1985; Coughlin and Thomas, 2002). This 'hidden' influence is said to be critical to the entrepreneur's success, since it assists with the development of one's human capital potential and one's access to financial resources, whether directly or indirectly through network links with others.

While a number of factors, namely: family, friends, religious and work affiliations, banks, lending agencies, government agencies, family, friends and associates, are said to provide role models, training experiences, advice, financial support, source of labor, clientele, business advice and possible access to contracts to improve market share (Fratoe, 1986; Molm et al., 2001; Weiss, 1990), it would be an astronomical task to detail all the variables and related factors. A few of these elements have been presented as critical dimensions of an entrepreneur's network structure in the current study, which sought to emphasize a sector of this kaleidoscope of what impacts on an entrepreneur's success. The specific dimensions looked at in this study include: the assistance received from family and friends when starting the business; ongoing assistance received from family, friends and organizations in operating the business; assistance received from other sources during both the start-up and operation of the business; the extent to which the women entrepreneurs have family members and friends who are business owners and the extent to which they have family members and friends providing paid or unpaid assistance in the business; the impact of their marital status on their pre-business ownership experiences; and the number of membership organizations the women entrepreneurs belong to.

Some of the proceeding dimensions have also been emphasized as part of the human capital dimensions. Figures 2.2 and 2.3 serve as a reminder that common elements appear as part of an entrepreneur's human capital potential as well as part of their network structure dimensions. These elements, which are common to both spheres, have also been looked at in this study, including: start-up assistance from family, friends and organizations; assistance from family, friends and organizations during the operation of the business; assistance from other sources during the operation of the business; having family members and friends who are business owners; and having memberships in formal organizations. Network structure results are presented in the following sections, beginning with assistance received from family and friends.

ASSISTANCE RECEIVED

Table 6.1 indicates that minority women entrepreneurs were more likely to have family members assist on a paid/non-paid basis (55.65%) as compared to their white counterparts (40.29%). The same was true when looking at paid/non-paid assistance received from friends (see Table 6.2). Minority women entrepreneurs were more likely to have received this assistance (34.68%) when compared to their white counterparts (28.78%).

A look at the level of assistance received from other sources indicates that white women entrepreneurs were more likely to receive such assistance from

Table 6.1   Family Members Working in Business on a Paid/Non-paid Basis

Response	Minority Women Entrepreneurs	White Women Entrepreneurs	Total
Yes	69 (55.65%)	56 (40.29%)	125 (47.53%)
No	55 (44.35%)	83 (59.71%)	138 (52.47%)
Total	124 (100.00%)	139 (100.00%)	263 (100.00%)

Notes: Chi-Square = 5.394, p = 0.020.

Table 6.2   Friends Working in Business on a Paid/Non-paid Basis

Response	Minority Women Entrepreneurs	White Women Entrepreneurs	Total
Yes	43 (34.68%)	40 (28.78%)	83 (31.56%)
No	81 (65.32%)	99 (71.22%)	180 (68.44%)
Total	124 (100.00%)	139 (100.00%)	263 (100.00%)

Notes: Chi-Square = 1.056, p = 0.304.

other sources at the start-up of the business (see Table 5.13). However, minority women entrepreneurs were more likely to receive assistance from other sources during the operation of their business (23.39% vs. 20.14%) (see Table 5.14). White women entrepreneurs were more likely to relate that their additional assistance came from banks, Certified Public Accountants (CPAs) and lawyers. They were also more likely to cite assistance from consultants, banks, CPAs, lawyers, professional organizations, educational institutions, network organizations and women's organizations. In contrast, the minority women entrepreneurs were more likely to cite assistance received from churches, membership organizations, conferences, workshops, former business owners and partners. An in-depth look at the minority women entrepreneurs showed that Asian women entrepreneurs were the most likely minority group to cite assistance from formal institutions when compared to other minority women. They were followed by Hispanic American, African American, American Indian entrepreneurs, in terms of obtaining assistance from formal institutions.

In the broader literature, family support was often seen by women entrepreneurs to be a contributing factor in their success (Deng et al., 1994). This support could take the form of assistance in the business, whether at the start-up or during the operation of the business, assisting with knowledge regarding managerial, supervisory, entrepreneurial or industrial experience or assisting by allowing the women entrepreneurs to use their family network structures to indirectly access their (family) links.

RELATIONSHIPS FOR NETWORK STRUCTURE DIMENSIONS

An individual's network structure and its encompassing network links have been described as the connection to others that the individual experiences in relation to those in her 'circle' (Moore, 2000a; Coughlin and Thomas, 2002), that is, those individuals and/or organizations that are acquainted with the individual in some form and assist her with connections to elements which the individual is not directly connected to, but can be connected to via their links to those in her network structure (see Figure 6.1). For an entrepreneur or business owner, the individuals and/or organizations that comprise their network structure are said to be made up of family, friends, banks, other business owners, customers and membership organizations. These links assist the entrepreneur or business owner in having indirect access to resources and to others that she herself would not directly have. Alternatively, this can be stated to mean a business owner would have access to person B, based on the business owner's relationship with person A, who knows person B (see Figure 6.1). A network structure and its impending links are said to be important to the start-up and survival of minority-

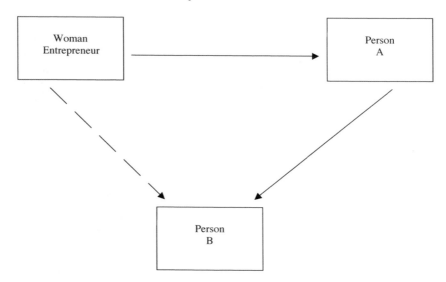

Figure 6.1   Indirect Relationships in Network Structures

owned businesses (Johnson, 1996). While the composition of the network structure of the business owner may change over time, it remains an important feature of the viability efforts of the business (Boyd, 1991; Beech, 1997).

Partners in Business

The relationship between the number of business partners the women had and their difficulty in obtaining financial capital or a bank loan was the first correlation coefficient that was examined. For white women entrepreneurs, the data revealed that there were significant correlation coefficients for both relationships. Table 6.3 displays values which show a value of −0.314 between having partners and the difficulty in obtaining financial capital and −0.193 for the difficulty in obtaining a bank loan. In essence, for white women entrepreneurs an increase in partners results in a decrease in the level of difficulty in obtaining a bank loan or financial capital.

For the minority women entrepreneurs, there was also a correlation coefficient value of −0.156 between the number of partners and the level of difficulty they experienced in trying to obtain financial capital, which was significant. In essence, an increase in partners for minority women entrepreneurs was also likely to result in a decrease in the level of difficulty encountered by minority women entrepreneurs when trying to obtain financial capital. A second correlation coefficient value assessed specifically male business partners. Table 6.4 shows that

Table 6.3   Correlation for Partners in Business and Difficulty in Obtaining Financial Capital/Obtaining Bank Loan

	Correlation Coefficients of Minorities	Correlation Coefficients for Whites
Difficulty in Obtaining Financial Capital	−0.156***	−0.314**
Difficulty in Obtaining a Bank Loan	−0.016	−0.193***

Notes: *** p = 0.10, ** p = 0.05, * p = 0.01.

Table 6.4   Correlation for Male Partners in Business and Difficulty in Obtaining Financial Capital/Obtaining Bank Loan

	Correlation Coefficients of Minorities	Correlation Coefficients for Whites
Difficulty in Obtaining Financial Capital	−0.002	−0.193
Difficulty in Obtaining a Bank Loan	−0.008	−0.322*

Notes: *** p = 0.10, ** p = 0.05, * p = 0.01.

white women entrepreneurs had a significant correlation coefficient value of −0.322 for the relationship between the number of male partners and the difficulty in obtaining a bank loan. This value indicates that for a white woman entrepreneur an increase in male partners was associated with a reduction in the difficulty she would have gaining access to a bank loan.

Difficulty in Obtaining Financial Capital and Bank Loans

Another dimension of network structure dimensions that was considered was in relation to the level of difficulty in obtaining financial capital (see Table 6.5). Specifically, minority women entrepreneurs had five significant relationships, while white women entrepreneurs had three significant relationships, noting that the assistance received from family and friends impacted favorably on the level of difficulty of obtaining financial capital for the women entrepreneurs.

Table 6.5   Correlation Coefficients of Network Structure Dimensions and Difficulty in Obtaining Financial Capital

Network Structure Dimensions	Correlations (Minorities)	Correlations (Whites)
Family Members Working in Business	−0.193**	−0.031
Friends Working in Business	−0.219**	0.049
Start-up Assistance from Family	−0.018	−0.155***
Start-up Assistance from Friends	−0.179***	0.008
Business Assistance from Family	0.039	0.079
Business Assistance from Friends	−0.209**	−0.242*
Assistance from Other Sources	−0.193**	0.064
Family Members Business Owners	0.032	0.022
Friends Business Owners	0.068	−0.051
Membership in Organizations	0.102	−0.210**
Marital Status	−0.152	−0.099

Notes: *** $p = 0.10$, ** $p = 0.05$, * $p = 0.01$.

The results indicated that assistance received from friends, family and other sources decreased the level of difficulty minority women entrepreneurs experienced when trying to access financial capital (correlation coefficient values of −0.179, −0.209, −0.193, −0.219 and −0.193). In a similar vein, assistance received by white women entrepreneurs from family, friends and their membership in organizations favorably impacted their ability to obtain financial capital, showing correlation coefficient values of −0.155, −0.242 and −0.210 respectively.

A look at the relationships between possessing certain network structure dimensions and the difficulty of obtaining a bank loan are presented in Table 6.6. There was one significant correlation coefficient value that was not shared by the two groups of entrepreneurs. The results indicated that minority women entrepreneurs who received assistance from friends had less difficulty obtaining a bank loan (correlation coefficient value = −0.239). One study to look at the issue of bank loans and women entrepreneurs assessed the proportions of bank loan officers and the characteristics they attributed to successful women entrepreneurs (Buttner and Rosen, 1988). The study looked at psychological characteristics such as need for achievement and not demographic or human capital characteristics as was done in this study.

A comparative look at Italian and American women entrepreneurs and their particular network structures when compared to their male counterparts yielded interesting results (Aldrich et al., 1989). The study's samples included active

Table 6.6   Correlation Coefficients of Network Structure Dimensions and Difficulty in Obtaining Bank Loan

Network Structure Dimensions	Correlations (Minorities)	Correlations (Whites)
Family Members Working in Business	−0.017	0.166
Friends Working in Business	−0.086	0.116
Start-up Assistance from Family	−0.122	−0.075
Start-up Assistance from Friends	−0.239*	−0.119
Business Assistance from Family	−0.065	−0.103
Business Assistance from Friends	−0.104	−0.109
Assistance from Other Sources	−0.176	0.110
Family Members Business Owners	0.125	0.046
Friends Business Owners	0.154	0.065
Membership in Organizations	0.082	0.139
Marital Status	0.147	0.154

Notes: *** p = 0.10, ** p = 0.05, * p = 0.01.

women entrepreneurs in the Research Triangle Area in North Carolina for the Americans and women entrepreneurs from Milan for the Italians. The authors concluded that networking activity (in terms of the size of the network structure and time spent) was very similar within each country. The males had almost no women in their network structures, while the women had primarily men in their network structures. The latter findings remained consistent in both countries. In addition, the majority of the samples (both men and women from both countries) had a self-employed parent. Finally, while most in the sample were married, marital status per se did not impact the network structures or the success of the businesses (Aldrich et al., 1989).

In the broader literature review, minority entrepreneurs, especially Blacks, have shown the least amount of assistance from those in their network structures (Fratoe, 1988; Bates, 1989) and are more likely to have individuals from a similar background (both economic and educational) in their networks when compared to their non-minority counterparts. The need for assistance, that can sometimes be lacking for minority women entrepreneurs, by those in their network structures was best expressed by Shirin, a minority woman entrepreneur from New York, who operated an advertising business:

> You definitely need assistance from others. You would be surprised at how much those in your network can help with referring you for instance to someone who can assist you with a business plan, writing a grant to obtain financial assistance or other

issues. It is so much easier if you are able to call someone and have them either assist you themselves or refer you to someone else that can actually help.

Stuart et al. (1999) indicate that, faced with great uncertainty about the quality of young companies, third parties (e.g., banks, financial institutions) rely on the prominence of the affiliates of those companies to make judgments about their quality. When young companies are endorsed by prominent exchange partners, it is expected that they will perform better and be given greater access to financial capital than otherwise comparable ventures that lack prominent associates. The authors also empirically demonstrated that much of the benefit of having prominent affiliates stems from the transfer of status that is an inherent by-product of interorganizational associations (Stuart et al., 1999). Role models have an enduring impact on influencing individuals to embrace entrepreneurship (Krueger et al., 2000; Scherer et al., 1989).

Years in Business

Another relationship that was looked at in terms of the correlation coefficient values was that of network structure dimensions and the number of years in business. Significant relationships were found between start-up assistance received from family and the number of years in business for minority women

Table 6.7   Correlation Coefficients of Network Structure Dimensions and Years in Business

Network Structure Dimensions	Correlations (Minorities)	Correlations (Whites)
Family Members Working in Business	0.031	0.011
Friends Working in Business	0.083	−0.072
Start-up Assistance from Family	0.222*	0.072
Start-up Assistance from Friends	0.028	0.174***
Start-up Assistance from Other Sources	−0.058	0.159***
Business Assistance from Family	0.064	0.090
Business Assistance from Friends	0.037	−0.063
Assistance from Other Sources	0.001	0.037
Family Members Business Owners	−0.011	−0.021
Friends Business Owners	0.005	0.081
Membership in Organizations	−0.052	−0.045
Marital Status	0.042	0.099

Notes: *** p = 0.10, ** p = 0.05, * p = 0.01.

entrepreneurs, with a correlation coefficient value of 0.222. In essence, an increase in the length of time in business for minority women entrepreneurs is correlated with increased assistance received from family members (see Table 6.7).

For the white women entrepreneurs, their longevity in business was correlated significantly with start-up assistance from friends and other sources, with correlation coefficient values of 0.174 and 0.159 respectively. These values indicate that the longer the white women entrepreneurs were in business, the more likely they were to have received start-up assistance from friends and other sources.

Previous Entrepreneurial Experiences

Table 6.8 details the relationship between the entrepreneurs' network structure and their previous entrepreneurial experience. There was a significant correlation coefficient value of 0.180 for the relationship between business assistance from family and their previous entrepreneurial experience for the minorities. This indicates that an increase in family assistance increases one's previous self-employment experience. For the white women entrepreneurs, there were significant correlation coefficient values of 0.245 and 0.196 respectively for the relationship between having friends and family members who are business owners and having previous self-employment experience.

Table 6.8   Correlation Coefficients of Network Structure Dimensions and Previous Self-Employment Experience

Network Structure Dimensions	Correlations (Minorities)	Correlations (Whites)
Family Members Working in Business	0.067	−0.038
Friends Working in Business	0.070	0.113
Start-up Assistance from Family	−0.082	−0.047
Start-up Assistance from Friends	0.044	−0.055
Business Assistance from Family	0.180**	0.030
Business Assistance from Friends	−0.053	0.019
Assistance from Other Sources	0.081	0.083
Family Members Business Owners	0.007	0.245*
Friends Business Owners	0.120	0.196**
Membership in Organizations	0.085	0.017
Marital Status	0.096	0.044

Notes: *** $p = 0.10$, ** $p = 0.05$, * $p = 0.01$.

Some studies have shown that women and men are embedded in different types of network structures. Women tend to include more relatives in their networks (Popielarz, 1999). However, this indulgence is viewed as a disadvantage (ibid.). Another showed that networking was not essential for business survival (Aldrich et al., 1995). A follow-up study by Renzulli et al. (2000) found that an increased number of relatives in one's network structure served as a disadvantage, regardless of the gender of the person. The study advocates an increase in the heterogeneous nature of one's network structure, which is said to benefit one's entrepreneurial position. The positive impact of a heterogeneous network structure is fuelled by the fact that such a composition increases the diversity of the links, which provides an overall improvement in one's network links.

Business as the Only Alternative

When looking at the human capital dimensions and the business owners who saw going into business as their only alternative, a few interesting relationships were found (Table 6.9). For minority women entrepreneurs, being married was less likely to result in them seeing going into business as their only alternative (correlation coefficient value = –0.165). One of the few studies to look at the relationship between marital status and entry into entrepreneurship was undertaken by Taniguchi (2002). The author used the National Longitudinal Survey

Table 6.9   Correlation Coefficients of Network Structure Dimensions and Business Ownership as Only Alternative

Network Structure Dimensions	Correlations (Minorities)	Correlations (Whites)
Family Members Working in Business	0.140	–0.041
Friends Working in Business	0.253*	–0.101
Start-up Assistance from Family	0.052	–0.033
Start-up Assistance from Friends	0.116	0.029
Business Assistance from Family	0.186**	0.054
Business Assistance from Friends	0.104	0.112
Assistance from Other Sources	0.121	–0.017
Family Members Business Owners	–0.049	–0.277*
Friends Business Owners	0.109	–0.119
Membership in Organizations	–0.035	–0.069
Marital Status	–0.165**	–0.134

Notes: *** $p = 0.10$, ** $p = 0.05$, * $p = 0.01$.

of Youth (NLSY79), specifically looking at white, African American and Hispanic American women born during the period from January 1, 1957 to December 31, 1964, to assess the factors that contributed to their entry into self-employment. The author found that for all three groups of women analyzed in the study, marital status was positive and significantly associated with the rate at which they became self-employed – twice as likely when compared to the rates for single women (Taniguchi, 2002).

The correlation results in Table 6.9 also show that obtaining assistance from family and having friends working in the business was more likely to result in the minority women entrepreneurs seeing going into business as their only alternative (correlation coefficient values of 0.186 and 0.253 respectively). As for white women entrepreneurs, having family members who were business owners was less likely to result in white women entrepreneurs seeing going into business as their only alternative (correlation coefficient value = –0.277).

Start-Up Capital

The assessment (see Table 6.10) showed that business and start-up assistance, assistance received from others and having friends who are business owners (significant correlation coefficient values of 0.252, 0.176 and 0.171) also increased the amount of start-up capital for minority women entrepreneurs. The

Table 6.10   Correlation Coefficients of Network Structure Dimensions and Amount of Start-up Capital

Network Structure Dimensions	Correlations (Minorities)	Correlations (Whites)
Family Members Working in Business	0.105	–0.089
Friends Working in Business	0.065	–0.129
Start-Up Assistance from Family	0.117	0.359*
Start-Up Assistance from Friends	0.081	0.162***
Start-Up Assistance from Others	0.252*	0.045
Business Assistance from Family	0.117	0.005
Business Assistance from Friends	0.076	0.172***
Assistance from Other Sources	0.176***	0.057
Family Members Business Owners	0.118	0.142
Friends Business Owners	0.171***	0.220*
Membership in Organizations	0.073	0.111
Marital Status	0.011	0.276*

Notes: *** p = 0.10, ** p = 0.05, * p = 0.01.

factors impacting the increases in start-up capital were slightly different for white women entrepreneurs. Start-up assistance received from family and friends and business assistance from friends (correlation coefficient values of 0.359, 0.162 and 0.172) had a positive impact on their start-up capital. Having friends who are business owners and being married also improved the amount of start-up capital of white women entrepreneurs (correlation coefficient values of 0.220 and 0.276 respectively).

Pre-business Ownership Experiences

The relationship between network structure dimensions and pre-business owner-ship experience for minorities showed seven significant correlation coefficient values (see Table 6.11). Start-up assistance from friends and having pre-business ownership hobby experience showed a positive and significant relationship (0.164), which indicates that having start-up assistance from friends is positively related to obtaining pre-business ownership in the form of a hobby. There were also significant relationships regarding assistance from friends and school edu-cation that was directly related to the business (correlation coefficient value = 0.200) as well as sales/marketing experience (0.174). This indicated that minor-ity women entrepreneurs who received business assistance from friends were more likely to have acquired pre-business ownership experience that was related to school education and sales/marketing experience. Individuals who had family members and friends who were business owners were also more likely to acquire school education directly related to the business (correlation coefficient values of 0.148 and 0.182), while having friends who were business owners had a positive impact on attending seminars/programs related to the business (0.149). For minority women entrepreneurs, school education that was directly related to the business was positively related (correlation coefficient value = 0.189) to obtaining start-up assistance from others.

The white women entrepreneurs (see Table 6.12) had positive correlation coefficient values that were significant in terms of the relationship between membership in organizations and the dimensions related to the pre-business ownership experiences, with corresponding values as follows: for a job in the same field as the business (correlation coefficient value = 0.189), school educa-tion directly related to the business (correlation coefficient value = 0.182), seminars/programs related to the business (correlation coefficient value = 0.292), having a related hobby (correlation coefficient value = 0.254), supervisory ex-perience (correlation coefficient value = 0.303), accounting experience (correlation coefficient value = 0.169) and sales/marketing experience (correla-tion coefficient value = 0.194).

They were also significant correlation coefficient values of 0.160 for white women entrepreneurs who had friends as business owners and had a hobby re-

Table 6.11 Correlation Coefficients of Network Structure Dimensions and Pre-business Ownership Experience (Minorities)

Network Structure Dimensions	Job in Same Field	School Education	Seminars/ Programs	Hobby	Supervisory	Accounting	Sales/ Marketing
Family Members Working in Business	0.069	0.038	0.026	0.010	0.121	0.058	0.026
Friends Working in Business	–0.021	–0.085	–0.090	0.105	–0.024	–0.005	0.100
Start-up Assistance from Family	0.121	0.087	–0.135	–0.018	–0.030	–0.093	–0.008
Start-up Assistance from Friends	0.051	0.067	–0.021	0.164***	0.080	0.047	–0.028
Start-up Assistance from Others	–0.056	0.189**	–0.060	–0.042	–0.029	0.060	–0.001
Business Assistance from Family	–0.086	–0.109	–0.128	0.110	–0.044	–0.122	–0.053
Business Assistance from Friends	–0.074	0.200**	–0.004	0.125	0.098	0.010	0.174**
Assistance from Other Sources	0.053	0.054	0.022	0.025	0.002	- 0.065	–0.020
Family Members Business Owners	0.016	0.148***	0.038	0.106	0.022	0.080	–0.014
Friends Business Owners	0.081	0.182**	0.149***	0.088	0.008	0.068	–0.125
Membership in Organizations	–0.033	–0.117	0.112	0.049	0.091	0.100	–0.039

Notes: *** p = 0.10, ** p = 0.05, * p = 0.01.

Table 6.12   *Correlation Coefficients of Network Structure Dimensions and Pre-business Ownership Experience (Whites)*

Network Structure Dimensions	Job in Same Field	School Education	Seminars/Programs	Hobby	Supervisory	Accounting	Sales/Marketing
Family Members Working in Business	−0.118	−0.102	−0.003	0.046	0.008	0.128	0.112
Friends Working in Business	0.066	0.011	0.092	0.001	0.182***	0.126	0.112
Start-up Assistance from Family	0.062	0.024	0.020	−0.006	−0.219**	−0.313*	−0.144
Start-up Assistance from Friends	0.048	0.017	0.034	−0.001	0.009	−0.034	0.038
Start-up Assistance from Others	0.035	−0.050	0.177***	0.028	0.126	0.089	0.142
Business Assistance from Family	−0.074	−0.110	0.044	0.104	−0.098	−0.020	0.129
Business Assistance From Friends	0.059	−0.037	0.158	0.110	0.109	0.058	0.323*
Assistance From Other Sources	−0.050	−0.110	0.051	−0.031	0.071	−0.032	−0.049
Family Members Business Owners	−0.140	−0.038	−0.002	−0.072	−0.056	0.108	−0.050
Friends Business Owners	0.073	−0.012	0.069	0.160***	0.082	0.019	0.109
Membership in Organizations	0.189**	0.182***	0.292*	0.254*	0.303*	0.169**	0.194**

Notes: *** $p = 0.10$, ** $p = 0.05$, * $p = 0.01$.

116

lated to the business. This indicates that those with friends who are business owners were also more likely to have a hobby in the related field (correlation coefficient value = 0.160). Start-up assistance from family was also negatively but significantly related to the white women entrepreneurs' supervisory (correlation coefficient value = –0.219) and accounting experience (correlation coefficient value = –0.313). This indicated that the entrepreneurs who received assistance from family were also less likely to have supervisory and accounting experience. Finally, having supervisory experience was more likely to result in the white women entrepreneurs having friends working in their business (correlation coefficient value = 0.182). The importance of pre-business ownership and other experiences was expressed by both groups of women entrepreneurs and captured in and supported by the following statements. The first is from Hazel, an African-American who owns a photo-finishing firm in Richardson, Texas and the second is from Sharon, who owns a retail store in New York city, New York:

> I realize that I need more marketing and management skills, something I never gave much thought to before I started in this business. You have to market yourself and you have to market your services in a way that appeals to different types of customers. You are also now responsible for hiring and keeping good employees and that's not always easy.

> You definitely need to do a lot of research before opening a business. Owning and operating a business requires a lot of passion. Once you start the business, you eat, live and breathe your business. You need experience, a good source of financial assistance and a good education.

A study undertaken to document the outcomes of entrepreneurship training given to 50 women entrepreneurs involved in a micro-enterprise program indicated that increased training – especially in regard to management and business-related skills – was critical in improving women's entrepreneurial financial position (Dumas, 2001). Correlation coefficient values in a study of 220 Israeli women business owners showed that marketing, financial and previous experience in the industry and previous entrepreneurial experience had positive and significant relationships with strategic planning of the business owners and thus indirectly impacted business performance (Lerner and Almor, 2002). The authors also found that most of the sample had parents who were business owners. This argument can be extended and related to the current study, which documented (see Table 6.8) that women entrepreneurs with family members and friends as business owners were also more likely to display pre-business ownership experiences.

An extensive theoretical review of the research related to gender and entrepreneurship conducted by Fischer et al. (1993) found that while women entrepreneurs were relatively highly educated (when compared to their male and mainstream labor market counterparts), they were significantly lacking in managerial and related experience in their field (Fischer et al., 1993). These deficiencies were apparently responsible in part for their less negative position in terms of financial success when compared to other entrepreneurial sectors (ibid.). These results were supported in a study by Barrett (1996), who confirmed that one of the deficiencies of entrepreneurship for women business owners was the lack of appropriate business skills. The current study's findings demonstrated that women entrepreneurs who have acquired experience, knowledge and skills through family, friends and affiliations are in a better position as entrepreneurs.

Hisrich and Brush (1986) suggested that to improve and successfully manage their businesses, minority entrepreneurs should acquire financial and marketing experience, attend relevant seminars and establish an appropriate network structure. Another study contended that minorities were more likely to have segregated network structures, less likely to have high corporate positions, or amass a great amount of wealth, compared to their white counterparts (Tang, 1995). Thus, it would be more difficult and take minorities longer to expand their network links, making them less competitive in the self-employment sector. Though women were analyzed as part of the overall sample, the results were not primarily broken down by gender.

Marital Status

The current study found no significant relationship with pre-business ownership experiences and marital status (see Table 6.13). Marital status as a stand-alone issue has seen mixed results in the literature. Robinson and Sexton (1994) and Connelly (1992) found highly significant positive effects for the presence of a husband on a woman entrepreneur's economic success. In contrast, Caputo and Dolinsky (1998) found no impact per se on the women entrepreneurs' choice to pursue entrepreneurship. However, the authors found that a husband's higher earnings and an increase in a husband's business knowledge and skills did increase the likelihood of the women becoming entrepreneurs. The most important determinant for women's pursuance of entrepreneurship was having a husband who was also engaged in an entrepreneurial venture (Caputo and Dolinsky, 1998).

A comparative look at Italian and American women entrepreneurs and their particular network structures as compared to each of their male counterparts yielded interesting results (Aldrich et al., 1989). The study's samples included active women entrepreneurs in the Research Triangle Area and North Carolina for the Americans and women entrepreneurs from Milan for the Italians. The authors concluded that networking activity (in terms of the size and time spent) was very similar within each country. The males had almost no women in their

Table 6.13   Correlation Coefficients for Marital Status and Pre-business Ownership Experiences

Pre-business Ownership Experiences	Correlation Coefficients of Marital Status for Minority Women Entrepreneurs	Correlation Coefficients of Marital Status for White Women Entrepreneurs
Previous Self-employment	0.096	0.044
Job in the Same Field	−0.019	0.016
School Education	−0.090	−0.026
Seminars, Programs	−0.018	0.013
Hobby/Personal Experiences	−0.038	−0.071
Supervisory Experiences	−0.046	−0.089
Accounting Experiences	−0.081	−0.014
Sales/Marketing Experiences	0.010	−0.064

Notes: *** $p = 0.10$, ** $p = 0.05$, * $p = 0.01$.

network structures, while the women had primarily women in their network structures. The latter findings remained consistent regardless of the country. In addition, the majority of the sample (both men and women from both countries) had a self-employed parent. Finally, while most of the sample were married, marital status per se had no impact on their network structures and ultimately their businesses' success.

CONCLUSION

This chapter has described how the two groups of women entrepreneurs used their network structure to their advantage, as a survival strategy for their business. In addition to looking at assistance from family and friends and other sources during the start-up and operational stages of the business, the chapter detailed the relationships between the women's network structures and the difficulty in obtaining financial capital and bank loans. Additional analyses on the relationships between the network structure dimensions and previous self-employment experiences, amount of start-up capital and pre-business ownership experience were also detailed.

Minority women entrepreneurs were more likely to report receiving work assistance from family and friends when compared to their white counterparts. While such support has been cited in other studies as a contributing factor in women entrepreneurs' success, one could argue that using family and friends as employees results from a lack of resources to pay 'regular' employees the required salaries (and benefits, etc.). For instance, it might be feasible to pay family members and friends less than going salary rates or use a sort of barter system to reciprocate for the assistance the women entrepreneurs receive in the business, while non-family members of staff would require salary payments.

Both groups of women entrepreneurs benefited from having assistance from family members and others in relation to the difficulty in obtaining financial capital. The results from the current study show an increase or decrease in one segment of the relationship having an opposite directional change in the other variable. In essence, an increase in assistance from friends, family members and others decreased the level of difficulty women entrepreneurs had in obtaining financial capital. A more in-depth look at the impact of obtaining a bank loan demonstrated that only minority women entrepreneurs showed a significant relationship in that area, with assistance from friends favorably impacting on the level of difficulty.

While there have been mixed results on the importance of network structures to women's entrepreneurial success, a study by Renzulli et al. (2000) showed that more kin in one's network structure was disadvantageous. It cannot be denied that having constructive assistance from others (including family, friends, acquaintances and organizational affiliations) can provide women entrepreneurs with much needed, but often lacking support. Findings that network structures are always beneficial have been refuted in other studies (Bates, 1994). For example, in a study of Korean, African American and non-minority-owned firms, Bates (1994) found that social resources available from peer and community support networks may have little impact on small business viability.

The relationships between network structure dimensions and years in business were significant for both groups, in particular the assistance received from friends for Whites and the assistance received from family for minorities. Years in business has been advanced in previous studies as a measure of success (Bowser, 1972; Moore and Buttner, 1997). One could therefore make the argument that such assistance has improved the success of entrepreneurial ventures for women. There were also significant relationships between network structure dimensions and previous self-employment experience for each group of women entrepreneurs. For minorities, it was assistance from family that was significant, while, for Whites, it was having family members and friends who were business owners. For the latter group, the results reconfirmed that having family members and friends as business owners has a positive impact on the entrepreneurial concern. In this case, it was in the form of acquiring pre-business ownership experience, which in turn was seen as an important feature of future entrepreneurial success. The women entrepreneurs' start-up capital had a positive influence for white women entrepreneurs in the form of friends (as business owners) and in overall assistance. And for minority women entrepreneurs, assistance was received from other sources.

The concept and actions of migration network theory can be applied to build substantial and sustainable network structures for minority and women entrepreneurs (Light et al., 1999). Migration network theory posits that networks makes it easier for immigrants to find jobs, housing, protection and companionship in the host country after leaving their home country (Light et al., 1999). Entrepreneurs must have an apex of formal and informal network structures to aid their start-up, development and continuous operation (Mason-Draffen, 2001). The author specifies that such structures should consist of knowledgeable and dependable people. While this study specifically focuses on black women entrepreneurs, the recommendations can be extended to include other minority entrepreneurs, as well as women entrepreneurs generally.

Major underlying network themes emerge from the present analysis. It is obvious that assistance received from family members, friends and membership organizations is important to the development of women's pre-business ownership experiences for both groups of women. For minority women entrepreneurs, assistance from family and friends was particularly important, while for white women entrepreneurs, membership in organizations surfaced as being important to their level of pre-business ownership experience and thus success.

7. Financial capital issues

Issues of financial capital and access to this entity are said to be extremely important for entrepreneurs, regardless of the size of the business or the type of industry in which the business operates (Nelton, 1997). It is essential to the long-term success of any business (Inman, 2000). Based on the recent coverage in the literature, there is no doubt that having access to financial capital, whether through loans, revolving credit, lines of credit or overdraft accounts, is a major concern for women entrepreneurs. A number of studies have indicated that women entrepreneurs are more likely than their male counterparts to experience this difficulty (Moore and Buttner, 1997; Nelton, 1997; Coughlin and Thomas, 2002). Studies have also shown that minority women entrepreneurs experience the same difficulty (Smith-Hunter, 2003; Inman, 2000).

FINANCIAL CAPITAL DIFFICULTIES

In looking at financial capital difficulties experienced by the women entrepreneurs when starting their businesses, a number of statistical analyses were used. This chapter begins with a look at the percentages, regarding source of funds, followed by an analysis that looks at the difficulty in obtaining financial capital and measures of success. The chapter ends with the results for the relationships between the measures of financial success and other pertinent variables, which provides an overall picture of the position of white and minority women entrepreneurs in this study.

Table 7.1   Difficulty Obtaining Financial Capital: Start-up Stage

Response	Minority Women Entrepreneurs	White Women Entrepreneurs	Total
Yes	76 (61.29%)	59 (42.45%)	**135 (51.33%)**
No	48 (38.71%)	80 (57.55%)	**128 (48.67%)**
Total	**124 (100.00%)**	**139 (100.00%)**	**263 (100.00%)**

Notes: Chi-Square = 7.000, p = 0.008.

At first glance, the straight percentages displayed results that showed that minority women entrepreneurs were more likely to face difficulties (see Table 7.1) when compared to their white counterparts at a rate of 61.29% versus 42.45%. The application of a chi-square test gave a value of 7.00, which had a p value of 0.008, indicating significance.

SOURCE OF START-UP FUNDS

In looking at the source of start-up funds for the women entrepreneurs, eight options were given. The question related to this issue sought to discover whether the start-up funds were from any of the following sources as well as what percentage was from each source: personal savings, gift from family, loan from family or friends, loan from previous owner of the business, credit card or personal loans, bank loans, money from business partners or other sources (see Table 7.2). The minority women entrepreneurs were more likely to use personal savings as their source of start-up funds when compared to their white counterparts (83.87% versus 74.10%). However, both groups of women relied heavily on personal savings as a source of start-up funding.

Table 7.2   Source of Start-up Funds

Source of Funds	Minority Women Entrepreneurs	White Women Entrepreneurs
Personal Savings	104 (83.87%)	103 (74.10%)
Gift from Family/Friends	8 (6.45%)	13 (9.35%)
Loan from Family/Friends	10 (8.06%)	24 (17.27%)
Loan from Previous Owner	2 (1.61%)	4 (2.88%)
Credit Card/ Personal Loan	31 (25.00%)	22 (15.83%)
Bank Loan	5 (4.03%)	15 (10.79%)
Money from Partners	6 (4.84%)	8 (5.76%)
Other	19 (15.32%)	11 (7.91%)

The use of personal loans or credit cards was the second most used source of start-up funding, particularly by minority women entrepreneurs (25.00% for minorities versus 15.83% for Whites). The six other main sources of funding were not heavily used by the women entrepreneurs, for example, gift from family or friends was reported by only 9.35% of the white women entrepreneurs in this study. The percentage of gifts from family and friends was even lower for minority women entrepreneurs (6.45%). Loans from family and friends fared slightly better as a funding source, being twice as likely for white women entrepreneurs (17.27%) as compared to minority women entrepreneurs (8.06%). Very few women entrepreneurs were able to obtain loans from the previous business owner. The white women entrepreneurs, however, were more likely to do so when compared to their minority counterparts (2.88% versus 1.61%). In addition, white women entrepreneurs were twice as likely as their minority counterparts to receive bank loans as a source of start-up funds (10.79% versus 4.03%). Also, the chance of receiving money from partners was higher for the white women entrepreneurs as compared to the minority women (5.76% versus 4.84%). However, this source of funds still represented a smaller portion of the types of funds accessed when compared to other sources, such as credit card/ personal loan and especially savings.

Other sources of start-up funds, accessed by 15.32% of the minority and 7.91% of the white women entrepreneurs, included sources such as loans from other financial institutions or from informal sources that are not partners, family and friends. An in-depth analysis showed that most of the women entrepreneurs – whether white or minority – used 100% of personal savings as their source of start-up funds. As for gifts from family and friends, more detailed analysis showed that most of the women entrepreneurs who used this source obtained less than 50% of their funds from this source. The same statement could be repeated for loans from family and friends, while the opposite statement would apply when discussing loans from the previous owner of the business. In the latter case, very few of the women entrepreneurs who accessed this source of income obtained most of their funding from this source.

Further analysis showed that women entrepreneurs who used credit cards or personal loans tended to limit the funds to 50% or less of the start-up costs. On the other hand, women entrepreneurs who accessed bank loans for additional funding used them for 50% or more of their start-up funds. For the women entrepreneurs who accessed the last category – money received from partners – 50% or less of their funds came from this source.

Two other studies to look specifically at the source of start-up funds for women entrepreneurs were by Burr and Strickland (1992) and Coleman (2000). A sample of women entrepreneurs in Wisconsin was analyzed to assess the source of their start-up funds (Burr and Strickland, 1992). The results showed that 68% used personal savings, 46% received funding from commercial bank financing, followed by 41% from family, friends and relatives, 10% from leasing companies and 8% from the Small Business Administration and 3% from private equity investors. Similar to the current study, respondents in this study could be identified by more than one source of funding in the questionnaire. The study results also reported that most of the women faced unfavorable loan and/or financial terms for the money received from the financial institutions (Burr and Strickland, 1992).

Coleman (2000) used data from the Federal Reserve Board and the United States Small Business Administration to assess the issues surrounding start-up and operational financial capital for male and female business owners. The author found that women-owned businesses were less likely to use external funding for the start-up and operation of their businesses and that they were more likely to rely on their personal funds. The author contends that lenders (banks and financial institutions) did not discriminate against the women business owners because of their gender, but rather because of firm size and age, and that holding such factors constant resulted in males and females having the same access to external credit. The difficulty women entrepreneurs faced in obtaining start-up capital was expressed by Carrie, a white woman entrepreneur operating a tax preparation service business in Georgia:

> I found that there were resources out there for women to obtain finances for start-up funding, but finding out where they were took a lot of work. When I finally got to the sources, what I needed to obtain the financial resources and how much financial resources I could actually get was almost not worth the effort. You would think that with all the talk about how important women business owners are to the economy, more would be done to help us.

DIFFICULTY OF OBTAINING FINANCIAL CAPITAL AND BANK LOAN: START-UP STAGE

In assessing the level of difficulty in obtaining bank loans, the results for the two group of women entrepreneurs showed great disparity (see Table 7.3). White women entrepreneurs were more likely to express having no level of difficulty – this at approximately two and a half times the rate (46.76%) expressed by minority women entrepreneurs (19.35%). This trend continued with white women entrepreneurs also less likely to have found it somewhat difficult when compared to their minority counterparts (17.99% versus 20.97%) and being

Table 7.3   Difficulty Obtaining Bank Loan: Start-up Stage

Response	Minority Women Entrepreneurs	White Women Entrepreneurs	Total
Not Difficult at All	24 (19.35%)	65 (46.76%)	**89 (33.84%)**
Somewhat Difficult	26 (20.97%)	25 (17.99%)	**51 (19.39%)**
Very Difficult	74 (59.68%)	49 (35.25%)	**123 (46.77%)**
Total	**124 (100.00%)**	**139 (100.00%)**	**263 (100.00%)**

Notes: Chi-Square = 18.505, p = 0.000.

much less likely to find it very difficult to obtain a bank loan (35.25% versus 59.65%) when compared to their minority counterparts. The results or level of difficulty of obtaining a bank loan for the two groups show a chi-square value of 18.505, which was significant at a p value of 0.000.

The majority results for each group of women entrepreneurs expressing financial capital and bank loan difficulties is congruent with a study done by Fabowale et al. (1995), who looked at the terms and treatment of male and female business owners when applying for financial credit. In looking at whether the terms of bank credit differ between men and women business owners, Fabowale et al. (1995) found surprising results. The authors found that while male and female business owners differed in systematic ways regarding the characteristics of the business owners and their businesses, after taking those differences into account, no differences in credit persisted. The study's conclusions went on to state that the women felt they were treated disrespectfully by bank loan officers, in the process of applying for their loans, which might account for their perceived unfair treatment.

Although financing and access to financing is frequently noted as a major problem, only a few authors (Fabowale et al., 1995) have looked directly at the possible causes of such problems. In response to previous research that subjectively viewed perceptions of bankers towards women business owners, Riding and Swift (1990) looked empirically at the terms of credit women business owners received from such institutions. The data were taken from an original study done through the Canadian Federation of Independent Businesses, where 153 women business owners were asked to complete a questionnaire. On the surface, the results indicated that the women entrepreneurs faced unfavorable terms of credit (Brush and Hisrich, 1991). However, a more in-depth look illuminated the underlying reasons. They included female business owners who operated smaller and newer firms in less profitable industries, with lower sales growth (Riding and Swift, 1990). Thus, the perception of women business owners as being discriminated against was ratified by more objective findings (ibid.). The perspective of this stance does not preclude the finding in this study and others that women entrepreneurs continue to perceive that they are being treated unfairly when they attempt to apply for formal sources of financial resources.

In another study by Bates (1991), the author found that black-owned firms received smaller loan amounts than white-owned firms possessing identical measure characteristics (such as educational levels, work experiences, equity capital). The author attributes the inequity to discriminatory practices by the financial institutions. Lack of available capital, especially from financial institutions and a lack of technical assistance were seen as the primary reason for the difficulties black-owned businesses faced (Wilson and Martin, 1982).

Loscocco et al. (1991) concluded that small firm size, lack of experience and concentration in the least profitable industries were the major reasons for women business owners' disadvantaged position in obtaining credit and government contacts and not the discriminatory practices that are often alleged. The lack of access to external capital has been reported by female business owners as a major problem, resulting in slow and sporadic growth of their businesses (Orser et al., 2000). One key study showed that black women entrepreneurs were entering and remaining in the entrepreneurial sector at lower rates when compared to their white counterparts (Sullivan and McCracken, 1988) and that a primary factor contributing to this overall lowered status was a lack of access to financial capital. However, other factors leading to financial success included employment of a business consultant and a business plan (Orser et al., 2000).

Buttner and Rosen (1988) studied 106 bank loan officers, who evaluated their perceptions of the characteristics of what created a successful woman entrepreneur. The results confirmed the hypothesis that the characteristics attributed to successful entrepreneurs were more commonly ascribed to men than to women. These results were confirmed in a follow-up study by the same authors (Buttner and Rosen, 1989) and by Sexton and Bowman-Upton in 1990 and Buttner and Rosen in 1992.

A number of other factors have been advanced for women business owners' reduced access to credit. First, adverse discrimination may result in women being unfairly denied credit or discouraged from applying (Brophy, 1989; Brush, 1992; Neider, 1987; Riding and Swift, 1990; Scherr et al., 1993). Second, women are more risk averse than men and thus less likely to take on debt (Brown and Segal, 1989; Chaganti, 1986; Collerette and Aubry, 1990; Olsen and Currie, 1992; Scherr et al., 1993). Third, women business owners use less debt because they don't need it, based primarily on the size of their business ventures and their conservative view of business expansion (Chaganti, 1986; Kallenberg and Leicht, 1991).

AMOUNT OF START-UP CAPITAL

The figures for the approximate start-up dollar amount at the inception of the business (see Table 7.4) showed that for each group of women entrepreneurs, there were women entrepreneurs that started with $0 – eight women for the white women entrepreneurs and 14 for the minority women entrepreneurs. The average start-up costs for the minority women entrepreneurs was $25,204, who had start-up costs ranging from $0 to $500,000. In contrast, the average start-up costs for the white women entrepreneurs was $122,961, which was almost five times the rate of their counterparts, with white women entrepreneurs having start-up costs ranging from $0 to $10,000,000.

Table 7.4   Amount of Start-up Capital

Amount of Funds ($)	Minority Women Entrepreneurs	White Women Entrepreneurs	Total
< $1, 000	27 (21.77%)	37 (26.62%)	**64 (24.33%)**
$1,001–$50,000	86 (69.35%)	86 (61.87%)	**172 (65.40%)**
$50,001–$100,000	5 (4.03%)	10 (7.19%)	**15 (5.70%)**
$100,001–$1 mil	6 (4.84%)	4 (2.88%)	**10 (3.80%)**
$1 mil–$10 mil	0 (0.00%)	2 (1.44%)	**2 (0.76%)**
Total	**124 (100.00%)**	**139 (100.00%)**	**263 (100.00%)**
Average	**$25,204**	**$122,961**	

MEASURES OF FINANCIAL SUCCESS

Three measures of financial success were applied in this study – sales/total revenue, net profit and personal income. Sales/total revenue values ranged from $0 to $10,000,000 for the minority women entrepreneurs and from $0 to $14,000,000 for the white women entrepreneurs. Average sales/total revenue figures (see Table 7.5) showed average figures at twice the rate for the white women entrepreneurs ($688,250) when compared to their minority counterparts ($313,501).

The overall results for net profits or net revenues (see Table 7.6) showed a range from –$20,000 (for a minority woman entrepreneur) to a high of $1,150,000 (for a white woman entrepreneur). The average for the net profit or net revenue figures for the white women entrepreneurs was also twice the rate ($87,088) of the minority women entrepreneurs ($44,689). Personal income (see Table 7.7), the final measure of economic success, had values ranging from $0 (for a minority woman entrepreneur) to $800,000 (for a white woman entrepreneur). Average values for the two groups were as follows: white women entrepreneurs at $69,440 and minority women entrepreneurs at $38,642.

Women business owners occupy a marginalized position when compared to male business owners and minority women entrepreneurs occupy an even more marginalized position when compared to their white counterparts in terms of income earned as business owners (Goffee and Scase, 1983a). A few studies that go against the norm show that black-owned firms in suburban areas have enjoyed more lucrative returns when compared to their urban-located counterparts (Cummings, 1999; Robinson-Jacobs, 2002). These findings run counter to the conclusions of Grogan (2000), Reilly (2001), Boston and Ross (1996), Villimez and Beggs (1984) and Bates and Osborne (1979) in articles that show

Table 7.5   Sales Revenue from Businesses

Amount of Funds ($)	Minority Women Entrepreneurs	White Women Entrepreneurs	Total
< $10, 000	18 (14.52%)	19 (13.67%)	**37 (14.07%)**
$10,001–$100,000	52 (41.94%)	40 (28.78%)	**92 (34.98%)**
$100,001–$1 mil	47 (37.90%)	63 (45.32%)	**110 (41.83%)**
$1,000,001–$10 mil	7 (5.65%)	16 (11.51%)	**23 (8.75%)**
$10,000,001–$14 mil	0 (0.00%)	1 (0.72%)	**1 (0.38%)**
Total	**124 (100.00%)**	**139 (100.00%)**	**263 (100.00%)**
Average	**$313,501**	**$688,250**	

Table 7.6   Net Profit or Revenue of Businesses

Amount of Funds ($)	Minority Women Entrepreneurs	White Women Entrepreneurs	Total
–$20,000–$1, 000	51 (41.13%)	38 (27.34%)	**89 (33.84%)**
$1,001– $50,000	46 (37.10%)	54 (38.85%)	**100 (38.02%)**
$50,001–$100,000	19 (15.32%)	18 (12.95%)	**37 (14.07%)**
$100,001–$1 mil	8 (6.45%)	28 (20.14%)	**36 (13.69%)**
$1 mil–$10 mil	0 (0.00%)	1 (0.72%)	**1 (0.38%)**
Total	**124 (100.00%)**	**139 (100.00%)**	**263 (100.00%)**
Average	**$44,689**	**$87,088**	

Table 7.7   Personal Income of the Business Owners

Amount of Funds ($)	Minority Women Entrepreneurs	White Women Entrepreneurs	Total
$0–$1, 000	28 (22.58%)	24 (17.27%)	**52 (19.77%)**
$1,001–$50,000	64 (51.61%)	64 (46.04%)	**128 (48.67%)**
$50,001–$100,000	22 (17.74%)	25 (17.99%)	**47 (17.87%)**
$100,001–$1 mil	10 (8.06%)	26 (18.71%)	**36 (13.69%)**
Total	**124 (100.00%)**	**139 (100.00%)**	**263 (100.00%)**
Average	**$38,642**	**$69,440**	

that minority business owners consistently experience fewer returns in terms of sales/gross revenue, net profit or personal income, when compared to their white counterparts.

RELATIONSHIPS FOR FINANCIAL CAPITAL DIMENSIONS

The three factors used to assess the women entrepreneurs' financial position, namely sales income, net profit and personal income were evaluated in the context of their relationship with other important dimensions in this study. These dimensions are commonly used to assess a business owner's or entrepreneur's success (Bowser, 1972). The relationships looked at for the current study were the network structure and human capital dimensions as related to the financial capital factors for both groups of women. In addition, factors such as difficulties experienced in securing financial capital, obtaining bank loans and drawing start-up capital were also analyzed as part of the relationships.

Difficulty of Obtaining Financial Capital or Bank Loans

An analysis of the relationship between the difficulty of obtaining financial capital and obtaining bank loans showed significant relationships for both groups of women entrepreneurs. As expected, there were positive relationships between difficulty in obtaining financial capital and the difficulty of obtaining bank loans for both groups of women, showing correlation coefficient values of 0.444 and 0.659 for the white and minority women entrepreneurs respectively (see Table 7.8).

Table 7.8   Correlation Coefficients for Difficulty in Obtaining Financial Capital and Bank Loan

Variables	Correlation Coefficients (Minorities)	Correlation Coefficients (Whites)
Difficulty in Obtaining Financial Capital and Bank Loan	0.659*	0.444*

Notes: *** p = 0.10, ** p = 0.05, * p = 0.01.

Business Location

Table 7.9 shows that there were significant results for the relationship between location of the business and the difficulty of obtaining financial capital or a bank loan for both the white and the minority women entrepreneurs. For the minority women entrepreneurs, there were positive relationships between both measures of difficulty of accessing financial resources and those responding 'yes' to locating their businesses inside their home. The significant correlation coefficient value of 0.215 indicated that the more likely a minority woman entrepreneur was to locate her business inside the home, the more difficulty she would have obtaining financial capital. In the same vein, a significant correlation coefficient value of 0.312 was found between locating the business in the home and the difficulty in obtaining a bank loan for minority women entrepreneurs. For white women entrepreneurs, only one relationship was significant: the difficulty of obtaining a bank loan was positively related to locating the business in the home for this group of women entrepreneurs (correlation coefficient value = 0.206).

Table 7.9   Correlation Coefficients for Business Location (Home/ Commercial Office) and Difficulty in Obtaining Financial Capital/ Obtaining Bank Loan

Variables	Correlation Coefficients (Minorities)	Correlation Coefficients (Whites)
Difficulty in Obtaining Financial Capital	0.215**	0.061
Difficulty in Obtaining a Bank Loan	0.312*	0.206**

Notes: *** $p = 0.10$, ** $p = 0.05$, * $p = 0.01$.

Type of Business

The correlation coefficient values for the relationships between the type of business (sole proprietor, etc.) and the difficulties in obtaining a bank loan or financial capital are displayed in Table 7.10. There was only one significant value and that was for the minority women entrepreneurs and the relationship between a sole proprietor and the difficulty in obtaining financial capital. The relationship had a positive value of 0.250, indicating that being a sole proprietor increased the level of difficulty in obtaining financial capital at the start-up of the business for minority women entrepreneurs.

Table 7.10   Correlation Coefficients for Type of Business and Difficulty in Obtaining Financial Capital/Obtaining Bank Loan

	Correlation Coefficients (Minorities)	Correlation Coefficients (Whites)
Difficulty in Obtaining Financial Capital (Sole Proprietorship)	0.250**	0.003
Difficulty in Obtaining Financial Capital (Partnership/Corporation)	−0.009	−0.046
Difficulty in Obtaining a Bank Loan (Sole Proprietorship)	0.101	0.084
Difficulty in Obtaining a Bank Loan (Partnership/Corporation)	−0.069	−0.089

Notes: *** p = 0.10, ** p = 0.05, * p = 0.01.

Network Structure Dimensions

A look at the relationships between the network structure dimensions and the three measures of financial success showed four significant relationships for white women entrepreneurs (see Table 7.11). Sales income had positive and

Table 7.11   Correlation Coefficients of Network Structure Dimensions and Measures of Income (Whites)

Network Structure Dimensions	**Sales Income**	**Net Profit**	**Personal Income**
Family Members Working in Business	0.110	−0.088	0.035
Friends Working in Business	0.063	0.073	0.052
Start-up Assistance from Family	0.223*	−0.088	−0.012
Start-up Assistance from Friends	0.023	0.034	0.078
Start-up Assistance from Others	0.090	0.087	0.058
Business Assistance from Family	−0.069	−0.070	−0.074
Business Assistance from Friends	0.039	0.059	0.109
Assistance from Other Sources	0.089	0.312*	−0.006
Family Members Business Owners	0.201**	−0.123	−0.123
Friends Business Owners	0.120	0.036	−0.073
Membership in Organizations	0.176**	0.011	−0.020

Notes: *** p = 0.10, ** p = 0.05, * p = 0.01.

significant relationships with the following variables: start-up assistance from family (correlation coefficient value = 0.223), family members who are business owners (correlation coefficient value = 0.201) and membership in organizations (correlation coefficient value = 0.176). The importance of membership organizations and the benefits they offer was explained by Shirley, a white woman entrepreneur from California who operated a beauty salon:

> Don't be afraid to take advantage of those membership organizations, especially after the dues and fees you pay. They can be helpful, but you have to ask the right questions and know what you expect from them or you will be wasting your money. From these organizations you can benefit from the help and knowledge of others in the same field or from others who are potential customers. The potential is there to really gain benefits, but as I said, you have to be aware of the potential assistance they can offer.

The results indicated that obtaining more start-up assistance from family, having more membership in organizations and having more family members who are business owners also increased your sales income/gross revenue. A fourth significant relationship indicated that obtaining more assistance from other sources also increased the net profit amounts of the white women entrepreneurs (correlation coefficient = 0.312).

Six significant relationships were found (see Table 7.12) between the network structure dimensions and the measures of income for minority women entre-

Table 7.12   Correlation Coefficients of Network Structure Dimensions and Measures of Income (Minorities)

Network Structure Dimensions	Sales Income	Net Profit	Personal Income
Family Members Working in Business	−0.037	0.011	0.055
Friends Working in Business	0.069	0.106	0.045
Start-up Assistance from Family	0.001	−0.108	−0.041
Start-up Assistance from Friends	−0.063	−0.002	0.018
Start-up Assistance from Others	0.0460	0.061	0.024
Business Assistance from Family	0.012	−0.078	−0.030
Business Assistance from Friends	0.139	0.160***	0.137
Assistance from Other Sources	0.100	−0.043	0.240*
Family Members Business Owners	−0.083	0.061	−0.014
Friends Business Owners	−0.033	0.158***	0.201*
Membership in Organizations	−0.028	−0.003	0.044
Number of Organizations	0.317*	0.280*	0.165

Notes: *** p = 0.10, ** p = 0.05, * p = 0.01.

preneurs. Business assistance from friends and other sources resulted in correlation coefficient values of 0.160 (for business assistance from friends and net profit) and 0.240 (for business assistance from other sources and personal income) respectively for the minority women entrepreneurs. These relationships indicate that the greater the assistance provided to those entrepreneurs by friends and other sources, the more economically successful they became (income they obtained). Also, having friends who were business owners positively impacted the minority women entrepreneurs' net profit (correlation coefficient value = 0.158) and personal income (correlation coefficient value = 0.201). Finally, having membership in a number of organizations had a positive impact on minority women entrepreneurs' sales income (correlation coefficient value = 0.317) and net profit (correlation coefficient value = 0.280).

Overall factors identified as important to their success by business owners included: personal determination, management, financial and sales/marketing skills, expert advice from others, and the encouragement of family and friends (Humphreys and McClung, 1981). Weiler and Bernasek (2001) contended that women's disadvantaged economic positions in the mainstream labor market and self-employment sectors were caused by gender discrimination in the former and customer and supplier discrimination in the latter. The conclusion was that women in both spheres occupied network structures that were limited in their abilities to help the women advance when compared to their male counterparts who occupied more advantaged positions.

In direct relation to the results from this study, Bates (1985) found that better educated minority entrepreneurs were more likely to effectively utilize their financial and human capital inputs. This utilization would result in higher returns on profits and they would be more likely to operate businesses outside of the retail and service sector. A number of studies have concluded that a high proportion of minorities utilize their network structure, both for business preparation and operation (Kim and Hurh, 1996; Sanders and Nee, 1996; Evans and Leighton, 1989; Fratoe, 1986; House, 2000). Findings that network structures are always beneficial have been refuted in other studies notably Bates (1994), who found that social resources available from peer and community support networks may have little impact on small business viability in a study of Korean, African American and non-minority-owned firms.

Obtaining Financial Capital and Bank Loans

The correlation coefficient value for the relationship between the difficulty in obtaining financial capital and measures of financial success showed one significant relationship which occurred with minority women entrepreneurs and was specifically related to obtaining financial capital and sales income/gross revenue (correlation coefficient value –0.210) (see Table 7.13). This indicates

Table 7.13 *Correlation Coefficients of Measures of Income and Difficulty in Obtaining Financial Capital*

Measures of Income	Correlation Coefficient (Minorities)	Correlation Coefficient (Whites)
Sales/Gross Revenue	−0.210*	−0.010
Net Profit	−0.072	0.088
Personal Income	−0.085	0.093

Notes: *** p = 0.10, ** p = 0.05, * p = 0.01.

Table 7.14 *Correlation Coefficients of Measures of Income and Difficulty in Obtaining Bank Loan*

Measures of Income	Correlation Coefficient (Minorities)	Correlation Coefficient (Whites)
Sales/Gross Revenue	−0.252*	−0.259*
Net Profit	−0.249*	0.045
Personal Income	−0.183**	0.038

Notes: *** p = 0.10, ** p = 0.05, * p = 0.01.

that the more difficulty minority women entrepreneurs had obtaining financial capital, the less success they experienced in sales income/gross revenue.

The results, which detailed the level of difficulty in obtaining bank loans for the women entrepreneurs, indicated that white women entrepreneurs who experienced difficulty in obtaining bank loans achieved lower sales income/gross revenue (correlation coefficient value = −0.259). In the same vein, minority women entrepreneurs who had difficulty obtaining bank loans achieved far less financial success in all three areas (see Table 7.14): with sales income (correlation coefficient value = −0.252), with net profit (correlation coefficient value = −0.249) and with personal income (correlation coefficient value = −0.183).

The finding that lack of access to financial capital and/or bank loans has a negative effect on the financial success of a business is logical and reiterates previous conclusions. Access is critical to financial success, both in the start-up and operational stages of the business. The difficulty of obtaining financial assistance for women entrepreneurs was reiterated by Lorraine, a white woman entrepreneur, who owned a consulting business in Texas:

Owning your own business is often difficult, you are always working and preparing
for the next step relentlessly. Having access to financial resources, whether from a
loan, income or savings, is critical. You have to remember that you no longer have a
steady paycheck from another source but are instead relying on yourself for income.
Getting access to financial resources, for example a bank loan, is very competitive
and you don't always have someone to rely on who can help you with completing
the forms, especially the first time you apply for a loan.

Start-Up Capital

A look at the measures of financial success and their relation to the amount of
start-up capital indicated one significant relationship (see Table 7.15). There
was a significant relationship between the amount of start-up capital and the
amount of net profit (correlation coefficient value = 0.182) for the white women
entrepreneurs. This indicates that the more start-up capital the white women
entrepreneurs had, the more net profit they achieved and vice versa. A related
look at the link between the amount of start-up capital and the difficulty in obtaining financial capital showed a correlation coefficient value of –0.203. This
appears to indicate that the more difficulty one has in obtaining financial capital,
the less start-up capital is available (not shown in any table).

*Table 7.15   Correlation Coefficients of Measures of Income and Amount of
            Start-up Capital*

Measures of Income	Correlation Coefficient (Minorities)	Correlation Coefficient (Whites)
Sales/Gross Revenue	0.015	0.065
Net Profit	0.028	0.182***
Personal Income	0.054	0.027

Notes: *** p = 0.10, ** p = 0.05, * p = 0.01.

Business Location

Table 7.16 depicts the correlation coefficient values for all three measures of
income and business location. The results indicate that all three relationships
were significant, with the correlation coefficient values for business location
and sales income, net profit and personal income at –0.226, –0.199 and –0.267
respectively for the minority women entrepreneurs and –0.287, –0.229 and
–0.329 for the white women entrepreneurs. The results can be interpreted to
mean that those locating their business in the home were less likely to achieve
economic success.

Table 7.16   Correlation Coefficients of Measures of Income and Business Location

Measures of Income	Correlation Coefficient (Minorities)	Correlation Coefficient (Whites)
Sales/Gross Revenue	–0.226*	–0.287*
Net Profit	–0.199*	–0.229*
Personal Income	–0.267*	–0.329*

Notes: *** p = 0.10, ** p = 0.05, * p = 0.01.

Human Capital Dimensions

The final set of tables of correlation coefficient values and measures of income looks at the human capital dimensions of the white and minority women entrepreneurs relating to measures of income (see Tables 7.17 and 7.18). For the minority women entrepreneurs (see Table 7.17), having pre-business ownership experience of a job in the same field as the business was positively related to sales/gross revenue (correlation coefficient vale = 0.171), as was pre-business ownership experience in accounting (correlation coefficient value = 0.170) and higher educational levels (correlation coefficient value = 0.189). Higher educational levels were also positively and significantly correlated with higher net profit levels (correlation coefficient value = 0.223) and personal income (correlation coefficient value = 0.172). The same was true for business assistance from friends (correlation coefficient value = 0.160), having friends who were business owners (correlation coefficient value = 0.158) and having a hobby/personal pre-business ownership experience (correlation coefficient value = 0.210) with higher net profit levels. Assistance from other sources (correlation coefficient value = 0.240), friends who were business owners (correlation coefficient value = 0.201), having pre-business ownership as a hobby (correlation coefficient value = 0.216) and having pre-business ownership experience in supervision (correlation coefficient value = 0.163) were positively and significantly related to personal income.

For white women entrepreneurs, 11 significant correlation coefficient values were noted in terms of the relationships between human capital dimensions and measures of financial success (see Table 7.18). All three measures of success (sales/gross revenue, net profit and personal income) were negatively correlated with years in the business (correlation coefficient values of –0.244, –0.227 and –0.150), indicating that more years in the business negatively impacted financial success for white women entrepreneurs. In addition, previous entrepreneurial experiences in the accounting, supervisory and personal experience areas had

*Table 7.17   Correlation Coefficients of Human Capital Dimensions and
Measures of Income (Minorities)*

Human Capital Dimensions	Sales/Gross Revenue	Net Profit	Personal Income
Years in Business	−0.104	−0.102	−0.059
Previous Self-employment	0.001	0.090	0.096
Educational Levels	0.189**	0.223*	0.172***
Age of Business Owner	−0.064	0.015	0.040
Start-up Assistance from Family	−0.001	−0.108	−0.047
Start-up Assistance from Friends	−0.063	−0.002	0.018
Start-up Assistance from Others	0.046	0.061	0.024
Amount of Start-up Capital	−0.015	−0.028	−0.054
Business Assistance from Family	0.012	−0.078	−0.030
Business Assistance from Friends	0.139	0.160***	0.137
Assistance from Other Sources	−0.100	−0.043	0.240*
Family Members Business Owners	−0.083	0.061	−0.014
Friends Business Owners	−0.033	0.158***	0.201*
Membership in Organizations	−0.028	−0.003	−0.044
Number of Organizations	0.317*	0.280*	0.165
PBOE: Job in Same Field	0.171***	0.154	−0.004
PBOE: School Education	0.088	−0.051	−0.131
PBOE: Seminars/Programs	0.034	0.114	0.054
PBOE: Hobby/Personal Experience	0.129	0.210*	0.216*
PBOE: Supervisory Experience	−0.080	0.069	0.163***
PBOE: Accounting Experience	0.170***	−0.120	0.047
PBOE: Sales/Marketing Experience	−0.052	0.035	0.116

Notes: *** p = 0.10, ** p = 0.05, * p = 0.01.

positive and significant correlation coefficients with various measures of income. Finally, membership in organizations had a positive impact on sales/gross revenue for white women entrepreneurs (correlation coefficient value = 0.176), while larger amounts of start-up capital positively impacted net profit figures for white women entrepreneurs.

A longitudinal study of women entrepreneurship spanned from 1967–84, following some from birth to self-employment, concluding that higher educational levels resulted in more women in the sample embracing entrepreneurship

Table 7.18   Correlation Coefficients of Human Capital Dimensions and Measures of Income (Whites)

Human Capital Dimensions	Sales/Gross Revenue	Net Profit	Personal Income
Years in Business	−0.244*	−0.227*	−0.150***
Previous Self-employment	0.029	0.129	0.084
Educational Levels	0.129	0.126	0.073
Age of Business Owner	0.004	0.033	0.086
Start-up Assistance from Family	−0.123	−0.088	−0.012
Start-up Assistance from Friends	0.023	0.034	0.078
Start-up Assistance from Others	0.090	0.087	0.058
Amount of Start-up Capital	0.065	0.182***	−0.027
Business Assistance from Family	−0.069	−0.070	−0.074
Business Assistance from Friends	0.039	0.059	0.109
Assistance from Other Sources	0.089	0.112	−0.006
Family Members Business Owners	−0.001	−0.123	−0.123
Friends Business Owners	0.120	0.036	−0.073
Membership in Organizations	0.176**	0.011	−0.020
PBOE: Job in Same Field	−0.071	−0.062	−0.165
PBOE: School Education	0.086	0.106	0.089
PBOE: Seminars/Programs	0.080	−0.029	−0.001
PBOE: Hobby/Personal Experience	0.170***	0.174***	0.148***
PBOE: Supervisory Experience	0.121	0.036	0.155***
PBOE: Accounting Experience	0.147***	0.156***	0.123
PBOE: Sales/Marketing Experience	−0.109	0.030	0.008

Notes: *** p = 0.10, ** p = 0.05, * p = 0.01.

(Dolinsky et al., 1993). The overall results indicated that initial entry, continuous stayer and re-entry status increased with increasing levels of educational attainment. Schwartz (1976) conducted a much earlier study on the emerging wave of women entrepreneurs, noting that management and specific industry experience impacted women entrepreneurs in a negative way.

LINKING FINANCIAL RESULTS TO CURRENT LITERATURE

The following sections detail the results from a number of studies that have looked at the factors impacting the financial success of women-owned businesses. The results reinforce the current study's findings, that previous experiences (especially in the field) and assistance from family, friends and others positively impact on the success of businesses owned by women.

Three main barriers to women business owners' success emerged from Loscocco and Robinson's (1991) study. These included a lack of: management skills, access to financial capital and access to government contracts, which were said to be directly related to the carry-over disadvantages attached to the mainstream labor market. These results are tantamount to the current study's findings, showing that previous experiences were appropriate and that there was a relevant and positive impact upon the economic success of the business.

Brush and Hisrich (1991) sampled a nationwide stratum of women entrepreneurs and concluded that higher educational levels and more business experience were positively correlated to the women entrepreneurs' economic success. One could extrapolate and state that economic success impacts and is dependent on easier access to financial capital and bank loans as seen in this study. Hisrich and Brush (1984) previously proposed that educational levels increased success levels for entrepreneurs. The authors indicated that it did so by providing increased knowledge and by helping communication factors.

In 1983, Cuba et al. profiled 58 female owners of small businesses in three eastern metropolitan areas and found three significant factors related to financial success, including: formal education, prior work experience and delegating more routine tasks to employees. The authors' study of female owners of small business indicated that the financially successful were more likely to delegate certain key tasks to employees and, in a direct parallel to the present study, were more educated and more likely to have prior work experience than their less successful counterparts.

Brush and Hisrich (1991) assessed the economic success of 344 women-owned businesses. The authors used discriminant analysis to analyze the data and concluded that women entrepreneurs who had previous industrial experience in their field of venture had a better chance of succeeding. Of lesser significance, yet still important, to the successful establishment of women-owned businesses were other business skills – dealing with people, idea generation and business operations skills. The authors went on to clarify that these characteristics were not particularly gender specific, but that women owners were less likely to possess the skills.

In contrast to the above findings, Collerette and Aubry (1990) used a Canadian sample to study the economic success of women entrepreneurs and determined that previous experience had no impact. While Schwartz (1976) found that the lack of management experience and the industry in which they operated contributed to business failures for women entrepreneurs. A profile of women entering self-employment, undertaken in recent years, shows that those entering self-employment were more likely to be wealthier, have young children, were better educated and that they had more years of work experience than their wage and salary counterparts (Boden and Nucci, 2000). Boden and Nucci (2000) analyzed longitudinal data from the Current Population Survey to arrive at their conclusions.

A theoretical model drawing on resource-based theory was developed and used to test Israeli women entrepreneurs' business performance empirically (Lerner and Almor, 2002). Analysis reveals that business performance is highly correlated with certain aspects of the business owners' skills, as well as their venture resources. The findings suggest that the performance of businesses owned by women depends heavily on marketing, financial and managerial skills, more so than on innovation. The authors conducted multiple regressions for each of the performance variables: sales volume, number of employees and income of the entrepreneur. Sales volume appears to be the most efficient measure of the three, correlating strongly with all items representing the owners' capabilities, which were demonstrated as: skills, resources, planning and previous experience in the field.

In terms of financial success factors impacting on the businesses of minority owners, the results were identical to those of their white counterparts in one study (Model, 1985). The authors first looked at a comparative perspective on blacks, Italians and jews in New York City, finding that previous experience in the field of their entrepreneurial venture increased survival rates for the firms. Other mechanisms utilized by the entrepreneurs to enhance their viability were: a reliance on partners, kin and friends with relevant backgrounds in business (Model, 1985).

Using Census Data, specifically the Characteristics of Business Owners Survey, the Survey of Minority Business Enterprises (SMOBE) and the State and Metropolitan Area Data Book, Christopher (1998) investigated the factors influencing small and minority-owned business ownership and viability. The author confirmed that the positive effects of years of work experience on business survival were lower for minority business owners, when compared to their non-minority counterparts. So too were previous managerial and executive experiences or increases in the impact of commercial bank financing and educational levels on business viability for minority owners (Christopher, 1998). Supervisory experience was also found to be positively related to business survival for all the entrepreneurs in the study (ibid.).

Gimeno et al. (1997) looked at why some firms survived, while others with equal economic performance did not. The authors contend that the entrepreneurs' human capital characteristics, which are said to determine the difference in the threshold, were a key factor impacting their success levels. Education, management experience and supervisory experiences are positively related to the economic performance of entrepreneurship ventures. The sample for this study was taken from the National Federation of Independent Business (NFIB). There is a large measure of agreement that a lack of equity finance represents a major constraint on the formation and development of enterprises (Mason and Harrison, 1995). Human capital (founder's education, career history, family, occupational background) are important to business survival (Bruderl et al., 1992).

Overall, a number of factors have been said to impact the success of women business owners, including: family support, knowledge of culture and language of the business region, communication and human relations skills, knowledge and quality of the product or service (Maysami and Goby, 1999). The authors also identify additional factors, such as: customer loyalty, quality of the business personnel, availability of professional services, technological advantage, availability of finance, presence of opportunities, a desire to succeed and the personal qualities of the business owner as factors contributing to the success of women business owners worldwide.

A study of male versus female home-based business owners found that five variables were significant when explaining the log of gross business income for both the men and the women business owners (Olson, 1997). The two that were positively associated with income were the number of hours worked per year and whether the home-based owner lived in an urban area. There were three variables that were negatively associated with income for both groups: whether the owner had another job, the amount of additional income beyond earnings from the home-based business and the percentage of females in the home-based business. For women, use of a sales representative and hiring help for household chores also significantly increased income. For men, education was an additional significant variable.

CONCLUSION

In this chapter, the factors related to the women entrepreneurs' financial position have been analyzed. Factors such as difficulty in obtaining financial capital, source of start-up funds and measures of economic success (net profits, sales income and personal income) were analyzed for both groups of women. The relationships between financial measures and the human capital or network structure dimensions of the two groups of women entrepreneurs were also analyzed. The minority women entrepreneurs were more likely to experience difficulties in obtaining financial capital, a deficiency that is said to be based on their accumulated wealth or lack thereof throughout their lifetime. They occupy lower positions in the mainstream labor market, which results in lower salaries and less collateralled capital, leaving them less likely to obtain financial assistance (Collerette and Aubry, 1990; Lerner and Almor, 2002).

The findings regarding the source of start-up funds showed that women overwhelmingly depended on their own savings. One reason for this dependence is their lack of ability to access finances from financial institutions. In addition, a lack of belief by others in their dreams has resulted in women entrepreneurs relying on their own savings. In addition, the weaker network structures of women when compared to their male counterparts (Aldrich et al., 1989) indicate that they are less likely to have friends and family who are able to assist in providing the women entrepreneurs with funds, through loans, gifts, etc.

Data from the current study consistently showed that white women entrepreneurs were more financially successful than their minority counterparts – in terms of sales/gross income, net profit and personal income. These results have been previously confirmed in other studies on women entrepreneurs (Smith-Hunter, 2003; Inman, 2000; DeCarlo and Lyons, 1979) and entrepreneurs in general (Boyd, 1996; Bates, 1995a; Christopher, 1998).

Women entrepreneurs who located their business in the home were more likely to have difficulty with financial capital and bank loans, a relationship which is logical and supports the idea that a lack of financial capital is said to result in women entrepreneurs locating their business in the home to take advantage of inexpensive costs and unpaid labor assistance from family members (Priesnitz, 1989; Furry and Lino, 1992; Field-Hendrey, 1990; Loscocco and Smith-Hunter, 2004). The results also showed that minority sole proprietors were more likely to have difficulty with financial capital.

The network structure relationships and measures of success showed that those receiving assistance from family and friends were also more likely to achieve increased financial success. White women entrepreneurs were more likely to receive assistance from formal institutions or organizations, while minority women entrepreneurs were more likely to obtain assistance from informal sources, such as family and friends. These findings are in keeping with reports from others (Inman, 2000; Smith-Hunter, 2003), who detailed that the network structures of minority women entrepreneurs were more likely to have informal forces in their network structures versus their white counterparts who had more assistance from formal sources.

Overall, the findings indicated that having difficulty in obtaining capital resulted in the women entrepreneurs being less successful financially. This occurred more frequently for the minority women entrepreneurs than for their white counterparts. Access to financial capital is said to be the key factor that impacts the entrepreneur's financial success (Ash, 1987; Begley, 1995; Boyd, 1990, Brush et al., 2001). The fact that minority entrepreneurs are often seen as having less access to financial capital compared with their white counterparts helps to explain their financial position (Bates, 1995a; Smith-Hunter and Nolan, 2003). White women entrepreneurs who start with more financial capital also experienced higher measures of financial success, specifically with regard to net profit figures.

The relationships between the human capital dimensions and the measures of economic success showed that those who had more experience and belonged to membership organizations were also more successful. A number of studies have detailed the positive influence of experience on an entrepreneur's success. This experience can take the form of previous entrepreneurial experience, business experience in the industry of the business enterprise and management experience. All of this is said to be critical and has a positive effect on an entrepreneur's measure of economic success.

8. The state of women entrepreneurs in the United States

INTRODUCTION

The last four chapters provided a solid sample of women entrepreneurs across racial lines in the United States. This chapter serves as an important and integral step in completing a composite of the state of women entrepreneurs. It begins by assessing the primary reasons why potential and future women entrepreneurs exit the mainstream labor market. It continues by assessing the statistical place of women entrepreneurs in America, then hones in on women entrepreneurs in certain diverse racial groups, specifically African Americans, Hispanic Americans, Asian Americans and Native Americans. The chapter ends by taking a comprehensive look at financial capital and what results from lack of access. Recently completed government reports reaffirm the need to take a closer look at the implications of access, especially across racial lines. There is thus a need to delve deeper into this important resource, as increasing numbers of new and diverse women entrepreneurs enter this field.

EXIT STRATEGIES FROM THE MAINSTREAM LABOR MARKET

During the last two decades and especially in the last 10 years, several sources have documented the barriers to women's advancement in corporate America and their resulting exit into one of the main alternatives – entrepreneurship (Moore and Buttner, 1997; Coughlin and Thomas, 2002; Catalyst Guide, 1998). The barriers highlighted included: stereotyping and misperceptions about women's abilities and their long-term commitment to business careers; exclusion from informal networks and channels of communication; lack of access to mentors; unwillingness of managers to 'risk' putting women in key developmental assignments; and salary inequities and sexual harassment (Catalyst Guide, 1998).

In an important study conducted by the Catalyst Guide Organization eight years ago, the organization investigated women entrepreneurs who had exited corporate America to start entrepreneurial ventures (Catalyst Guide, 1998). The study found that the main reason most of the women exited corporate America was because of the flexibility offered by owning and operating their own businesses (Catalyst Guide, 1998). The second most common reason for the exit was the glass ceiling effect. The women were also unhappy with the work environment and felt unchallenged in the mainstream labor market (Catalyst Guide, 1998).

The study also found that the women entrepreneurs craved flexibility in their world. This was defined as having the opportunity to fulfill child-care and elder-care obligations; participate in community affairs; personal health concerns and to satisfy their family obligations (Catalyst Guide, 1998). The study noted that women were not necessarily seeking reduced hours, but more flexibility in when they actually worked – a flexibility that they felt was offered by entrepreneurship.

Moore and Buttner (1997) noted this exodus in their book on women entrepreneurs. Like the Catalyst Guide report, Moore and Buttner (1997) did not have a diverse racial sample of women entrepreneurs. However, they found similar results, with five themes emerging as the reasons why women entrepreneurs exit from the mainstream labor market. The themes, in order of importance, are:

- Challenges: comprising items related to the attraction of operating one's own business; respect towards the business owner; the opportunity to be in charge; regaining feelings of excitement about work; and recognition and reward for accomplishments.
- Self-determination: comprising items related to trying to make it on one's own; self-esteem from becoming an entrepreneur; and freedom from bureaucracy.
- Family Concerns: comprising two related items such as balancing family and work; and gaining control of time.
- Blocks to Advancement: comprising items related to discrimination career barriers; and a feeling of not fitting into the corporate culture.
- Organizational Dynamics: comprising items related to organizational obstacles; to getting work accomplished, namely, others failing to share critical information, lack of urgency in completing tasks; demotivating aspects of the organizational climate; and low quality standards.

The preceding factors have previously been described as 'push factors' for leaving the mainstream labor market (Orhan and Scott, 1999). And 'pull factors' attract women to the field of entrepreneurship (ibid.). The Catalyst Guide study found that the top seven 'pull' factors for women entrepreneurs in order of importance are: being one's own boss, setting one's own hours, controlling one's destiny, pleasing customers, having independence and freedom, making decisions and achieving goals (Catalyst Guide, 1998).

A final important study assessing women's entry into entrepreneurship was completed recently by Coughlin and Thomas (2002). The authors looked at women entrepreneurs embracing entrepreneurship in terms of three broad categories of motivation, including economic (need to generate income), social (work–family conflict issues and obligations) and personal (self-fulfillment). Such factors propelling women to be 'pushed' from the corporate world and 'pulled' into the entrepreneurial sphere were echoed in the study which was conducted on women entrepreneurs from diverse racial backgrounds by Inman (2000) and in a study by Orhan and Scott (1999) which did not analyze women entrepreneurs from diverse backgrounds.

THE OVERALL STATUS OF WOMEN ENTREPRENEURS IN THE UNITED STATES

The Center for Women's Business Research provides the most up-to-date information currently available on privately held, 50% or more, women-owned businesses in the United States. The Center's reports give estimates for privately held firms owned 50% or more by a woman or women, and provides the most complete picture of women's business ownership currently available. These data presented in separate fact sheets focus on segments representing the crux of the business ownership data on women entrepreneurs at a national level. The data include privately held firms that are majority (51% or more) owned by women, and firms equally (50-50) owned by women and men.

The United States Census Bureau is currently working to update data for the Characteristics of Women Business Owners Survey, which is slated for publication in 2005. The Center for Women's Business Research works directly with the United States Census Bureau. The data that is bulleted below is taken from the Center for Women's Report (The Center, 2004a). Analyzing data provided by the US Bureau of the Census, the Center projects the following statistical portrait of privately held, 50% or more women-owned businesses in 2004:

- As of 2004, there were an estimated 10.6 million privately held, 50% or more women-owned firms in the US, accounting for nearly half (47.7%) of all privately held firms in the country (see Table 8.1). Both women-owned and all US privately held firms with paid employees and firms without paid employees are included. These exclude publicly held, foreign-owned and non-profit businesses.
- Privately held, 50% or more women-owned firms in the US generate $2.46 trillion in sales and employ 19.1 million people nationwide.
- Of the 10.6 million privately held, 50% or more women-owned firms, 2.4 million are employer firms. Both women-owned employer firms and US

Table 8.1   *Privately-held 50% or More Women-owned Firms in the United*
               States

Total US	1997	2004	% Change 1997–2004	Share of All Privately Held Firms, 2004
Total				
Number of Firms	9,058,297	10,630,045	17.4	47.7
Number of Employer Firms	1,876,249	2,403,201	28.1	43.8
Employment	15,360,618	19,083,277	24.2	29.0
Sales ($000)	1,762,549,668	2,455,137,953	39.3	21.9
Agriculture Services				
Number of Firms	173,410	215,477	24.3	39.8
Number of Employer Firms	41,310	60,410	46.2	
Employment	201,869	284,858	41.1	
Sales ($000)	17,814,352	27,961,224	57.0	
Mining				
Number of Firms	50,460	33,297	−34.0	40.8
Number of Employer Firms	6,013	5,456	−9.3	
Employment	54,272	49,654	−8.5	
Sales ($000)	11,622,661	11,015,071	−5.2	
Construction				
Number of Firms	502,334	652,807	30.0	23.9
Number of Employer Firms	217,066	274,389	26.4	
Employment	1,364,005	1,960,818	43.8	
Sales ($000)	184,928,608	317,305,911	71.6	
Manufacturing				
Number of Firms	259,577	261,904	0.9	39.9
Number of Employer Firms	101,167	121,480	20.1	
Employment	1,768,773	1,815,398	2.6	
Sales ($000)	215,579,338	247,755,668	14.9	
TCPU				
Number of Firms	315,202	403,926	28.1	36.7
Number of Employer Firms	86,079	119,022	38.3	
Employment	703,374	774,842	10.2	
Sales ($000)	75,215,136	101,917,696	35.5	

Table 8.1   concluded

Total US	1997	2004	% Change 1997–2004	Share of All Privately Held Firms, 2004
Wholesale Trade				
Number of Firms	286,762	298,721	4.2	37.1
Number of Employer Firms	124,328	165,620	33.2	
Employment	1,024,050	1,235,999	20.7	
Sales ($000)	375, 364, 771	532,295,342	41.8	
Retail Trade				
Number of Firms	1,656,442	1,781,172	7.5	61.2
Number of Employer Firms	508,367	601,441	18.3	
Employment	4,382,764	5,298,332	20.9	
Sales ($000)	404,786,694	550,212,226	35.9	
FIRE				
Number of Firms	859,071	966,662	12.5	46.4
Number of Employer Firms	133,823	186,421	39.3	
Employment	553,780	482,100	−12.9	
Sales ($000)	111,777,783	135,721,176	21.4	
Services				
Number of Firms	4,300,205	4,876,991	13.4	53.1
Number of Employer Firms	657,045	901,431	37.2	
Employment	5,301,716	7,409,732	39.8	
Sales ($000)	345,979,206	524,813,153	51.7	
Industries Not Classified				
Number of Firms	660,646	1,351,756	104.6	51.8
Services				
Number of Employer Firms	7,033	893	−87.3	
Employment	6,015	977	−83.8	
Sales ($000)	19,481,119	36,730,407	88.5	

Source: The Center for Women's Business Research (2004a).

privately held employer firms include only those firms with paid employees. These exclude publicly held, foreign-owned and non-profit businesses.

- The 10.6 million privately held, 50% or more women-owned firms are comprised of 6.7 million privately held, majority (51% or more) women-owned firms and 4.0 million privately held, equally (50-50) women and men-owned firms. Differences between the total and sum of the two segments are due to rounding. These two segments account for 29.9% and 17.8% of all privately held firms in the country.
- Of the 10.6 million privately held, 50% or more women-owned firms, 62.6% are majority (51% or more) women-owned firms and 37.4% are equally (50-50) women- and men-owned firms.
- Between 1997 and 2004, the growth in the number of 50% or more women-owned firms is nearly twice the rate of all firms (17.4% vs. 9.0%). Employment grew at more than twice the rate (24.2% vs. 11.6%), and revenues increased at a similar rate (39.3% vs. 33.5%). The 1997 data include C corporations that are not publicly traded; therefore, the 2004 estimates also include these firms.
- The Center estimates that the number of privately held, 50% or more women-owned employer firms grew by 28.1% from 1997 to 2004 – three times the growth rate of all US privately held employer firms (9.1%).
- The percentage of privately held, 50% or more women-owned firms and all US firms with employees is similar. Nearly 23% (22.6%) of privately held, 50% or more women-owned firms and 24.6% of all US firms have employees.
- The largest share of privately held, 50% or more women-owned firms is in the service sector. Nearly half (45.0%) of these firms (4.9 million) are in services; 16.4% (1.8 million) are in retail trade; 8.9% (966,662) are in finance, insurance or real estate; and 6.0% are in construction (652,807). Another 12.5% (1.4 million) are in industries that are not classified.
- Privately held, 50% or more women-owned firms are diversifying into non-traditional industries. The greatest growth in the number of these firms during the 1997 to 2004 period has been seen in:
  - Construction (30.0% growth)
  - Transportation, communications, and public utilities (28.1% growth)
  - Agricultural services (24.3% growth)
- The top 10 states for privately held, 50% or more women-owned firms based on an average rank of the number of firms, employment, and sales in 2004 are: California, Texas, Florida, New York, Illinois, Ohio, Michigan and Pennsylvania (tied), North Carolina and Washington.
- The top 10 fastest growing states based on an average rank of 1997 to 2004 growth rates in the number of privately held, 50% or more women-

owned firms, employment, and sales are: Utah, Arizona, Nevada, Idaho, Kentucky and New Mexico, South Carolina, North Carolina, Arkansas and Oregon.

THE STATUS OF MINORITY WOMEN ENTREPRENEURS

Analyzing data published by the US Census Bureau and the Center for Women's Business Research yielded the following statistical portrait of majority-owned, privately held firms owned by women of color in 2002 (The Center, 2004b). In 2002, there were an estimated 1.2 million majority-owned (see Tables 8.2 and 8.3), privately held firms owned by women of color in the US, employing over 822,000 people and generating $100.6 billion in sales (The Center, 2004b). Firms owned by minority women represented 20% of all privately held, majority-owned women-owned firms in the US – in other words, one in five women-owned firms were owned by a woman or women of color (The Center, 2004b). Between 1997 and 2002, the number of minority women-owned firms increased by 32%, employment grew by 6% and sales rose by 19% (The Center, 2004b). In 1997, there were nearly 10,700 majority-owned, privately held firms owned by women of color with $1 million or more in revenues, and over 80 with 100 or more employees (The Center, 2004b). Based on recent growth rates, there were 14,116 minority women-owned firms with revenues of $1 million or more, and 111 with 100 or more employees in 2002 (The Center, 2004b).

In terms of overall minority women business ownership, the Center for Women's Business Research detailed the following additional figures. Over one-third (39%) of minority women-owned firms were owned by Hispanics (470,344), 30% by African Americans (365,110), 30% were Asian or Pacific Islander owned (358,503) and 6% were owned by women of Native American or Alaska Native heritage (77,483) (The Center, 2004b). The 10 states with the greatest number of minority women-owned firms in 2002 are: California, New York, Texas, Florida, Illinois, Georgia, Maryland, New Jersey, Virginia and North Carolina (The Center, 2004b).

Geographically, the 10 states with the fastest growth in the number of minority women-owned firms from 1997 to 2002 were: Montana, North Dakota, Maine, Oklahoma, South Dakota, Vermont, West Virginia, Idaho, New Hampshire and Alaska (The Center, 2004b). The 10 states where minority women-owned firms comprise the greatest share of all women-owned firms are: Hawaii (60%), District of Columbia (40%), California (35%), New Mexico and New York, Texas (29%), Maryland and Florida (tied –28%), Alaska, Georgia and Oklahoma (tied – 24%) (The Center, 2004b). Nearly one-third (31%) of all of the firms owned by minorities are owned by women; minority women-owned firms employ 13% of the workers in minority-owned firms and generate 11%

Table 8.2 *Minority-owned Firms in the United States, 2002*

	Minority Women-owned Firms	All Minority-owned Firms	% Change 1997–2002	Share of All Firms
All Minorities:				
Number of Firms	1,214,309	3,941,536	31.5	30.8
Employment	822,357	6,223,536	5.7	13.2
Sales ($000)	$100,571,001	$945,110,859	18.8	10.6
African American:				
Number of Firms	365,110	1,035,514	16.7	35.3
Employment	197,151	787,332	16.6	25.0
Sales ($000)	$14,485,453	$94,379,957	6.9	15.3
Asian and Pacific Islander				
Number of Firms	358,503	1,258,806	44.6	28.5
Employment	370,101	3,654,527	18.0	10.1
Sales ($000)	$49,069,703	$543,079,183	28.8	9.0
Hispanic:				
Number of Firms	470,344	1,560,583	39.3	30.1
Employment	197,868	1,685,528	-15.7	11.7
Sales ($000)	$29,410,201	$277,478,239	7.7	10.6
Native American and Alaska Native				
Number of Firms	77,483	272,041	44.6	28.5
Employment	87,466	495,427	18.0	17.7
Sales ($000)	$8,700,015	$60,767,210	28.8	14.3

Source: The Center for Women's Business Research (2004b).

Table 8.3   *Number, Employment and Sales and Percentage Change among Minority Women-owned Firms by Industry, 1997–2002*

	1997	2002	% Change 1997–2002
Total US			
Number of Firms	923,403	1,214,309	31.5
Employment	777,999	822,357	5.7
Sales ($000)	$84,666,144	$100,571,001	18.8
Agriculture			
Number of Firms	7,404	7,903	6.7
Employment	5,943	8,166	37.4
Sales ($000)	$459,500	$554,187	20.6
Mining			
Number of Firms	622	508	−18.3
Employment	1,395	1,395	0.0
Sales ($000)	$131,056	$131,056	0.0
Construction			
Number of Firms	18,227	18,990	4.2
Employment	36,521	24,362	−33.3
Sales ($000)	$4,243,591	$3,293,827	−22.4
Manufacturing			
Number of Firms	16,099	15,573	−3.3
Employment	66,131	62,939	−4.8
Sales ($000)	$5,269,373	$5,200,811	−1.3
TCPU			
Number of Firms	23,855	28,891	21.1
Employment	29,299	77,913	165.9
Sales ($000)	$2,488,391	$5,068,095	103.7
Wholesale Trade			
Number of Firms	16,642	15,442	−7.2
Employment	37,723	33,893	−10.2
Sales ($000)	$16,628,051	$15,129,447	−9.0
Retail Trade			
Number of Firms	133,924	131,617	−1.7
Employment	176,246	158,318	−10.2
Sales ($000)	$16,172,247	$17,034,316	5.3
FIRE			
Number of Firms	48,432	42,679	−11.9
Employment	18,952	10,032	−47.1
Sales ($000)	$3,640,761	$2,350,139	−35.4
Services			
Number of Firms	531,532	708,540	33.3
Employment	354,925	391,668	10.4
Sales ($000)	$29,456,109	$41,971,189	42.5

Notes: TCPU = Transportation, Communications and Public Utilities; FIRE = Finance, Insurance and Real Estate.

Source: The Center for Women's Business Research (2004b).

of the sales (The Center, 2004b). More than one-half of minority women-owned firms (58%) were in the service sector (see Table 8.3), 11% were in retail trade and 4% were in goods-producing industries (The Center, 2004b). The greatest growth by industry in the number of minority women-owned firms from 1997 to 2002 came from the services industry (33% growth), followed by transportation/communications/public utilities (21%) and agriculture (7%) (The Center, 2004b).

THE STATUS OF AFRICAN AMERICAN WOMEN ENTREPRENEURS

Analyzing data published by the US Bureau of the Census, the Center detailed the following statistical portrait of majority-owned, privately held firms owned by African American women in 2002 (The Center, 2004c). As of 2002, there were an estimated 365,110 majority-owned, privately held firms owned by African American women in the US (see Table 8.4), employing nearly 200,000 people and generating almost $14.5 billion in sales (The Center, 2004c). Between 1997 and 2002, the number of African American women-owned firms increased by 17%, employment grew by 17% and sales rose by 7% (The Center, 2004c). Nearly one-third (30%) of minority women-owned firms were owned by African Americans. Firms owned by African American women represented 6% of all privately held, majority-owned women-owned firms in the US (The Center, 2004c). The 10 states with the greatest number of African American women-owned firms in 2002 are: New York, Florida, Illinois, California, Georgia, Texas, Maryland, North Carolina, Michigan and Virginia (The Center, 2004c).

The 10 states with the fastest growth in the number of African American women-owned firms from 1997 to 2002 were: Illinois, New York, Wisconsin, Florida, Indiana, Delaware, Georgia, Massachusetts, North Carolina and Oregon (The Center, 2004c). The states where African American women-owned firms comprise the greatest share of all women-owned firms are: District of Columbia (30%), Maryland (16%), Mississippi (15%), Georgia (14%), Louisiana and New York (tied – 12%), Illinois and South Carolina (tied – 11%) and Delaware, Alabama and North Carolina (tied – 10%) (The Center, 2004c).

More than one-third (35%) of all African American firms are owned by women. These women-owned firms employ 25% of the workers in African American owned firms and generate 15% of the sales (The Center, 2004c). Three-quarters (75%) of African American women-owned firms are in the service sector and 7% are in retail trade (The Center, 2004c). The greatest growth by industry in the number of African American women-owned firms from 1997 to 2002 was in the services industry (29% growth), (The Center, 2004c).

Table 8.4   Number, Employment and Sales and Percentage Change among African American Women-owned Firms by Industry, 1997–2002

	1997	2002	% Change 1997–2002
Total US			
Number of Firms	312,884	365,110	16.7
Employment	169,038	197,151	16.6
Sales ($000)	$13,550,983	$14,485,453	6.9
Agriculture			
Number of Firms	1,139	782	−31.3
Employment	750	1,417	89.0
Sales ($000)	$56,103	$93,793	67.2
Mining			
Number of Firms	44	14	−67.4
Employment	D	D	D
Sales ($000)	D	D	D
Construction			
Number of Firms	3,294	2,157	−34.5
Employment	4,971	3,174	−36.1
Sales ($000)	$509,604	$330,408	−35.2
Manufacturing			
Number of Firms	2,567	1,859	−27.6
Employment	2,975	1,613	−45.8
Sales ($000)	$289,881	$183,597	−36.7
TCPU			
Number of Firms	7,810	6,388	−18.2
Employment	10,011	44,623	345.7
Sales ($000)	$493,113	$860,677	74.5
Wholesale Trade			
Number of Firms	1,840	1,011	−45.1
Employment	1,974	793	−59.9
Sales ($000)	$1,002,928	$617,458	−38.4
Retail Trade			
Number of Firms	35,366	26,175	−26.0
Employment	17,607	9,924	−43.6
Sales ($000)	$1,961,236	$1,573,200	−19.8
FIRE			
Number of Firms	12,671	9,359	−26.1
Employment	3,873	2,618	−32.4
Sales ($000)	$632,227	$439,425	−30.5
Services			
Number of Firms	211,353	272,260	28.8
Employment	124,258	178,945	44.0
Sales ($000)	$7,869,760	$10,951,455	39.2

Notes: D = Data withheld by Census Bureau to avoid disclosing data of individual companies; TCPU = Transportation, Communications and Public Utilities; FIRE = Finance, Insurance and Real Estate.

Source: The Center for Women's Business Research (2004c).

THE STATUS OF HISPANIC AMERICAN WOMEN ENTREPRENEURS

Analyzing data published by the US Bureau of the Census, the Center projected the following statistical portrait of majority-owned, privately held firms owned by Hispanic women in 2002 (The Center, 2004d). In 2002, there were approximately 470,344 majority-owned, privately held firms owned by Hispanic women in the US, employing nearly 198,000 people who generated $29.4 billion in sales (The Center, 2004d). Between 1997 and 2002, the number of Hispanic women-owned firms increased by 39% and sales grew by 8% (see Table 8.5); employment has decreased by 16% during this period (The Center, 2004b). Nearly four in ten (39%) minority women-owned firms were owned by Hispanics. Hispanic women represented 8% of all privately held, majority-owned women-owned firms in the US (The Center, 2004d). The 10 states with the greatest number of Hispanic women-owned firms in 2002 were: California, Texas, Florida, New York, Arizona, Illinois, New Jersey, Massachusetts, New Mexico and Colorado (The Center, 2004d).

The 10 states with the fastest growth in the number of Hispanic women-owned firms from 1997 to 2002 are: West Virginia, North Carolina, Arkansas, North Dakota, Alabama, Georgia, Massachusetts, Minnesota, New York and Pennsylvania (The Center, 2004d). The states where Hispanic women-owned firms comprise the greatest share of all women-owned firms were: New Mexico (20%), Texas (18%), California (17%), Florida (16%), New York (14%), Arizona (13%), New Jersey, Nevada and Colorado (tied – 7%) and Massachusetts, Rhode Island and Hawaii (tied – 6%) (The Center, 2004d).

Nearly one-third (30%) of all Hispanic-owned firms are owned by women. Hispanic women-owned firms employ 12% of the workers in Hispanic-owned firms and generate 11% of the sales (The Center, 2004d). More than half (55%) of Hispanic women-owned firms are in the service sector, 12% are in retail trade and 5% are in goods-producing industries (The Center, 2004d). The greatest growth by industry in the number of Hispanic women-owned firms from 1997 to 2002 was transportation/communications/public utilities industry (57% growth), services (36%) and construction (18%) (The Center, 2004d).

THE STATUS OF ASIAN AMERICAN AND PACIFIC ISLANDER WOMEN ENTREPRENEURS

Analyzing data published by the US Bureau of the Census, the Center projected the following statistical portrait of majority-owned, privately held firms owned by Asian and Pacific Islander women in 2002 (The Center, 2004e). In 2002, there were approximately 358,503 majority-owned, privately held firms owned

Table 8.5   Number, Employment and Sales and Percentage Change among Hispanic Women-owned Firms by Industry, 1997–2002

	1997	2002	% Change 1997–2002
Total US			
Number of Firms	337,708	470,344	39.3
Employment	234,591	197,868	−15.7
Sales ($000)	$27,319,361	$29,410,201	7.7
Agriculture			
Number of Firms	3,504	3,450	−1.5
Employment	3,468	3,675	6.0
Sales ($000)	$225,761	$183,455	−18.7
Mining			
Number of Firms	292	277	−5.0
Employment	D	D	D
Sales ($000)	D	D	D
Construction			
Number of Firms	10,041	11,891	18.4
Employment	20,463	13,521	−33.9
Sales ($000)	$2,069,539	$1,422,673	−31.3
Manufacturing			
Number of Firms	6,023	6,164	2.3
Employment	22,900	19,507	−14.8
Sales ($000)	$2,282,556	$2,536,517	11.1
TCPU			
Number of Firms	10,575	16,581	56.8
Employment	9,762	18,805	92.6
Sales ($000)	$1,027,842	$2,381,221	131.7
Wholesale Trade			
Number of Firms	5,546	4,553	−17.9
Employment	10,130	5,884	−41.9
Sales ($000)	$4,263,226	$2,794,346	−34.5
Retail Trade			
Number of Firms	48,860	54,136	10.8
Employment	45,123	28,600	−36.6
Sales ($000)	$4,485,430	$3,638,348	−18.9
FIRE			
Number of Firms	17,204	17,465	1.5
Employment	8,855	6,111	−31.0
Sales ($000)	$1,534,622	$1,277,028	−16.8
Services			
Number of Firms	189,800	258,932	36.4
Employment	104,717	98,542	−5.9
Sales ($000)	$9,971,881	$16,015,973	60.6

Notes: D = Data withheld by Census Bureau to avoid disclosing data of individual companies; TCPU = Transportation, Communications and Public Utilities; FIRE = Finance, Insurance and Real Estate.

Source: The Center for Women's Business Research (2004d).

Table 8.6   Number, Employment and Sales and Percentage Change among Asian and Pacific Islander Women-owned Firms by Industry, 1997–2002

	1997	2002	% Change 1997–2002
Total US			
Number of Firms	247,966	358,503	44.6
Employment	313,603	370,101	18.0
Sales ($000)	$38,100,770	$49,069,703	28.8
Agriculture			
Number of Firms	1,678	2,858	70.3
Employment	1,750	3,759	114.8
Sales ($000)	$133,715	$259,107	93.8
Mining			
Number of Firms	140	129	−8.2
Employment	D	D	D
Sales ($000)	D	D	D
Construction			
Number of Firms	2,972	3,418	15.0
Employment	4,622	3,127	−32.3
Sales ($000)	$711,228	$562,784	−20.9
Manufacturing			
Number of Firms	6,240	6,774	8.6
Employment	37,730	41,218	9.2
Sales ($000)	$2,443,344	$2,510,094	2.7
TCPU			
Number of Firms	5,628	8,803	56.4
Employment	7,578	18,400	142.8
Sales ($000)	$757,811	$1,296,468	71.1
Wholesale Trade			
Number of Firms	8,185	9,963	21.7
Employment	24,275	31,041	27.9
Sales ($000)	$11,019,906	$13,022,510	18.2
Retail Trade			
Number of Firms	48,089	54,370	13.1
Employment	107,776	128,815	19.5
Sales ($000)	$9,318,712	$11,504,824	23.5
FIRE			
Number of Firms	18,757	17,171	−8.5
Employment	5,600	1,975	−64.7
Sales ($000)	$1,362,952	$729,524	−46.5
Services			
Number of Firms	133,721	185,314	38.6
Employment	119,079	121,897	2.4
Sales ($000)	$11,106,181	$14,333,170	29.1

Notes: D = Data withheld by Census Bureau to avoid disclosing data of individual companies; TCPU = Transportation, Communications and Public Utilities; FIRE = Finance, Insurance and Real Estate.

Source: The Center for Women's Business Research (2004e).

by Asian and Pacific Islander women in the US (see Table 8.6), employing over 370,000 people and generating $49.1 billion in sales (The Center, 2004e). Between 1997 and 2002, the number of Asian and Pacific Islander women-owned firms increased by 45%, employment grew by 18% and sales rose by 29% (The Center, 2004e). Nearly one-third (30%) of minority women-owned firms were owned by Asian or Pacific Islanders (The Center, 2004d). Firms owned by Asian and Pacific Islander women represented 6% of all privately held, majority-owned women-owned firms in the US (The Center, 2004e).

The 10 states with the greatest number of Asian and Pacific Islander women-owned firms in 2002 are: California, New York, Texas, Florida, Hawaii, New Jersey, Virginia, Illinois, Washington and Georgia (The Center, 2004e). The 10 states with the fastest growth in the number of Asian and Pacific Islander women-owned firms from 1997 to 2002 are: Maine, Tennessee, Montana, Oklahoma, Kentucky, West Virginia, Wyoming, Vermont, Alabama and Idaho (The Center, 2004e). The states where Asian and Pacific Islander women-owned firms comprise the greatest share of all women-owned firms are: Hawaii (55%), California (14%), New York (11%), Virginia (9%), Nevada, New Jersey, Maryland and Washington (tied – 8%) and Texas, Georgia, Alaska and the District of Columbia (tied – 6%) (The Center, 2004e).

More than one-quarter (29%) of all Asian and Pacific Islander-owned firms are owned by women. Asian and Pacific Islander women-owned firms employ 10% of the workers in Asian and Pacific Islander-owned firms and generate 9% of the sales (The Center, 2004e). More than half (52%) of Asian and Pacific Islander women-owned firms are in the service sector, 15% are in retail trade and 4% are in goods-producing industries (The Center, 2004e). The greatest growth by industry in the number of Asian and Pacific Islander women-owned firms from 1997 to 2002 was in the agriculture/forestry/fishing industry (70% growth), transportation/communications/public utilities (56%) and services (39%) (The Center, 2004e).

THE STATUS OF NATIVE AMERICAN AND ALASKA NATIVE WOMEN ENTREPRENEURS

Analyzing data published by the US Bureau of the Census, the Center projected the following statistical portrait of majority-owned, privately held firms owned by Native American and Alaska Native women in 2002 (The Center, 2004f). In 2002, there were approximately 77,483 majority-owned, privately held firms owned by Native American and Alaska Native women in the US (see Table 8.7), employing nearly 88,000 people and generating $8.7 billion in sales (The Center, 2004f). Between 1997 and 2002, the number of Native American and Alaska Native women-owned firms increased by 45%, employment grew by 18% and

*Table 8.7   Number, Employment and Sales and Percentage Change among
Native American and Alaska Native Women-owned Firms by
Industry, 1997–2002*

	1997	2002	% Change 1997–2002
Total US			
Number of Firms	53,593	77,483	44.6
Employment	74,114	87,466	18.0
Sales ($000)	$6,755,233	$8,700,015	28.8
Agriculture			
Number of Firms	1,363	2,322	70.3
Employment	375	805	114.8
Sales ($000)	$48,411	$93,809	93.8
Mining			
Number of Firms	178	163	−8.2
Employment	D	D	D
Sales ($000)	D	D	D
Construction			
Number of Firms	2,271	2,612	15.0
Employment	6,883	4,656	−32.3
Sales ($000)	$1,031,765	$816,420	−20.9
Manufacturing			
Number of Firms	1,727	1,875	8.6
Employment	3,497	3,820	9.2
Sales ($000)	$393,116	$403,856	2.7
TCPU			
Number of Firms	1,030	1,611	56.4
Employment	2,525	6,131	142.8
Sales ($000)	$256,155	$438,232	71.1
Wholesale Trade			
Number of Firms	1,383	1,683	21.7
Employment	1,549	1,981	27.9
Sales ($000)	$418,481	$494,530	18.2
Retail Trade			
Number of Firms	5,012	5,667	13.1
Employment	7,865	9,400	19.5
Sales ($000)	$641,238	$791,668	23.5
FIRE			
Number of Firms	1,170	1,071	−8.5
Employment	742	262	−64.7
Sales ($000)	$151,836	$81,271	−46.5
Services			
Number of Firms	13,190	18,279	38.6
Employment	16,671	17,066	2.4
Sales ($000)	$974,030	$1,257,042	29.1

Notes: D = Data withheld by Census Bureau to avoid disclosing data of individual companies;
TCPU = Transportation, Communications and Public Utilities; FIRE = Finance, Insurance and Real
Estate.

Source: The Center for Women's Business Research (2004f).

sales rose by 29% (The Center, 2004f). Six percent (6%) of minority women-owned firms were owned by Native American or Alaska Natives. Firms owned by Native American and Alaska Native women represented 1% of all privately held, majority-owned women-owned firms in the US (The Center, 2004f).

The 10 states with the greatest number of Native American and Alaska Native women-owned firms in 2002 were: Oklahoma, California, Texas, Florida, New Mexico, Arizona, North Carolina, Alaska, Michigan and Kentucky (The Center, 2004f). The 10 states with the fastest growth in the number of Native American and Alaska Native women-owned firms from 1997 to 2002 were: Maine, Tennessee, Montana, Oklahoma, Kentucky, West Virginia, Wyoming, Vermont, Alabama and Idaho (The Center, 2004f). The states where Native American and Alaska Native women-owned firms comprise the greatest share of all women-owned firms were: Oklahoma (18%), Alaska (16%), New Mexico (11%), Montana (8%), South Dakota (5%), Maine, Arizona and Wyoming (tied – 4%) and Kentucky, Vermont and Idaho (tied – 3%) (The Center, 2004f). More than one-quarter (29%) of all Native American and Alaska Native-owned firms were owned by women. Native American and Alaska Native women-owned firms employed 18% of the workers in Native American and Alaska Native-owned firms and generated 14% of the sales (The Center, 2004f).

Nearly one-quarter (24%) of Native American and Alaska Native women-owned firms were in the service sector, 9% were in goods-producing industries and 7% were in retail trade (The Center, 2004f). Due to the separation of Native American and Alaska Native firms from Asian and Pacific Islander firms in the 1997 census, 49% of Native American and Alaska Native women-owned firms did not have easily identifiable industry codes and were included by the Census Bureau in the 'industries not classified' grouping (The Center, 2004f). The greatest growth by industry in the number of Native American and Alaska Native women-owned firms from 1997 to 2002 was in the agriculture/forestry/fishing industry (70% growth), transportation/communications/public utilities (56%) and services (39%) (The Center, 2004f).

METHODOLOGY FOR THE CENTER FOR WOMEN'S BUSINESS RESEARCH NATIONAL DATA

Due to changes in the way that the Census Bureau defines a woman-owned business, the 1997 Survey of Women-Owned Business Enterprises did not count those firms in which a woman owned 50% of the business (The Center, 2004a). They also did not count publicly traded women-owned firms (The Center, 2004a). The data were not directly comparable to data gathered previously because the agency counts only privately held, majority-owned firms (the Center, 2004a). Thus, the Census Bureau provided the Center with reconfigured 1992 data based on the 1997 definition and provided growth rates during that span of time for women-owned firms and all firms (including sole proprietorships, partnership, and subchapter S corporations) (The Center, 2004a). The revised 1992 to 1997 data was then used to calculate growth rates at the national and state levels for privately held, majority (51% or more) women-owned firms and for all privately held firms (The Center, 2004a).

In this reconfiguration, the Census Bureau excluded C corporations from the 1992 data in order to approximate the effect of excluding publicly traded firms in 1997 (The Center, 2004a). This approximation produced slightly different rates compared to the Census Bureau's previously published growth rates at the national level for privately held, women-owned firms and for all privately held firms (The Center, 2004a).

The Center derived the 2004 estimates by using the Census Bureau's unpublished revised rates for the national and state levels while controlling by the published national growth rates for privately held, women-owned firms and all privately held firms. Controlling by the published national growth rates is an additional step that the Center implemented for the 2004 estimates. Therefore, these 2004 estimates for numbers and growth are not directly comparable to the Center's 2002 estimates. To calculate the 2004 estimates and growth rates of privately held, 50% or more women-owned firms, the Center followed these steps: (1) estimates for privately held, majority (51% or more) women-owned firms were projected to 2004; (2) estimates for privately-held, equally (50-50) women- and men-owned firms were projected to 2004; (3) estimates for the majority (51% or more) women-owned firms and equally (50-50) women- and men-owned firms were added for both 1997 and 2004 estimates; and (4) growth rates for privately held, 50% or more women-owned businesses were derived based on the differences between 1997 combined counts and 2004 combined estimates (The Center, 2004a).

The Center for Women's Business Research projects these trends forward into 2004 using the following general assumptions: (1) growth rates between 1992 and 1997 would continue at similar rates through 2004 (growth rates are projected linearly); (2) differences between the approximated growth rates and the actual growth rates for privately held firms at the industry and state levels would be the same as the proportional differences between the approximated and published national growth rates; and (3) growth rates for privately held, equally (50-50) women and men-owned firms were the same as for all privately held firms.

In some instances, the Census Bureau did not report a 1992 to 1997 growth rate because the confidence interval for the rate included zero (0). In these cases, as noted, the assumption was made that the growth rate was zero (0). Comparisons between women-owned firms and all firms are made to all privately owned firms.

THE KEY RESOURCE FOR WOMEN ENTREPRENEURS IN THE UNITED STATES – FINANCIAL CAPITAL

The entrance of women as an important contributing sector of the labor market impacted the growth, productivity and development of the United States economy with an unparalleled force. There is no doubt that women's labor force participation in the mainstream labor market not only revolutionalized the productivity of the economy, but also had a major impact on women's place as it is viewed from a wider societal perspective. This revolutionary stance is advancing as women continue to make inroads into the field of entrepreneurship. The increasing and heightened awareness of women entrepreneurs' vital contribution has led to a number of studies – both from the private and the governmental sector – looking at the most important element needed to promote and support women's entrepreneurial ventures. Studies have resoundingly agreed that financial capital – and the level of access to capital – is the most critical factor to current women entrepreneurs in the United States. With this illumination in mind, the current section looks at financial capital issues for women entrepreneurs in the United States.

The section begins with the Milken Institute and the National Women's Business Council (NWMC) report on women business owners' access to financial capital, focusing on some best practices in the financial markets. It continues with a look at a second report from The National Women's Business Council describing nationwide training programs that assist women in their efforts to achieve access to and to manage financial capital. The section ends with the Diana Project, which strives to dispel the myths regarding women business owners and equity capital.

The 2000 report procured by the Milken Institute and the National Women's Business Council addressed issues related to economic prosperity and access to credit for women business owners. Its main focus was to examine best practices initiated by government not-for-profits and financial institutions to address the demand for credit by women business owners in the United States (National Women's Business Council, 2000). The report emphasized that while women business owners' access to credit has improved over the years, a void still remains. Women received approximately 12% of all credit provided to small businesses in the United States even though they own almost 48% of all privately held businesses (The Milken Institute and NWBC, 2000).

Overall, the report indicated that women were most likely to operate small, local, low-collateral enterprises in the service and retail sectors and that they face more difficulty when gathering start-up capital. The report also highlighted three additional issues. First, women entrepreneur business owners were more likely to apply for smaller loans, of the type considered by banks to be money-losers. Second, women business owners are often unaware of the credit sources and information networks available to them. Third, occupational segregation disadvantaged women entrepreneurs, who had fewer experiences personally, professionally and financially (The Milken Institute and NWBC, 2000).

The report raised concern about the future of the banking sector and how changes in the industry would impact on their response to the needs of women entrepreneurs. More specifically, the report indicated that a high proportion of the banks did not meet the capital funding needs of the women and instead they sought other financial help, including finance companies and family and friends (The Milken Institute and NWBC, 2000). The report further extrapolated by predicting that the move towards bank centralization, mergers and regulations in the banking industry would lead to depersonalized customer services. The move was expected to negatively impact women entrepreneurs, who were more likely to operate small enterprises – a sector that would be hardest hit by the changes (The Milken Institute and NWBC, 2000).

The report's most critical contribution lies in the recommendations made regarding the issue of access to financial capital by women entrepreneurs in the United States marketplace. Some of these challenges were met through programs such as those offered through the Small Business Administration, federal and state programs from banks and financial institutions-created incentives for lenders who provided funding to women business owners. The challenges were also met by special marketing programs where loan officers were educated on the particular needs of women business owners. There were also programs that offered educational and training expertise in management and financing experience assisting women business owners who received financial assistance (The Milken Institute and NWBC, 2000).

The Milken Institute and NWBC made five recommendations in their final report regarding the future of women business owners. In it they address financial issues centered around government regulations including amendment of the Federal Reserve Regulation B – Equal Credit Opportunity Act. According to the report, the Act was counterproductive to women entrepreneurs by preventing the collection of demographic information from borrowers. It was believed that a revision would open the market to underrepresented individuals: those previously stunted by such official measurements (The Milken Institute and NWBC, 2000).

A second recommendation was to create new credit scoring policies that incorporate data relevant and specific to the unique features of women business owners. The report also recommended the implementation of a national Capital Access Program (CAP), which would create a reserve insurance pool, giving banks the leverage to make loans that would not otherwise be approved, such as loans to women and minority businesses. Also the report recommended exploiting securitization, with financial institutions pooling standardized small business loans and selling them as securities to institutional investors. The report indicated that such a move would serve to increase each bank's liquidity, lower their transaction costs and improve their ability to make additional loans.

Finally, the report recommended institutionalizing various government statistical reports, such as: The Economic Census, The Survey of Women-Owned Business Enterprises, The Survey of Minority-Owned Business Enterprises, The Characteristics of Business Owners' Survey and The Survey of Small Business Financing and not to allow such programs and their continuing funding be at the whim of legislators. It further recommended that Congress should include such programs in their budget allocation decisions (The Milken Institute and NWBC, 2000).

A 2002 report by the National Women's Business Council identified programs nationwide that focused on helping women entrepreneurs gain access to financial capital. The report highlighted nine nationwide programs that assisted women business owners in this respect. They were: ACCION New York, The Coleman Foundation, Dingman Center for Entrepreneurship, The Ewing Marion Kauffman Foundation, The Institute for Social Economic Development, Minnesota Women's Business Center, The Wachovia Corporation, Women's Business Center of Northern Virginia and Women's Growth Capital Funds. Of the nine programs presented, five in particular were highlighted as being particularly effective in successfully addressing the needs of women entrepreneurs nationwide.

ACCION New York's micro-enterprise program helped more than 3,000 low-income New York city residents access capital for business start-ups and expansions (NWBC, 2002). The Ewing Marion Kauffman Foundation's overall goals were to increase the number of child-care businesses (NWBC, 2002). The Institute for Social and Economic Development, which fosters micro-enterprise development as a strategy to alleviate poverty, provided hundreds of Iowans with start-up loans of up to $35,000 for small businesses (NWBC, 2002). In 1999, the Wachovia's Women Program began helping women businesses develop successful enterprises through a commitment of $5 billion. Loans were granted to women business owners over a 10 year period. Finally, the Women's Growth Fund began providing venture capital to women-owned firms if the firms had been in business for at least two years; had revenues of at least $500,000; and had submitted a business plan that supported a projected annual growth rate of at least 20% (NWBC, 2002).

The report found that the best practices of these latter five programs fostered a number of key elements. These comprised a focus on women entrepreneurs, using community liaisons to supplement their program initiatives, with special attention given to and programs revised in the light of feedback received from these women entrepreneurs; having realistic expectations for the women-owned enterprises and having a staff that possessed the background and experience to demonstrate the commitment needed to assist women in business enterprises.

A final report done from a national perspective that deserves special mention was conducted by a number of researchers from various institutions. Sponsored by the Kauffman Center for Entrepreneurial Leadership, the United States Small Business Administration and the National Women's Business Council and authored by Brush et al. (2001), the Diana Project strove to dispel the common myths regarding women business owners and equity capital. The report looked at eight common myths and dispelled them by using data from applicants and participants of the Springboard 2000 venture firms, two volumes of Pratt's Guide for 1995 and 2000 and data on the portfolio of 20,000 companies; 34,000 executives, 120,000 company investments provided by 4,500 private equity firms having 7,000 private equity funds obtained from the National Venture Capital Association (NVCA) between 1957 and 1998 (Brush et al., 2001).

The myths dispelled by the report are as follows:

- Women don't want to own high growth businesses.
- Women don't have the right educational backgrounds to build large ventures.
- Women don't have the right types of experience to build large ventures.
- Women aren't in the network and lack the social contacts to build a credible venture.
- Women don't have the financial savvy or resources to start high growth businesses.
- Women don't submit business plans to equity providers.
- Women-owned ventures are in industries unattractive to venture capitalists.
- Women are not a force in the venture capital industry.

While a cautionary note needs to be sounded regarding the sample source and the lack of representativeness of the sample regarding all women entrepreneurs across the United States, the results also serve an important function: reminding us that all women entrepreneurs are not the same, and serving to emphasize that women entrepreneurs are making significant strides towards improving the overall picture for the woman entrepreneur.

CONCLUSION

Women business owners in the United State are overwhelmingly clustered in two industries, namely services and retail trade. Many of the businesses in these industries offer easy access and low barriers to entry through the minimal skills needed, the low level of start-up financial resources needed and the personal knowledge women have regarding the needs of their customers through themselves being women, wives and mothers. Even across racial lines, the concentration of women entrepreneurs in industries such as retail trade and services remains consistent. Like the current study, other studies accessing various sources of samples repeatedly echo this industry concentration for women business owners. This concentration of women entrepreneurs in these industries spans decades, centuries and geographic regions.

The major reasons cited by women for exiting the mainstream labor market to pursue entrepreneurial opportunities center around a general theme of disappointment or frustration with their mainstream labor market circumstances. 'Push' factors including the glass ceiling, wage gap effects and lack of autonomy, have caused women to see entrepreneurship as a viable and more pleasant situation in which to earn an income. 'Pull' factors, such as the level of independence achieved, the opportunity to earn money and be involved in the major decision-making components of an organization, have also spurred women into the entrepreneurial sector in the United States.

Blatantly put, access to financial resources, whether at the start-up or during the operation of the business, remains the number one problem for women entrepreneurs, even across racial lines. Other critical areas include lack of experience, whether in the field of the business, in the entrepreneurial world or in other appropriate areas relevant to business ownership. Finally, the lack of appropriate network structures to aid women entrepreneurs as they navigate through this sector has come to be seen as a critical issue, especially in the last decade. It has been recommended that women entrepreneurs focus on intimate but effective networks instead of manifesting a number of ineffective network links. While minority women entrepreneurs focus on more informal network links, white women entrepreneurs are seen to focus on more formal connections to aid their entrepreneurial journey.

The issue of financial deficiency for women entrepreneurs is being somewhat alleviated by a few organizations that focus either exclusively on women as a part of their general umbrella. Such organizations aid women entrepreneurs in different areas such as training, financing and networking. These organizations also assist women entrepreneurs who manage different sized enterprises and who are present in different industries.

While women entrepreneurs have significantly increased their numbers in non-traditional industries such as construction, mining, engineering and wholesale trade in the last decades, they remain concentrated in lower paying industries such as services and retail trade. Finally, a number of women's organizations offer membership through paying and non-paying means, with the aim of disseminating information to women entrepreneurs, to government agencies and society at large in order to raise awareness about the various dimensions critical to this twentieth and twenty-first century phenomenon.

Statistical information on women entrepreneurs in the preceding sections indicates that women entrepreneurs, even across racial lines, are clustered in industries such as the retail trade and the services industries. However, there are strong indications that women are making rapid inroads into previously unchartered areas, such as construction, mining and wholesale trade (The Center, 2004a).

The reports reviewed above consistently show that financial capital and access to this resource remains a critical area of concern for women entrepreneurs and has done so historically. Several organizations (the Diana Project, ACCION and the Catalyst Guide) have been operating to help women across racial lines, across various industries and women who operate various sizes and forms of business organizations. While progress is being made, much more needs to be done, especially as the number of women entrepreneurs continues to increase. This trend is expected to continue into the near future.

In its 2000 report, the Milken Institute and National Women's Business Council issued a call to action to modify federal laws related to loan programs that cater to women entrepreneurs. A statement by one of the women entrepreneurs (Terry from Michigan, a white woman entrepreneur), interviewed during the course of the current study, supports such action:

> One of the things that could definitely be helpful for our type of business is to obtain additional tax breaks, maybe something specifically geared towards small businesses. Anything that allows you an avenue to keep more of the money you make will definitely help you with the business.

Some changes are being made by the current president of the United States, who has called on Congress to support his proposal on tax concessions. These breaks would be granted to small businesses that are primarily owned by women. While these are steps in the right direction, more needs to be done to address the significant place occupied by women entrepreneurs in the marketplace.

9. The state of women entrepreneurs in the global marketplace

INTRODUCTION

Entrepreneurship as a legitimate occupational source of income for women can be found worldwide. In some regions, it is institutionalized and represents a viable source of employment for women and an income bearing source for their families. While women working as self-employed individuals date back to much earlier centuries (Oppedisano, 2000; Boyd, 1996), their formalization as business owners or as a sector requiring their place and contribution to a country's gross national or domestic product has taken prominence primarily in the last two to three decades, and for some countries only in the last five years. Accounting for and documenting exact worldwide figures on women in the entrepreneurial sector remain illusive, but there is no doubt that women's place as a part of the entrepreneurial field is becoming more assured. This phenomenon is seen as a necessary development and a vital component of a country's advancement. Vital, since women represent approximately 50% of most countries' population and thus 50% of the potential workforce. Vital still, since the latter portion of the workforce is often marginalized, existing on the peripheral boundaries of a country's mainstream labor market – facing obstacles and being denied their rightful place as contributing income earners in their society.

Some have suggested that this documentation should mainly occur at the micro level (Shane et al., 1991), others have emphasized the need to conduct studies that address the informal versus the formal economic sector (Weiling et al., 2001), while others have advocated a theoretical and empirical understanding of home-based employment, especially as it impacts and is impacted by the contributions of women as independent income earners for their families (Hennon and Locker, 2000; Hennon et al., 1998).

This chapter focuses primarily on the contributions and issues of women entrepreneurs worldwide. It addresses issues such as their motivations for embracing entrepreneurship, the obstacles and opportunities they face, the factors that impact the problems they face during the operation of their business and highlights areas that need improving by appropriate organizations, institutions and government agencies. While a number of studies have explored immigrant women entrepreneurs and their performance in their host countries (Gilbertson,

1995; Dallafar, 1994), that dimension will not be the major thrust of the presentation in this chapter. Instead, this chapter's main purpose is to address the place of women entrepreneurs on a worldwide platform. The analysis is presented in various sections traveling from country to country and continent to continent. The chapter culminates with a comparison of the various issues for women entrepreneurs on an international and national level and how this relates to the findings in the current study.

In a (1992) article, McGrath and Macmillan contended that there existed a basic set of beliefs that entrepreneurs worldwide shared, a set of core values and that these values transcend cultures. Be that as it may, a more pertinent question is what are the characteristics of and dominant issues that women entrepreneurs face worldwide. The answer to this question can only be adequately answered by providing snippets of studies that have been conducted on women entrepreneurs worldwide. The following sections begin with a look at Asian women entrepreneurs and continue by assessing important issues for women entrepreneurs in 12 other regions.

ASIAN WOMEN ENTREPRENEURS

Godbout (1993), who looked at women entrepreneurs a little over a decade ago, found that, except for Japan, women had a greater effect on employment growth than men and that much of the growth came from changes in the labor market. The subservient position of Asian women as a labor market contributor was also acknowledged in a later article by Lee (1995) who studied the exploitation of women as labor market commodities in factories. While Asian women have occupied less favorable positions in the mainstream labor market in their home countries, there is evidence that the same does not occur for Asian women entrepreneurs, especially those operating as immigrants in a foreign country.

A study conducted by Dhaliwal in 1998 highlighted the contributions that Asian women entrepreneurs made to both the field of entrepreneurship and the management of family enterprises in Britain. The women interviewed were grouped into two categories of 'independent' (women entrepreneurs who were self-employed) and 'hidden' (women working in the background as joint owners of the business, alongside their spouses or family members). The latter group of women entrepreneurs were primarily in the background of the business compared with their male family counterparts, who took a more prominent role and the women were thus classified as 'hidden' entrepreneurs.

Through in-depth interviews with 10 women entrepreneurs, the author ascertained that 'independent' women entrepreneurs were more likely to be motivated by the need to provide for their children (Dhaliwal, 1998). This group of women entrepreneurs were also more educated than their 'hidden' counterparts and more likely to be married to affluent men and while they consulted with male family members on business issues, it was in an advisory capacity. The 'hidden' women, apparently caught up in a sense of duty to their families, dealt with more routine tasks as opposed to more prominent roles related to decision making. In spite of the differences between the two groups, the authors sought to show that Asian women entrepreneurs are involved and play an important role in entrepreneurship ventures.

CARIBBEAN WOMEN ENTREPRENEURS

A very different picture emerges for women entrepreneurs in the Caribbean. Browne (2001) provides a cross-cultural, interdisciplinary and comparative study of three countries – Puerto Rico, Martinique and Barbados – and shows how female entrepreneurship is patterned according to a society's particular configuration of gendered institutions and ideologies. The author believes that against a backdrop in which women are strongly represented in the workforce, yet lack the economic mobility and decision-making authority of men, female entrepreneurship offers a unique and under-examined analytical vantage point for the said women.

With this in mind, Browne (2001) and her research associates conducted 30 two-stage interviews with female entrepreneurs from the three countries. The study concluded that in societies which are strongly gender-stratified and where male authority is not easily negotiated in households, such as Puerto Rico, women with entrepreneurial ambitions may prefer to live alone or in non-traditional households. In addition, the author contended that women in welfare-oriented economies such as Martinique and Puerto Rico are likely to be less risk-oriented and more conservative in their entrepreneurial undertakings because of the lack of resources and accumulated wealth. Finally, the study concluded that cross-culturally the women entrepreneurs shared a key set of priorities for their business, priorities that centered primarily on the need to exercise their femininity regardless of the size or type of business. This was critical to their overall self-esteem and development and done in order to render workplace settings more nurturing and effective.

ITALIAN WOMEN ENTREPRENEURS

A cross-cultural study of male and female entrepreneurs in Italy and the United States showed more similarity than differences between women entrepreneurs in the two countries (Aldrich et al., 1989). The study assessed the differences in network structures of women and men across the two countries. The samples were taken from the Research Triangle Council for Entrepreneurial Development (CED) in North Carolina and from entrepreneurs in the Gemini Project in Italy, which was part of an entrepreneurship training program conducted by SDA Bocconi, a Milan-based business school. The study found that the women entrepreneurs in the American sample were older (39 versus 29), more likely to be married (66% versus 35%), but their level of education was equal to their Italian counterparts (Aldrich et al., 1989). However, the two groups shared similar levels of networking activities and characteristics and composition, with the women in the study (regardless of country) having mostly men in their network structures compared with the men in the study (regardless of country), who had almost no women in their network structures (Aldrich et al., 1989).

ISRAELI WOMEN ENTREPRENEURS

The factors affecting the performance of Israeli women entrepreneurs were analyzed by Lerner et al. in a 1997 study. The demographic characteristics from the sample showed that the women were on average 50.5 years old, tended to be married, had two to three children and had high levels of education. The sample consisted of women who had studied liberal arts (67%), some who had previous management experience before starting their businesses and a low percentage (22.3%) who had previous entrepreneurial experience before starting their current business. A high percentage (51.6%) of the women had previous experience of working in the business sector.

The authors also looked at five theoretical explanations for entrepreneurs' business performance, including their networks, human capital, environment, theories of social learning theory and the motivational influence and goals in a sample of 220 women business owners. The analysis examined the influence of different variables from the previously mentioned five theoretical explanations on performance measures, such as profitability, revenue, income and number of employees (Lerner et al., 1997, Figure 1).

The results from the study showed that motivation had a significant effect on the business performance of the women entrepreneurs and that economic necessity motives were most highly correlated with profitability. In addition, the findings indicated that Bandura's (1977) Social Learning theory had no power in explaining the business performance of women entrepreneurs (cited in Lerner et al., 1997). While the effect of human capital factors on performance was not as evident, the actual level of the women entrepreneurs' education had no direct effect on business performance. However, previous salaried employment and previous experience in the industry and business skills were highly correlated with performance. A comparison of the women entrepreneurs in the different industry sectors showed that those in the service industries had significantly high levels of education and higher levels of previous business experience than their colleagues in other sectors. In addition, network theory offered the greatest explanations for differences in the performance of the Israeli women entrepreneurs.

POLISH WOMEN ENTREPRENEURS

Countries that have transitioned to a market economy in the last few decades have also been influenced dramatically by the contribution of women entrepreneurs in the form of small and medium-sized business enterprises. Poland is an example of such a transitioning economy, where many of the country's economic sectors are under development. An article in 2001 looked at the women entrepreneurs in Poland and presented a framework regarding the characteristics of the women entrepreneurs (Bliss and Garratt, 2001). The article said that the growth of Poland's private sector was fostered by an explosion of small businesses that came after 1989. Polish women entrepreneurs were identified as having a significant role in this growth, but from a less disadvantaged position when compared to their male counterparts. A look at the statistics from 1989 to 1995 in that country showed that while women led in the number of jobs they occupied in the public sector, they lagged behind their male counterparts in the private sector, as self-employed individuals and as employers. Since then, growth in the latter three sectors has been remarkable, moving from a low of 2.7% for women employers in 1989 to a high of 39% in 1995.

While there has been growth in various areas of Poland, the marketplace was not always favorable to women, resulting in them suffering from discriminatory practices, in both society and the workplace, especially in the early days of Poland's move to a free market (Bliss and Garratt, 2001). Based on these disadvantageous positions, the article proposed that there was a need for a support organization for women entrepreneurs in transitioning economies such as Poland. The need for such an organization was said to be based on the fact that there was, in general, little governmental support for entrepreneurs in the Polish economy and that the needs of women entrepreneurs were different than those of their male counterparts. In addition, the authors stated that the women entrepreneurs in transitioning economies differed from their male counterparts in the obstacles they faced, their reasons for starting a business, their goals and the factors they perceived as important. Such special needs of women entrepreneurs in a transitioning economy included: obtaining credit, obtaining a collateral position, work–family conflict issues, having fewer mentors, the culture's lack of respect for women in business and women's insufficient business training.

In response, the Polish Association of Women Entrepreneurs (PAWE) was established in 1998 to address the needs of women entrepreneurs in that country. A new set of recommended objectives focused on meeting the business development needs of women entrepreneurs in Poland by (Bliss and Garratt, 2001):

- providing a forum where women entrepreneurs could come together to exchange experiences and network;
- offering an educational and informative program and activities to help develop the leadership and managerial skills of women entrepreneurs;
- promoting women entrepreneurs and their businesses in order to enhance their position and influence their economic and public life in Poland.

SINGAPOREAN WOMEN ENTREPRENEURS

Articles looking at what motivates Singaporean women in particular to set up new ventures as well as the various factors contributing to the success of women entrepreneurs from this geographic sphere have provided some rich results. The five major factors which motivate Singaporean female business owners were as follows (Teo, 1996):

- the perceived presence of a business opportunity;
- the desire to put knowledge and skills to use;
- the need for freedom and flexibility;
- the desire to achieve personal growth and recognition;
- the need to make more money to achieve financial independence.

The most critical start-up problems for female business owners in Singapore were (Teo, 1996):

- difficulties in finding good labor;
- difficulties in obtaining finance;
- competing with others;
- establishing credibility;
- coping with high business costs.

Factors that Singaporean business women cited as contributing to their success were (Teo, 1996):

- product and service qualities;
- personal qualities;
- quality of personnel;

- adequate knowledge of products and services;
- customer loyalty.

Teo (1996) also found that successful Singaporean business women seemed to be more educated and had more up-to-date knowledge of available technologies, which aided their business development. They were also more aware of how the business world operated and were able to apply their skills and knowledge. The author found that approximately three-quarters of the successful women business owners in Singapore stated that a good networking system was an important success factor in their business enterprise, compared to the less successful women. Finally, Teo (1996) found that most of the female Singaporean business owners had at least 10 years of formal education and 35% held first or postgraduate degrees.

CROSS-CULTURAL STUDIES

A 1999 article by Maysami and Goby looked at studies that assessed Singaporean women entrepreneurs and compared the results to those from the United States, Canada, the Netherlands, Asia and Australia (see Table 9.1). The results indicated that, in relation to their demographic profiles, women business owners in Canada ranged in age from 31–45 years, were more likely to be married and had on average 2.4 children (Maysami and Goby, 1999). Meanwhile women business owners from the United States were described as being under 51 years old, more likely to be married with a few children, while Asian and Australian women business owners were in their thirties to early forties, and the Singaporean women business owners were on average 41 years, most were married and had an average of two children.

In terms of educational levels, 25% of the female business owners who participated in a 1995 study in Australia held a university degree, with another 18.2% also holding a higher degree (Breen et al., 1995 as cited in Maysami and Goby, 1999). The authors concluded that the majority of the female business owners in the study from various countries had prior business experience (Maysami and Goby, 1999). However, the women from the United States had work experience similar to their current venture, while the Australian women had worked in industries that were different than their current venture.

The motivational factors (see Table 9.2) for the women entrepreneurs from the other countries were similar to those of the Singaporean women entrepreneurs (Maysami and Goby, 1999). Like the Asian women entrepreneurs, they were motivated primarily by the desire for autonomy, freedom and flexibility offered in operating one's own business (Deng et al., 1995). And the Australian women business owners' motivating factors included general dissatisfaction

Table 9.1   Characteristics of Women Business Owners

Personal profiles	Singapore – Teo (1996)	Netherlands – Leo-Gosselin and Grise (1990)	Canada – Collerette and Aubry (1991)	Asia – Deng, Hassan and Jivan (1995)	Australia – Breen, Calvert and Oliver (1995)	Singapore – Rashid (1996)	USA – Burdette (1990)	Australia – Williams (1986)	Australia – MacDiarmid and Thomson (1991)
Average Age	41	31–45	37	30s and 40s		30–39	< 51		
Marital Status	M	M	M			M			
Education									
University Degree	35%			55%	25%				
Professional/ Polytechnic	15%								
Higher Degree					18.2%				
Secondary Level	50%								
Below Secondary Level					15.3%				
Typical Business Experience	Y		Y		Y	Y	Y		
Typical Business Profile									
Service and Retail Industry	Y			Y	Y				
Small Size	Y			Y	Y			Y	
Personal Savings (Initial Capital)	Y			Y	Y				Y

Notes: M – married women entrepreneurs; Y – characteristics that women business owners possess.

Source: Maysami and Goby (1999).

with previous employment and lack of promotional opportunities (Breen et al., 1995 as cited in Maysami and Goby, 1999).

Overall, the authors indicate that women business owners from the countries studied were concentrated in the retail or professional services sectors, motivated by the low start-up capital required for such industries (Maysami and Goby, 1999). In addition, the principal problems (see Table 9.3) for women business owners regardless of their country's location were a lack of start-up capital, and the lack of confidence they faced from those in their network structures (family, friends, suppliers, banks and clients alike). Success (see Table 9.4) was primarily determined by the personal skills and abilities of the women entrepreneurs regardless of the country they operated in. Factors contributing to the women entrepreneurs' success across countries included: family support, customer loyalty, quality of personnel, availability of professional services among others (see Table 9.4) (Maysami and Goby, 1999).

An earlier study that looked at new firm formation across various countries and genders was conducted by Shane et al. (1991) in Great Britain, Norway and New Zealand. The number of female entrepreneurs participating in the study were Great Britain (17), New Zealand (16) and Norway (31) and represented 8%, 12% and 12% respectively of the sample of entrepreneurs studied from the three countries. Overall, the authors found that there was no dominant factor documented as a universal reason(s) leading to new business formation across gender and national boundaries. One factor that dominated as a reason for new business formation was the desire for job freedom (Shane et al., 1991). For the females in the study, the primary factors for business formation for the aggregate group included the need for independence, such as control over time and work being performed. A cross-country comparison in the same study indicated that women entrepreneurs from Britain were more likely to crave this independence, followed by women in New Zealand and ending with Norway. Other factors that showed high values across countries were: learning on the job for women entrepreneurs in Britain and Norway, as well as for women entrepreneurs from New Zealand (Shane et al., 1991).

Demographic profiles of the sample of women entrepreneurs from the previously mentioned study showed them dominating in the services industry with approximately two partners or employees and primarily located in rural or minor city areas. The educational levels and ages of the women entrepreneurs varied across countries, with New Zealand having the oldest women entrepreneurs (43.1 years), followed by Britain (41.2 years) and Norway (38.1 years). The highest level of education for all the women entrepreneurs was at the professional level, with Norway showing the highest education level of the three countries.

Table 9.2 *Major Motivating Factors for Female Business Owners*

Factors	Breen, Calvert and Oliver (1995)	Teo (1996)	Leo-Gosselin and Grise (1990)	Deng, Hassan and Jivan (1995)	Hisrich and Brush (1986)	Rashid (1996)	Fried (1989)	Capowski (1992)
Job Satisfaction					*	*		
Presence of Opportunities		*			*	*	*	
Desire to be One's Own Boss			*				*	*
Freedom and Flexibility	*	*		*				
Need to Make More Money		*		*		*	*	
Independence	*		*	*		*		
Desire to Realize an Ambition	*		*					*
To Put Knowledge into Use		*	*				*	
Personal Challenge	*				*		*	
Achievement		*	*					

Source: Maysami and Goby (1999).

Table 9.3 *Major Problems Faced by Female Business Owners*

Major Problems	Breen, Calvert and Oliver (1995)	Teo (1996)	Leo-Gosselin and Grise (1990)	Neider (1989)	Brown and Segal (1989)	Collerette and Aubry (1991)	Hisrich and Brush (1984)	Rashid (1996)	Stoner, Hartman and Arora (1990)
Obtaining Credit		A, B				C	A	B	
Lack of Collateral							A	A	
Lack of Capital			A					A	
Competition	C	A, B							
Establishing Credibility		A	A						
Coping With Costs		A			C				
Labor		A	B						
Personal		A	A	C					
Making Business Profitable					C				
Administrative Work					C				
Delegating Authority				C					
Lack of Experience							B		
Lack of Respect/Acceptance	C					C			
Work–Home Conflict	C			C		C			C

Notes: A – problems encountered during the start-up stage; B – problems encountered after the launch of the business; C – other major problems.

Source: Maysami and Goby (1999).

179

Table 9.4   Factors that Contributed to the Success of Women Business Owners

Factors	Teo (1996)	Deng, Hassan and Jivan (1995)	Rashid (1996)	Hisrich and O'Brien (1981)	Kelly (1985)	Leo-Gosselin and Grise (1990)	Bachemin (1989)	Woodward (1988)	Kotter (1982)
Family Support		*		*					
Knowledge of Culture and Language		*							
Communication Skills			*					*	*
Human Relation Skills			*						
Personal Qualities	*	*		*		*			
Knowledge of Product and Service	*								
Quality of Product and Service	*					*			
Customer Loyalty	*								
Quality of Personnel	*								
Availability of Professional Services					*				
Technological Advantage	*								
Availability of Finance	*								
Presence of Opportunities				*			*		
Desire to Succeed					*		*		

Source: Maysami and Goby (1999).

VIETNAM WOMEN ENTREPRENEURS

In Vietnam, only one-fifth of the women entrepreneurs in all sectors are said to have received training, compared with nearly one-half of their male counterparts (Lan, 2001). In response to this deficiency, a new project was established to improve the women's livelihoods by training women entrepreneurs in the food-processing sector. The focus of the project was to teach 25 trainers food-processing technology, management and marketing skills, so that they, in turn, could teach at least 300 women entrepreneurs. The project was a direct response to some of the challenges put forward by the government's strategy for the advancement of women, including promoting employment, reducing poverty and strengthening vocational training.

PAKISTANI WOMEN ENTREPRENEURS

One study which looked at women entrepreneurs from a developing country's standpoint was carried out with women entrepreneurs in Pakistan. The authors departed from other studies by looking at actual and potential women entrepreneurs in the urban formal sector by using a symbolic interactionist approach (Shabbir and Di Gregorio, 1996). This approach focuses on women's perceptions and the way they define their goals and the advantages and constraints they face in starting a business at a micro level. Data for the study are gathered through in-depth interviews of 33 participants in an Entrepreneurship Development Program (EDP) in Pakistan.

The study revealed that the women entrepreneurs wanted to start a business in order to achieve three types of personal goals, namely: personal freedom, security and satisfaction. The impact of structural factors on the women's ability to start a business varied according to the dominant personal goal the women chose. Structural factors influencing start-up were divided into three categories: internal resources – qualifications and/or work experience; external resources –finance and location; and relational resources – family, employees, suppliers and customers (Shabbir and Di Gregorio, 1996).

SAUDI ARABIAN WOMEN ENTREPRENEURS

More recent research has documented the rise of women business owners in Saudi Arabia (Pope, 2002). They operate businesses such as computing companies, boutiques and other small, mostly retail ventures. This new tolerance shown to women business owners does have limits. Some of the women entrepreneurs are seen as stand-ins for their civil servant relatives, who aren't allowed to own or operate private business or the women are heiresses, divorced from day-to-day management of their operations. Quite a number of the women, however, are involved in the actual operation of their businesses and thus the torturous job of navigating the path of business ownership in that society (Pope, 2002).

FRENCH WOMEN ENTREPRENEURS

A study by Orhan and Scott (2001) developed a model of the factors which motivated women to start their own businesses. They used a qualitative research method that involved 25 French women entrepreneurs. The research was conducted in three regions of Paris and the women entrepreneurs were identified by using business directories as well as by using a snowball sampling technique. The sample was biased in favor of large industrial firms, with 48% employing 10 employees or more. The research identified a range of reasons why females become entrepreneurs, namely: dynastic compliance, they had no other choice, entrepreneurship by chance, natural succession, forced entrepreneurship, informed entrepreneurship and pure entrepreneurship (see Table 9.5).

There were a number of cases that fell into the 'entrepreneur by chance' category, which associates the characteristics of the 'evolution of women' with push factors, individual or environmental. Three of the women entrepreneurs were leading or co-leading their businesses, either by succession because it was a family business or acquisition upon attaining sufficient experience. In some cases, the business itself might have been created with a combination of the husband's technical expertise and the wife's commercial and administrative experience.

For the pure entrepreneurs, running their own businesses occurred as a natural progression from their previous experience (Orhan and Scott, 2001). The authors contended that five women entrepreneurs represented the 'evolution of women' trend and that they had chosen entrepreneurship for 'pull' reasons, claiming environmental influences. In some cases, business succession circumstances, role models, or business partners ensured expertise and/or financial backing. Only two women entrepreneurs represented the 'evolution of women' characteristics, having started their businesses as a result of necessity factors.

A 2002 Executive Report, entitled the Global Entrepreneurship Monitor (GEM), completed by Reynolds et al. stated that more than 460 million adults around the world were engaged in entrepreneurial activity in 2002. It was reported that men were twice as likely to be involved in processes that led to entrepreneurial activity than women (Reynolds et al., 2002). In developed countries, women were more involved where there was equality in career opportunities; however, in developing countries women's participation reflected

Table 9.5 Typology of Identified Motivations for Women to Become Entrepreneurs

Motivations	Male Domination	Evolution of Women	Women's Identity
Influence of Environment	Dynastic Compliance	Natural Succession	
Influence of Environment and Push Factors		Entrepreneur by Chance	
Push Factors	No Other Choice	Forced Entrepreneur	
Pull Factors		Informed Entrepreneur	Pure Entrepreneur

Source: Orhan and Scott (2001).

the lack of jobs in the mainstream labor market and inadequate education. The report identified two main types of entrepreneur that exist worldwide, and defined them as follows:

- 'opportunity entrepreneurs', who perceive a business opportunity (electing to start a business as one of several possible career options);
- 'Necessity entrepreneurs', who see entrepreneurship as a last resort (feeling compelled to own a business because all other options are either absent or unsatisfactory).

The report indicated that both gender and age play a major role in predicting participation rates in entrepreneurial activity (see Table 9.6). Overall, the report showed that men are about 50% more likely to be involved in entrepreneurial activity than women (13.9% to 8.9%). This ratio is even greater for opportunity-based entrepreneurship (9.3% to 4.9%), but becomes more equal with necessity-based entrepreneurship (4.2% for men and 3.8% for women). The prevalence rates peak at 25 to 34 years of age for both men and women involved in all types of entrepreneurial activity. The next most active age groups are those who are 18 to 24 and 35 to 44 years of age. Participation is generally lowest for those aged 55 and older and entrepreneurial activity is almost non-existent among those of 65 years of age and older (Reynolds et al., 2002).

The report also documents that there is no country where women are more active than men, but there are a number of countries where the difference is not statistically significant. This occurs most often in countries where prevalence rates are quite low and the dearth of activity leads to small sample sizes and large standard errors. While, in general, men are about twice as likely to be involved in entrepreneurship as women, there is substantial variation from country to country. Participation is almost equal in a number of developing countries (e.g., Thailand, China, South Africa and Mexico) but the ratio exceeds 3:1 in some European and developed Asian countries (e.g., Croatia, Israel and Japan).

Correlations between several national characteristics believed to impact the status of women overall, and opportunity and necessity entrepreneurship in particular, are presented in Tables 9.7 and 9.8. The results are presented in such a way as to facilitate two comparisons: (1) women with men and (2) high per capita income countries with low per capita income countries. Reviewing these tables, it is immediately apparent that there is a substantial difference between the two types of country. Clearly, there are more statistically significant correlations in the nations with low per capita income and in addition, the patterns of correlations differ between the two countries (Reynolds et al., 2002):

- Population growth is associated with more female entrepreneurship only in developing countries.
- Unregistered (i.e., 'black market') economic activity is associated with less entrepreneurship in high per capita income countries and more entrepreneurship in low income per capita countries.
- Greater economic security is associated with less entrepreneurship in all countries for both men and women.
- Higher female-to-male participation in the labor force is associated with reduced participation in entrepreneurship, particularly in developing countries.
- More female participation in public or private administrative roles is associated with more entrepreneurship in high income countries, but with less entrepreneurship in low income countries.
- A higher proportion of women working in industry (manufacturing, wholesale and construction) is associated with less entrepreneurship. More women working in agriculture is positively correlated with more entrepreneurship in low income countries. Greater numbers of women working in services is related to higher levels of entrepreneurial activity in high income countries.
- Female unemployment, short or long term, is associated with less entrepreneurship in low income countries.
- Illiteracy in low income countries seems to be associated with higher levels of entrepreneurial activity.

Table 9.6   *Entrepreneurial Activity by Gender and Age*

By Age and Category	Women (Number per 100)	Men (Number per 100)
TEA All		
18–24 years	7.7	13.2
25–34 years	12.8	19.7
35–44 years	10.2	14.6
45–54 years	6.2	11.2
55–64 years	5.0	6.8
TEA Opportunity		
18–24 years	5.6	10.8
25–34 years	7.6	13.3
35–44 years	5.2	9.8
45–54 years	3.2	7.1
55–64 years	2.5	3.7
TEA Necessity		
18–24 years	1.9	1.8
25–34 years	5.0	6.0
35–44 years	4.8	4.3
45–54 years	3.0	4.1
55–64 years	2.4	2.8
Nascent Firms		
18–24 years	4.1	8.1
25–34 years	7.3	10.6
35–44 years	6.0	7.9
45–54 years	3.7	6.2
55–64 years	3.0	3.8
New Firms		
18–24 years	3.7	6.1
25–34 years	6.1	10.3
35–44 years	4.7	7.0
45–54 years	2.8	5.3
55–64 years	2.2	3.3

Note: TEA Total Entrepreneurial Activity.

Source: Reynolds et al. (2002).

Table 9.7   Correlations between Entrepreneurial Activity and Selected Factors Believed to Affect Women's Participation in Entrepreneurship High per Capita Income Countries (more than $18,000/year)

Correlations	Women TEA Overall	Women TEA Opportunity	Women TEA Necessity	Men TEP Overall	Men TEA Opportunity	Men TEA Necessity
Population Growth 1996–2002	0.06	0.09	0.21	0.25	0.22	0.46*
Unofficial Economy as % of GDP	-0.19	-0.38	0.16	-0.14	-0.22	-0.30
Social Security as % of GDP	-0.46*	-0.49*	-0.32	-0.50*	-0.50*	-0.54*
Female/Male Labor Force Participation Ratio	0.12	0.22	-0.42*	0.04	0.11	-0.29
% Women in Public Agency Management	0.37	0.43*	0.04	0.15	0.24	-0.10
% Women in Private Management	0.52**	0.31	0.51**	0.39	0.32	-0.24
% Women Work in Agriculture	-0.09	-0.23	-0.14	-0.14	-0.20	-0.28
% Women Work in Industry	-0.42*	-0.50*	0.12	-0.27	-0.40	-0.14
% Women Work in Services	0.42*	0.52*	-0.02	0.32	0.37	0.28
Female Current Unemployment	-0.11	-0.24	-0.01	-0.24	-0.31	-0.42*
Female Long-term Employment	-0.30	-0.47*	0.07	-0.34	-0.44*	-0.38
Female Illiteracy Rate	N/A	N/A	N/A	N/A	N/A	N/A

Notes: TEA = Total Entrepreneurial Activity; TEP = * < 0.05, ** < 0.01, *** < 0.001.

Source: Reynolds et al. (2002).

186

Table 9.8 Correlations between Entrepreneurial Activity and Selected Factors Believed to Affect Women's Participation in Entrepreneurship Low per Capita Income Countries (less than $18,000/year)

Correlations	Women TEA Overall	Women TEA Opportunity	Women TEA Necessity	Men TEA Overall	Men TEA Opportunity	Men TEA Necessity
Population Growth 1996–2002	0.63**	0.50**	0.49**	0.77***	0.76***	0.49*
Unofficial Economy as % of GDP	0.18	0.17	0.11	0.17	0.11	0.18
Social Security as % of GDP	−0.42*	−0.42*	−0.19	−0.47*	−0.56*	0.14
Female/Male Labor Force Participation Ratio	−0.34	−0.05	−0.54*	−0.47*	−0.32	−0.55*
% Women in Public Agency Management	0.20	−0.23	−0.07	−0.13	−0.15	−0.02
% Women in Private Management	−0.36	−0.22	−0.42	−0.58*	−0.46	−0.56*
% Women Work in Agriculture	0.52*	0.68*	0.04	0.15	0.25	−0.06
% Women Work in Industry	−0.47*	−0.29	−0.56*	−0.55*	−0.46	−0.52*
% Women Work in Services	−0.28	−0.49*	0.20	0.09	−0.03	0.27
Female Current Unemployment	−0.58*	−0.51*	−0.35	−0.56*	−0.57*	−0.31
Female Long Term Employment	−0.64*	−0.55	−0.72*	−0.58	−0.55	−0.48
Female Illiteracy Rate	0.49*	0.34	0.49*	0.45*	0.51*	0.24

Notes: TEA = Total Entrepreneurial Activity; TEP = * < 0.05, ** < 0.01, *** < 0.001.

Source: Reynolds et al. (2002).

There are a number of instances where the correlations are different for opportunity-motivated females than they are for those motivated by necessity, including: in the face of higher female/male labor force participation ratios, in sectors in which women are employed, and with high female illiteracy rates. This suggests that dissimilar processes led to opportunity and necessity entrepreneurship among women – a finding that holds for men as well.

In addition to the clear differences in many factors associated with the level of national per capita income, there are a number of differences associated with gender. There are differential impacts between males and females related to population growth, women in management and administrative positions, and the types of sectors where women are working. However, the impact on men and women is largely uniform with regard to: female/male labor force participation rates, presence of unofficial economic activities, social security payments, unemployment, and female illiteracy.

In sum, the report indicates that women make up a substantial proportion of those pursuing entrepreneurship (Reynolds et al., 2002). However, the process of involvement appears to differ significantly in comparison to the processes that affect men. This is particularly true in countries where there is a shortage of entrepreneurs, and where the overall participation of women should be especially encouraged. Their report suggests that any national effort to be more inclusive may be greatly facilitated by a more complete understanding of the unique experience of entrepreneurial females.

AFRICAN WOMEN ENTREPRENEURS

A report sponsored by the United Nations Conference on Trade and Development, published in 2001, highlighted the predicament of women entrepreneurs from a number of African countries. The report indicated that the failure of economic structures to provide viable sources of income for women often causes them to embrace the world of entrepreneurship, thus relying on their own initiatives to develop a business enterprise and sources of income (Radhakishun, 2001). The first section of the report looks at interviews with 235 women entrepreneurs in six African Least Developed Countries (LDCs), namely, Burkina Faso (48), Zambia (35), Ethiopia (27), Gambia (40), Madasgascar (75) and the United Republic of Tanzania (120). For the majority of the women entrepreneurs in the study (see Table 9.9), the idea to start a business was their own, and the type of businesses to operate was generally an extension of their home or work experience (Radhakishun, 2001).

The businesses surveyed in this study were small and in general, the women often used their personal savings and did not rely on any form of institutional support. The majority of the women had some secondary or high school education, with 15% of the sample completing higher education. The results were more dubious with regard to market research, with most of the women entrepreneurs lacking such experience, resulting in women entrepreneurs being less likely to be exposed to the international market, especially when compared to their male counterparts (Radhakishun, 2001).

The problems faced by women entrepreneurs in the study from the LDCs included access to financial capital, land, production inputs, adequate business premises to operate the business and helpful information on business opportunities. The women entrepreneurs in the six countries were not aware of the advantages of networking and rarely implemented networking practices with others in their circle. They also lacked business and management skills and needed training focused on business development services. Where the latter services did exist, the women entrepreneurs were often not aware of their existence. In addition, a lack of confidence, the absence of role models and the public's poor image of a woman entrepreneur were also described as key factors or problems from the study. Participation and assistance by government agencies relevant to the development of women's entrepreneurship while judged insufficient did exist in these countries (see Tables 9.10 and 9.11) (Radhakishun, 2001).

A second study detailed in the same report looked at women entrepreneurs in industrial developed countries, such as Cote d'Ivoire, Ethiopia, Mali, Morocco, Senegal and Zimbabwe (de Groot, 2000). The author found that the problems faced by women entrepreneurs to be similar to the ones faced by their counterparts in Radhakishun's 2001 report. The report showed that the women entrepreneurs were poorly educated and had low skill levels; that they had limited access to funding and information; inadequate infrastructures and training; and that they had limited access to appropriate production sites (de Groot, 2001). There were also strong barriers to women's enterprise development based on the countries' applicable laws and policies regarding women as business owners, as well as a lack of networking and training. This second paper from the report also contended that socio-cultural factors were levied against women entrepreneurs by various cross-sections of the society (de Groot, 2001).

These findings were also asserted in an earlier paper by Takyi-Asiedu (1993) who stated that the social structure in some African countries has placed women in a subservient position to the men in their society. In support of this statement, de Groot's paper explained that, while women in those countries engaged in enterprising ventures, it was done with a restriction on their mobility and advancement. The paper ended by recommending that changes be made in regard to government policies and strategies, institutional support and the level of involvement of women in their network structures to aid women's entrepreneurial advancement.

Table 9.9   Profile of Women Entrepreneurs in African LDCs (in percentage points)

Category	Burkina Faso	Ethiopia	The Gambia	Madagascar	Zambia
Sector and Industry					
Manufacturing	60	31	55	47A	70B
– Textile and Garment Manufacturers	25	–	10C	–	–
– Food and Beverage Production	35	–	–	–	–
– Trading	17	46	25D	28	–
– Other Services	23	23	20E	53	–
Level of Education					
– Primary School	8	–	3	–	10
– Secondary School	37	–	49	F	70
– High School/Higher Education	15	–	48	–	15
– Not Specified	40	–	10	–	5
Affiliation with Business Associations	–	–	25	28G	0.4
Number of Entrepreneurs Interviewed	48	27	40	75	35

Notes:

A   Of which 9% industrial manufacturing and 38% handicraft, textile and garment manufacturing.
B   Of which 30% are trading enterprises.
C   Trading included.
D   Of which 10% trading in agricultural products and 15% retail trading.
E   Includes production and trading of food and beverages.
F   The majority of Madagasi women entrepreneurs interviewed had completed at least secondary education.
G   Of medium-sized enterprises only.
–   No data available.

Source: Radhakishun (2001).

Table 9.10   Economic Empowerment of Women: Review of Policies and Governmental Framework

BURKINA FASO

Administrative Structure	• Ministry for the Promotion of Women.
Policy	• National action plan for follow-up to the Beijing Platform for Action.
	• Incorporation of gender concerns in policy planning.
Laws and Regulations	• Economic role of women: Investment code amended (1992).
Gender Awareness	• Initiated: Focused awareness creation at policy levels.

ETHIOPIA

Administrative Structure	• Minister-headed Central Coordinating Bureau on Women (1993).
	• Women's bureaus mandatory in national and regional ministries.
Policy	• National policy on women (1993).
	• Incorporation of gender concerns in policy planning.
	• Planned: Women-specific micro, small and medium-sized enterprise development strategy (Ministry of Trade and Development).
Laws and Regulations	• Enabling legal framework for SMEs: planned.
Gender Awareness	• Initiated: focused awareness creation at policy levels.
Women's Access and Involvement	• Access to business financing/support and to markets: some improvement for women entrepreneurs.

THE GAMBIA

Administrative Structure	• Western Bureau established.
	• Department of Community Development.

Table 9.10   concluded

Policy	• Prepared: draft national policy for the advancement of women. • Component on women's entrepreneurship included in industrial development policy. • Component on women's entrepreneurship included in enterprise development policy.

MADASGASCAR

Administrative Structure	• Secretariat of State for Women's Affairs (1996).
Policy	• Women in development policy.
Laws and Regulations	• Improvement of legal status of women: rules amended and adopted.

UNITED REPUBLIC OF TANZANIA

Administrative Structure	• Ministry for Women's Affairs (1990).
Policy	• Women in development policy (1992). • Component on women's SMEs included in industrial development policy. • Component on women included in community development policy.

ZAMBIA

Administrative Structure	• Gender in Development Division, GIDD (1996). • Gender focal points appointed in all ministries, provinces, districts and some specialized agencies.
Women's Access and Involvement	• Appointment of women to boards of the central bank and trade fair.

Source: Radhakishun (2001).

*Table 9.11   Enhancing Women's Entrepreneurship: Government,
Multilateral Bodies and NGOs*

BURKINA FASO

Credit Provision
- PAPME (Projet d'Appui aux Petites et Moyennes Enterprises).
- FAARF (Fonds d'Appui aux activités remuneratrices des femmes).

Credit and Training Programmes
- BA (Bureau des artisans).
- BAME (Bureau des artisans et de moyennes entreprises).
- PERCOMM (Promotion des entreprises rurales de construction metallique et des mecaniciens).
- CAPEO (Cellule d'appui à la petite entreprise de Ouagadougou).
- BAME
- DGAPME (Direction Générale de l'artisanat et des petites et moyennes entreprises).

Business Development Services
- PERCOMM

ETHIOPIA

Credit Provision
- SFPI (specialized financial and promotional institutes): focus on micro-credit (75% women clients).

Credit and Business Development Services
- UNICEF integrated service packages.

Training Programmes
- Handicraft training (pottery, carpet weaving, leather processing).
- Garment and textile manufacturing.
- UNCTAD's Entrepreneurship Development Programme (EMPRETEC).

Market Information and Networking
- UNCTAD's Trade Points Programme.
- UNCTAD's ETOS (Electronic Trading Opportunities) Programme through the Trade Points Programme.

Table 9.11   continued

	THE GAMBIA
Credit and Training	• AFET (Association of Farmers, Educators and Traders). • IDRC (international Development Research Centre , Canada). • IBAS (Indigenous Business Advisory Services). • CRS (Catholic Relief Services).
Credit,Training and Business Support	• Enterprise Development Project, IDAC (International Development Agency). • IBAS Government, ILO and UNDP. • WID (Women in Development Project), World Bank. • Social Development Fund, ABD, GWFA (African Development Bank/Gambia Women's Finance Association).
Entrepreneurship Development and Income Generation Projects	• ASP (Agriculture Services Project), UNDP. • Women's Programme, Department of Community Development – handicraft, home management and income generation.
Networking	• AATG (Action Aid the Gambia). • GCCI (Gambia Chamber of Commerce and Industry).
Legal Aid	• AATG.
	MADAGASCAR
Training Programmes	• Development of women's SMEs (UNDP, ILO). • Programme for Technological Development.
MSME Development Programmes	• ILO and UNIDO.

Table 9.11   concluded

	UNITED REPUBLIC OF TANZANIA
Credit Provision	● Presidential Trust Fund.
	● Women Development Fund
	● Women's Credit Scheme, MCDWCA (Ministry of Community Development).
	● SIDO (Small Industrial Development Organization).
	● Cooperative and Rural Development Bank.
Training Programmes	● MCDWCA (small entrepreneurs, textile sector, food technology).
	● VETA (Vocational Education and Training Authority), ABD and Government and bilateral donors.
Entrepreneurship Development Programmes	● SIDO, UNIDO.
Access to International Markets	● Special technical assistance programme for export development, BET (Board of External Trade), ITC, UNDP and Government.
	ZAMBIA
Credit Provision	● Micro-bankers trust.
Networking	● Business networking facilities established.

Source: Radhakishun (2001).

EUROPEAN WOMEN ENTREPRENEURS

It has been argued that family business enterprises in particular and the overall area of entrepreneurship in general can be an adaptive response to the transformations that have been characterizing various European countries (Hennon et al., 1998). It is also said to be at the center of changes in Eastern Europe and in the Commonwealth of Independent States (CIS) (Ruminska-Zimny, 2002). This phenomenon of entrepreneurship is characterized as an important source of job creation and opens up career opportunities for men and women alike. Factors motivating women to start their own business (see Table 9.12) include: a quest for independence, the need for reasonable earnings and an innate spirit of enterprise (Ruminska-Zimny, 2002; Lisowska, 2002).

The level of inequality between the two genders in Europe has resulted in women entrepreneurs facing barriers in starting their businesses, gaining access to information, utilizing networks and obtaining collateral (Ruminska-Zimny, 2002). Some of the problems faced by women entrepreneurs in Poland and Lithuania (see Table 9.13) include: instability of tax regulation, lack of operating capital and additional problems in the marketplace (Ruminska-Zimny, 2002; Lisowska, 2002). The report by Ruminska-Zimny also indicated that women entrepreneurs need these difficulties to be eliminated and to be able to obtain

Table 9.12   Factors Motivating Women to Set Up their Own Business in Poland, Ukraine and Lithuania (in percent)

Factors	Poland	Ukraine	Lithuania
Quest for Independence	90	79	87
Need for Reasonable Earnings	83	84	46
Innate Spirit of Enterprise	70	80	69
Experience Gained in Previous Jobs	62	73	64
Opportunity to Make Money	56	73	44
Values Inculcated at Home	49	68	23
Inclination to Take Risk	46	66	60
Acquired Profession	43	70	63
Desire to Prove Worth to Husband/ Partner	40	33	40
Parental Example	35	60	29
Threat of Unemployment	35	19	25
Family and/or Social Pressures	30	47	48
Depreciation of Savings	21	16	27

Source: Lisowska (2002).

Table 9.13   Problems Reported by Women Entrepreneurs in Poland and Lithuania (Percentages)

Problems	Poland	Lithuania
Instability of Tax Regulation	79	92
Lack of Reliable Banks	21	79
Lack of Operating Capital	37	77
Lack of Market Research	26	48
Dishonesty and Lack of Principle in the Marketplace	35	39
Lack of Opportunities to Enter Foreign Markets	18	42
Lack of Stable Staff	26	42

Source: Lisowska (2002).

financial assistance, to find business partners and access markets. The report claimed that difficulties in achieving the latter were caused by the uneven distribution of assets under privatization, work–family conflict issues regarding time allowed to women and negative attitudes towards women entrepreneurs based on discriminatory practices and attitudes and traditional views of gender roles in these societies (Ruminska-Zimny, 2002).

The number of women entrepreneurs in Hungary constitutes almost one-third of the total number of entrepreneurs and 11% of employed women (Lisowska, 2002). The figures for women entrepreneurs in Poland (see Table 9.14) are similar to those in Hungary. In other transition countries, the share of women entrepreneurs varies between 9% in Turkey and almost 50% in the Republic of Mohdova. In the transitional countries, women entrepreneurs are usually reported to have an average age of 40 years or more, they are more likely to be married, with one or two children and have longstanding experience of work in the public sector. A high percentage of women entrepreneurs possess tertiary, college or secondary level education and they often set up enterprises in the trade industries. Women entrepreneurs in Poland, Lithuania and Ukraine cite a quest for independence, an innate spirit of entrepreneurship and aspirations to achieve a high income as the three most important factors motivating them to become entrepreneurs (Lisowska, 2002).

The burden of expanding small and medium-sized businesses in the Russian Federation, developing entrepreneurial activity and boosting employment fell on women entrepreneurs to a large extent (Politova, 2002). The discriminatory practices faced by women entrepreneurs, especially in regard to access to financial capital would need to be alleviated according to Politova's report. Women entrepreneurs in the Russian Federation, Slovenia, The Czech Republic and

Table 9.14   Entrepreneurs in Poland in 1989–1999 (Outside Individual Agriculture)

| Year | Dynamics of Growth/ Decrease in the Number of Own-account Workers Outside Agriculture Previous Year = 100 | | | % of Women Entrepreneurs in Total of Employed Women | % of Women in Total of Entrepreneurs |
	Total	Women	Men		
1989	130.6	120.5	134.6	3.7	27.1
1990	124.4	132.4	125.5	5.3	28.1
1991	120.8	143.5	112.1	7.9	33.3
1992	101.9	109.5	98.1	8.9	35.8
1993	112.5	108.2	114.8	9.6	34.5
1994	73.9	70.2	75.8	6.7	32.8
1995	97.4	109.5	91.4	7.3	36.9
1996	96.1	91.1	99.0	6.4	35.0
1997	115.0	116.8	114.0	7.2	35.5
1998	102.8	116.4	95.4	8.3	40.2
1999	97.0	84.4	105.5	7.2	35.0

Source: Lisowska (2002).

Croatia also needed improved technological access, which in turn would aid their networking efforts to communicate with other women entrepreneurs in other geographic regions (Turk, 2002; Putnova, 2002; Politova, 2002 and Perkov, 2002).

CANADIAN WOMEN ENTREPRENEURS

A number of articles have chronicled the position of women entrepreneurs in Canada and their findings will be presented in the following sections. These begin with a look at the early 1990s and range from assessments of home-based employment, to ethnic enterprises, to women entrepreneurs' access to financial credit. Riding and Swift (1990) employed a sample of 153 women entrepreneurs and found on aggregate that they received credit on less favorable terms than their male counterparts. The study also found that female-owned firms tended to be younger, smaller and less likely to be incorporated businesses when compared to their male counterparts. In addition, the women entrepreneurs' enterprises were characterized by lower rates of sales growth than their male counterparts. The authors found that these differences in the business characteristics of the two groups contributed to the differences in credit terms between the two groups and was not so much the result of a straight gender bias (Riding and Swift, 1990).

The preceding results were confirmed in a later article by Cliff (1998) who sought to explain the typically small sizes of enterprises operated by women entrepreneurs when compared to their male counterparts. In looking at attitudes towards growth of their businesses of 141 male business owners and 88 female business owners, the author found sharp differences in the two groups' perceptions of growth. The women in the sample were more likely to head service firms and less likely to head manufacturing and wholesale firms and operated small-sized firms that they had owned for fewer years than their male counterparts. Although both groups desired growth, the findings indicated that the women entrepreneurs were more likely to establish maximum thresholds with regard to their business size beyond which they would prefer not to expand (Cliff, 1998). Such maximum sizes were dependent on achieving a work–family balance, a lowering of risk and a limiting relevance on large debt to operate their businesses. Cliff (1998) concludes that the findings are important for policy-makers and government programs interested in seeing women's businesses expand and should be taken into account as such areas are addressed.

A general portrait of women entrepreneurs in the province of Quebec, Canada in the late 1980s to the early 1990s showed a varying profile. A total of 303 women entrepreneurs from the nine administrative regions of Quebec were surveyed. Half of the women entrepreneurs surveyed had been in business for less than five years and had participated in the funding of the business (Collerette and Aubry, 1990). The start-up capital invested by approximately half of the women business owners at the business's inception was around $10,000 and when she borrowed money from a financial institution, she needed a co-signor in 35% of cases, twice as often as her male counterparts (Collerette and Aubry, 1990).

The women entrepreneurs in the sample were relatively young, with an average age of 37 years, married and had 2.3 children. They were also primarily involved in a partnership and were concentrated in small businesses of five employees or less. The major factors that motivated the female entrepreneurs to go into business in this instance were the desire to be their own boss, to achieve financial independence and to improve their self-esteem. Only 40% of the women entrepreneurs had prior work experience in the sector they chose to operate their businesses in and they faced two major problems during the operation of their business: work–family conflict issues and access to financial capital (Collerette and Aubry, 1990).

A study which looked at Canada's most successful women entrepreneurs was conducted by Belcourt (1990) at approximately the same time as the preceding study. The article's main thrust was a look at the motivating factors leading to the 36 women entrepreneurs in the sample embracing entrepreneurship. The sample portrayed businesses that had more than eleven employees, had been in operation for 6–10 years and with sales or gross revenue values of $2–5 million. In addition, most of the sample was concentrated in the services sector (33%), followed by manufacturing (31%), retail (17%), wholesale (14%) and real estate (6%) (Belcourt, 1990).

A focus on immigrant women who owned and operated their own enterprises in Canada was also studied. An article by Marger and Hoffman (1992) showed that Chinese immigrants are the most dominant sector, operating mainly in the Toronto metropolitan area. This was based on strong 'push' and 'pull' factors in the host country which propelled them into seeing entrepreneurship as a viable source of income. The dominance of Chinese immigrants' involvement in entrepreneurship in Canada was confirmed in a follow-up study by Wong and Ng (1998). Most of the participants in this latter sample were male, but women were also interviewed. The average age of all the entrepreneurs was 46 years, businesses were small in size, with a level of education beyond the secondary level. The authors argues that for many Chinese immigrant entrepreneurs in Vancouver, there are structural constraints and blocked mobility in the non-ethnic/open market that relegate entrepreneurs to ethnic enclaves (defined as a community and thus income source and economy, for a particular minority group, Boyd, 1996; Phizacklea, 1988; Raijman, 2001) in order to achieve success (Wong and Ng, 1998).

CONCLUSION

After reading the preceding section, it can be universally acknowledged that women entrepreneurs worldwide for the most part share similar features. They are primarily in their forties, with some in their fifties, have approximately two children and are more likely to be married. In addition, numerous research studies have showed that women entrepreneurs are well educated, have business and not necessarily entrepreneurial experience in their sector and tend to concentrate in the services or retail services areas that are often an extension of their roles as women, wives and mothers.

The articles cited above also highlight the fact that the formation of entrepreneurial ventures is an effective way to relocate labor and capital and have far-reaching effects on any economy. This is particularly true for developing economies in the Caribbean and African countries and transitional economies such as those in some parts of Europe and some former communist countries.

It is also pertinent to recognize that women as income earners represent a viable source of income for their families, capable of procuring such income in entrepreneurial ventures.

While the importance of women entrepreneurs to an economy cannot be overstated, it is obvious that their progress has been held back by a combination of factors, such as resistance to change in prevailing bureaucratic-administrative business culture, underdeveloped legal and financial infrastructure, lack of access to financial capital, lack of pertinent entrepreneurial and at times managerial skills and restrictive beliefs from societal members on a personal and business level about the roles that women should occupy in their countries.

The studies on women entrepreneurs in various parts of the world have grown over the years with a particularly large volume of contributions surfacing over the past 10 to 15 years. For the most part, these research studies looked at the motivating factors leading to women entrepreneurship, the demographic profiles of the women entrepreneurs in the samples, the challenges they face while operating their entrepreneurial ventures and the factors impacting their entrepreneurial success. At times, such studies have taken comprehensive looks from the standpoint of all four areas or from the perspective across countries, across periods in time from the same country or across gender lines in the same geographic region.

Much of the earlier literature on women entrepreneurs in the global marketplace was reminiscing in character, detailing the failures of outdated economies to respond politically, economically and societally to the plight of the early women entrepreneurs in their regions. Later studies have highlighted the concentration of women entrepreneurs in industries with low returns, emphasizing the need to remove them from such difficult positions.

The very essence of entrepreneurship is the degree of freedom it affords its participants. For women entrepreneurs this is particularly potent since they often face additional difficulties in occupying subservient positions in the mainstream labor market and wider society when compared to their male counterparts. Such subservient positions include lowered wages, work–family conflict issues, lack of movement into management positions and a lack of mentors on the job. While these factors and others (lack of access to financial capital and infrastructure) also classify their entrepreneurship paths, the entrepreneurial occupational route provides a sense of freedom and autonomy to make their own decisions.

As we look towards a new world order that needs to include more women in the income-earning arena over the next several decades, certain factors must be addressed for those involved in the entrepreneurship field. Government regulations and policies must be changed to address the specific needs of women entrepreneurs. The absence of an adequate financial market to overcome the difficulties women entrepreneurs face when striving to access financial resources will need to be addressed. The lack of women's entrepreneurial and business skills needs to be overcome in certain countries if their foray into entrepreneurship is to remain viable. It is only by building this framework of needed solutions that these recommendations can provide credence to the place held by women entrepreneurs in today's global marketplace and their ultimate impact on the development of various countries' economies worldwide.

10. Conclusion

INTRODUCTION

The rise of women entrepreneurs over the last few decades across countries with varying infrastructures, resources and support for their inception and continuance is nothing less than remarkable. Contributing greatly to this rise in the number of women entrepreneurs is the increase in minority women entrepreneurs (DeSimone, 2002; Hovey, 2001; Jackson, 2001; Kirby, 2001; McCrea, 2001; Laverdy, 1995, Neese, 2000; Ojito et al., 2001). Across the globe, women are starting businesses in record numbers in every field imaginable (Blanchflower and Meyer, 1994; Blau, 1987). Although the United States remains one of the most reported countries in studies on women entrepreneurs, women-owned businesses are on the rise everywhere (Chatterjee, 2001). Profound structural changes in various nations, as well as recognition by various facets of society of the advantageous position offered women by the entrepreneurial sector, has contributed to and boosted the importance of this employment sector for all – especially women who sometimes lack opportunities in the mainstream labor market (Furry and Radhakrishna, 1992; Highman, 1985; Himelstein and Anderson, 1997) or who were striving to combine their work and family life (Heck, 1992; Heck et al., 1992; Huff, 2003).

This profound effect of the role of women entrepreneurship is attributable to the fact that women entrepreneurs are more likely than other sectors to operate small business enterprises (Carroll and Mosakowski, 1987; Clarke, 1999; Curran and Blackburn, 1991; Gundry et al., 2002). Recent reports on the increases in women business owners worldwide have been documented with surprising results. In Eastern Germany, women have created a third of the new enterprises since reunification in 1990, providing one million new jobs and contributing US$5 billion to the German Gross National Product (Coughlin and Thomas, 2002). Female entrepreneurs in other transition economies, like Russia, Hungary, Romania and Poland, are making a similar impact. In Latin American countries, according to the World Bank, fully half of all economic growth in the last decade throughout the region is attributable to the creativity and hard work of female entrepreneurs (Browne, 2001). In the Caribbean, a recent study has detailed the importance of entrepreneurship to female's income earning potential (ibid.). In Southeast Asia, female-owned businesses have been at the forefront of that region's economic turnaround since 1997 (Coughlin and Thomas, 2002). In Africa, entrepreneurship has been heralded as a long overdue, but critical component of women's advancement in the income earning sector and in the reduction of their poverty levels (de Groot, 2000). Numerous other studies continue to advocate the importance to continuous economic development of entrepreneurship in general and women's entrepreneurship in particular (Krueger and Brazeal, 1994; Lachman and Brett, 1997; Kloosterman and Van Der Leun, 1999).

In turn, small business enterprises are said to be a critical component of the important cyclical patterns that aid in the financial development of a country's economy (Bollard, 1983; Burkett, 2000; Bird, 1988; Curran et al., 1986; Haskins and Gibb, 1987; Dugan, 1996; Daunis, 1992; Johnson, 1991). In addition to providing income for women business owners, women-owned businesses play a vital role in creating opportunities for employees and increasing the expenditure of affected citizens and thus overall wealth for various economies. As the world embarks on a new century, there remains a strong but almost one-sided call for the continuous support of women entrepreneurs. This one-sided chant speaks of the opportunities, challenges and factors impacting women entrepreneurs' success. Three areas that have come under the spotlight are human capital, financial capital and network structure issues.

HUMAN CAPITAL ISSUES

Human capital has focused on the educational levels, various skills, knowledge and training acquired by an individual and used to determine their worth from an income earning perspective. Earlier in this book, we looked at the elements of a business owner's human capital, which ranged from formal education levels acquired in the classroom to knowledge gained from those in their 'circle' – individuals who were family, friends or acquaintances. What was important to note was that this knowledge base was transformable into income based on the owner's application of the knowledge base and the worth the society applied to such knowledge or human capital. The worth of the knowledge was in part determined (in particular in this case) by what the woman entrepreneur chose to do with this knowledge and, more specifically, how it was applied in the entrepreneurial sector.

Overall, white women entrepreneurs were more likely to have acquired human capital skills when compared to their minority counterparts. The former group did so by having more years of formal academic education and by acquiring more pre-business ownership experience in the form of seminars, programs and entrepreneurial experience. The minority women entrepreneurs were also less likely to have acquired sales, accounting and management experience. In fact, the only area in which the minority women entrepreneurs showed a favorable level of knowledge was that of having school education in the area of the business.

A number of explanations can be advanced for this discrepancy in levels of knowledge acquisition. First, labor market disadvantage theory posits that disadvantaged labor market groups are less likely to be able to accumulate human capital experiences when compared to others because of a lack of mentorship among other challenges. While this proposition has been applied to women and minorities in the past, one could argue that minority women are more likely to have suffered labor market disadvantages when compared to their white counterparts. These disadvantages would have resulted in the former group having accumulated fewer human capital assets when compared to their white counterparts.

This 'doubly-disadvantaged' position of minority women entrepreneurs (Haddleston-Mattai, 1995; Smith and Tienda, 1988) has also had a threefold effect. First, they lack skills acquired from the mainstream labor market. Second, this deficient skill level has resulted in them being less likely to occupy higher paying positions and to have the chance to accumulate wealth. Third, the lack of skill acquisition from the mainstream labor market carries over to the entrepreneurial sector, serving as a disadvantage.

Substantial evidence from this study indicates that this lowered human capital potential of minority women entrepreneurs versus their white counterparts is in part responsible for their lowered profit/income earning position. The fact that human capital and its accumulated worth translates into income for its owner is a critical portion of the argument as to why minority women entrepreneurs earn less than their white counterparts. The current study has provided substantial evidence in that respect.

The lack of and undervaluing of the human capital potential of women entrepreneurs has been further documented in studies that have assessed women in the international marketplace. The importance of human capital to a woman entrepreneur's earning potential has also been documented worldwide. Repeatedly, reports from across the world document how important such an asset is to the development of and earnings acquired by women entrepreneurs worldwide. Education and experience are significant factors in self-employment because the field is one which requires accumulated experiences, skills and material resources to survive (Boyd, 1991).

NETWORK STRUCTURE ISSUES

Described as the 'hidden hand' or the 'blind force', network structures and various related parameters are said to be at the core of an entrepreneur's success.

Network structures, network links and/or social capital have been shown to be important in a number of contexts (Lee and Croninger, 2001; Wilson and Stanworth, 1987; Ramierez-Beltran, 2002; Teixeira, 2001; Tian and Cox, 2002; Wen et al., 2002) and have been conclusively linked to access to financial capital for entrepreneurs (Uzzi, 1999). Such prominence probably derives from the nature of what this element represents, especially for an entrepreneur. One could make a convincing argument that with the entrepreneur at the helm of the business, a lot depends on the entrepreneur's ability to develop contacts (Wilkins, 1980b; Krackhardt and Kilduff, 2002; Woolcock, 2001; Wortman, 1986). These contacts would enable the entrepreneur to gain knowledge, have access to financial resources and provide them with a potential market for their products or services.

The results for the current study showed that minority women entrepreneurs as well as white women entrepreneurs had both developed a network structure consisting of various elements. The minority women entrepreneurs were more likely to have a network structure that comprised friends, family and informal links to social organizations such as churches or women's organizations. The more informal nature of the minority women entrepreneurs' network structure is confirmed in a recent study by Mason-Draffen (2001). In contrast, white women entrepreneurs were more likely to belong to membership organizations and be affiliated to institutions that were more formal. In addition, while the latter group belonged to women's organizations, they also were involved in other organizations that had a mainly male membership. Historically and carefully utilized by immigrants, networks have traditionally been shown as important to an entrepreneur's development and success (Light et al., 1999).

Women entrepreneurs who had an adequate network structure were able to benefit from a variety of factors. Similar to the findings in other studies (Warbington, 2000; Westwood and Bhachi, 1988; Minniti and Bygrave, 1999; Littnen, 2000; Minkes, 1987; Morrison, 2000), individuals who figure prominently in a woman entrepreneur's network structure are: other women entrepreneurs, family, friends, financial advisers and legal advisers. One of the most important factors was having less difficulty in obtaining financial capital or a bank loan when they received assistance from those in their network structures. Networking, in this case, fosters an environment in which the women entrepreneurs receive assistance to complete forms, additional contacts and information that allow them assistance in accessing financial resources and a shared sense of community with those who have been through the process, who know someone who can help with the process or can refer them to someone who can help them through the process.

Networking fosters self-help, allows a forum in which information can be exchanged, improves productivity and provides a web of shared resources. The main concept behind networking is that a group of individuals form links or relationships based on common interests and that these related members help each other in the form of contacts, leads or advice. Clearly, networking is a key ingredient in the development of an entrepreneur's success.

One key factor for women entrepreneurs and the development of their network structures is first understanding what exactly it is that they are trying to achieve. In essence, what are their goals in developing relationships and to what end? With this backdrop in mind, women entrepreneurs can then begin to pursue avenues and outlets that will bring them the specific resources they crave. Based on the findings from the current study, one could trumpet the idea of 'mini-networks'. That is, in the formation of relationships, the quality and not the quantity of the relationships is a factor. By focusing on smaller, but more effective links, women entrepreneurs are able to gain valuable and rich experiences from network structures that are meaningful, but which are subparts of larger network associations. By adopting such a 'nano' focus, the women are able to benefit from the environment offered by network structures, but with a more concentrated level of assistance.

Moore (2000a) spoke of networking activities as a precursor and prerequisite for business ownership. A precursor, since the author stated that such activities should begin before opening a business and serve as a necessary build-up to the start of a business. Networking is important since it provides the potential market and serves as a source of a 'web of contacts' for women entrepreneurs as they progress through their enterprise's development. Moore (2000a) emphasizes the importance of a carefully constructed network plan. The author states that an entrepreneur's network structure is not developed by chance, but is one that should be carefully nurtured and maintained, in order to be beneficial to women entrepreneurs.

One could go further and speak of different types of networks that are important and in fact needed by women entrepreneurs. It would thus not be overly imperative to speak of 'social networks', 'business networks', 'knowledge networks' and 'financial networks'. Each of these networks are different in their composition, but they are also different in the assistance they provide to their members. Network structures can be construed as an example of resources since they are the basis on which contacts that assist the business are built.

Networks and their importance to an entrepreneur's development can never be overrated. The web of contacts in one's network can provide moral support, act as sounding boards and provide business guidance for women entrepreneurs. It has been recommended that women entrepreneurs construct a pre-venture network structure before embarking on a new enterprise (Moore, 2000a). This pre-business development network is said to be critical in providing an extra advantageous position for new entrepreneurs that will continue to provide them with benefits throughout their venture pursuance.

FINANCIAL CAPITAL ISSUES

The overall focus by researchers on small business enterprises and thus women's entrepreneurial ventures is one that is multifaceted and whose investigation needs to be carefully crafted because of the unique problems faced by these small businesses (Finnerty and Krzystofik, 1986; Goldsmith and Blakely, 1992; Ireland and Van Auken, 1987). At the core of these problems is a lack of access to financial resources (Fried, 2002; Johnson, 1990; Joyce, 1988; Kao, 1989; Learned, 1992). Of critical significance is the importance of financial capital at the start-up stage of the business and this has been well documented (Williams-Harold, 1998; Schollhammer and Kuriloff, 1979; Scase and Goffee, 1980; Nelton, 1997; Naffziger et al., 1994). The amount of start-up capital determines the size of the start-up enterprise, the type of industry the entrepreneur will venture into (some industries require larger capital outlays than others) and the circumstances under which the entrepreneur will start the venture (will they need a partner for instance?).

The enterprises of women entrepreneurs have been characterized by lower levels of initial start-up capital, especially as compared to their male counterparts. Minority women entrepreneurs in turn have been characterized by lower levels of start-up capital when compared to their white female counterparts. The causes and reasoning behind this trend have been identified in previous sections, but can again be briefly restated in a twofold perspective. First, there is less access to accumulated wealth for more disadvantaged groups who are also less likely to have held highly financially beneficial positions in the mainstream labor market. Second, more disadvantaged groups are less likely to have access to financial resources (from friends, family or institutions).

This initial lowered access to financial capital has led to women entrepreneurs and especially minority women entrepreneurs relying on their own personal savings to serve as an initial investment in their business. In addition, women entrepreneurs have also relied on assistance from family and friends, with white women entrepreneurs being more likely to do so. The underlying assumption is that white women entrepreneurs are more likely to have stronger network links to individuals who can support and assist their ventures financially. Securing continuous access to financial is tremendously important for the viability, expansion and contribution to wider economic society of female entrepreneurial ventures (Williams-Harold, 1998; Woodcock, 1986). It has also been asserted that women entrepreneurs are less likely to obtain formal financial assistance when compared to their male counterparts (Buttner and Rosen, 1989). Meeting personally with loan officers to 'present their specific case' and answer any unclear questions has been recommended as an effective strategy to overcome this difficulty (ibid.).

One woman entrepreneur in this study lamented the lack of assistance on the local and state level. Bates' (1995a) study did not support such an observation and spoke of loans being given disproportionately to women-owned businesses. Since Bates' (1995a) study, there is no doubt that more financial institutions have become more committed to providing assistance to women entrepreneurs. In recent years such major banks as First Union, Bank of America, Wells Fargo, National City, Fleet and Zions have recognized the potential of the women's small-business owners market and have pledged to lend billions to this group (Kessler, 2001). For African American women seeking help with funding, business plans, networking, expansion and other strategies, over 90 centers nationwide of the Small Business Association of Women Business Ownership are providing assistance (McCrea, 2001). While a step in the right direction, more needs to be done to aid women entrepreneurs across racial lines, especially as their numbers continue to increase.

The issue of economic success is linked to the three other factors that have been prominent in the story that has been told in this book – namely human capital, financial capital and network structures. Figure 2.5 in Chapter 2 of this book proposed a relationship between all four of the preceding factors based on the current literature. The proposition had human capital, network structures and access to financial capital each impacting the women entrepreneur's success. The strong link between human capital and access to financial capital and the

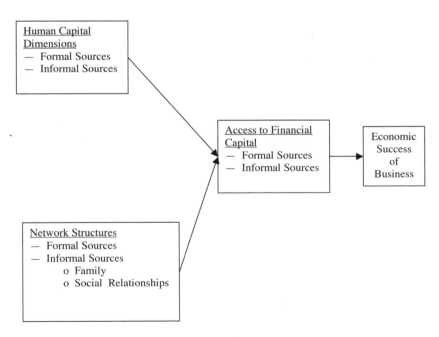

Figure 10.1   Model of Entrepreneurial Success

link between network structures and access to financial capital suggests a transformation of the links between these four factors, with human capital and network structure factors being linked to access to financial capital, which is in turn linked directly to economic success (see Figure 10.1).

Support for the link between human capital and access to financial capital comes to us from Bates (1990), who felt that entrepreneurs with college education have greater access to traditional financial capital sources such as commercial banks. Support for the link between network structures and access to financial capital comes to us from Inman (2000), who described women's financial resources as being intricately entwined with their human capital resources that are also identified in the network structure dimensions. The author added that individuals' relationships provided avenues to wealth, trust in lending and collateral support.

APPLICATIONS OF FINDINGS TO THEORETICAL PERSPECTIVES

Theoretical applications of these links would derive strong arguments for why minority women would be in a more disadvantaged position when it comes to access to financial resources. First, rational choice theory, when applied to minority and white women entrepreneurs, would propose that, based on the circumstances they are in currently, each group of women entrepreneurs would pursue rational choices.

In terms of social embeddedness theory, one could propose that the social networks minority women are embedded in will be less lucrative than the social networks of their white counterparts, thus leading to less accumulated human capital and weaker network structures, which independently and in turn affect their access to financial capital. The resources theory of entrepreneurship, which focuses on the cultural, demographic or economic characteristics or advantages a single group has that aid members who become business owners, details the uneven access to resources of minority versus white women entrepreneurs. In the current study, the application of this theory would posit that minority women entrepreneurs, through their social and business contacts and their work experiences, would be less likely to have strong contacts to help them in their ultimate access to financial resources.

The disadvantage theory, which posits that minority groups will face fewer returns to their labor market contributions because of their less fortunate position, is also applicable in this instance (Bates, 1991; Boyd, 1998, 2002a, 2002b; Blalock, 1967). The more disadvantaged position occupied by minority women in the mainstream labor market has resulted in them being less likely to be compensated for their human capital contributions (Misra, 1999; McGuire and

Reskin, 1993; Bonacich, 1989). It has also resulted in them being less likely to acquire human capital skills, such as management or key decision experiences, which are applicable and necessary in the entrepreneurial world. This less than advantageous position of minority women has followed them into the entrepreneurial world where they are less likely to be compensated for their contributions. The cause of this can be partly explained by their less than needed human capital potential, as well as their weaker network structures when compared to their white counterparts (Butler, 1991). However, this is also partly explainable by the lower value assigned to their contributions.

In the current study, the results indicated that minority women entrepreneurs were less likely to have acquired pre-business ownership experiences when compared to their white counterparts. It was also shown that the former group was more likely to obtain assistance from informal sources (such as friends) and less likely to have obtained assistance from formal sources (such as membership organizations). There is no question that human capital in the form of experiences, education or experiences gained from others and other sources are important to one's financial returns after presenting their work outputs (MaCurdy, 1999; Maffezzoli, 2000; Palme, 2000). The disadvantageous position of the minorities, and other minority classified groups such as immigrants, has been linked to overall lowered accumulated wealth and access to various resources, whether directly or indirectly through their network links (Light and Rosenstein, 1995; Goo, 2001; Green and Pryde, 1990; Hacker, 1995; Heckman and Payner, 1989; Keefe, 2002). The vast difference in access to resources has been documented over the last several decades (Dominguez, 1976; Jenkins, 1985; Portes and Zhou, 1992; Woodard, 1997; Schreiner, 1999). One could state that human capital is in turn determined by a society and the value it places on the work output of various groups (Sabirianova, 2001; Sorger, 2001; Wu, 2002).

The theory of niches, which has its roots in the population ecology model (Hannan and Freeman, 1977), can also be applied to the current study. Ethnic niches are ethnic enclaves or occupations that lend themselves to self-employment (Boyd, 1996; Phizaclea, 1988; Auster and Aldrich, 1984). One could make a strong argument that women entrepreneurs are concentrated in the personal services and retail trade industry because they are filling particular niches to aid a certain market. This market is primarily catering to other women, wives and mothers. However, by focusing on particular areas, the women entrepreneurs can obtain and maintain a competitive advantage in their area of expertise. This filling of these particular niches by women entrepreneurs is tantamount to the fulfillment of ethnic markets or enclaves by various immigrant groups (Cobas, 1989; Lee, 1999; Light and Sanchez, 1987; Aldrich and Waldinger, 1990) or minority groups throughout history (Boyd, 2001, 2002a).

Closely related to the theory of niches, is the concept of a protected market hypothesis (Aldrich et al., 1985) which speaks of the 'protection' of certain entrepreneurial groups from competition due to the unique services they offer. In this case, services that cater for women.

Overall, some of the findings in this study are said to support the liquidity constraint theory that posits that less educated individuals are less likely to have accumulated assets and hence are more likely to face liquidity constraints that make it relatively difficult to pursue entrepreneurship, that is, to access financial resources (Evans and Jovanovic, 1989). This theory is in contrast to the disadvantage theory that posits that individuals who possess limited wage labor skills (or face discrimination) are more apt to earn higher incomes being self-employed than working for wages (Light, 1972, 1979; Min, 1988; Evans and Leighton, 1987 as cited in Dolinsky et al., 1993).

While access to multiple sources of financial capital, the development of an effective network structure and a broad accumulation of human capital dimensions have been cited as important factors in attaining economic success in this and other studies, other factors have also been cited as important variables impacting an entrepreneur's success. They include: multiple methods of establishing customers, effective communication ability, the ability to delegate authority, having varied competitive strategies and developing a long-term plan for company continuation (Maxwell and Westerfield, 2002; Mason-Draffen, 2001; Milne and Thompson, 1986; Miner, 1997).

LINK BETWEEN CURRENT STUDY, NATIONAL RESEARCH AND INTERNATIONAL RESEARCH

The current study found that the motivation for women to embrace entrepreneurship as a viable income alternative was based primarily on the need to earn more family-compensated income, the need to have more autonomy in their career and work–family conflict issues. These findings have been repeated and reaffirmed on a national scale through various studies on women entrepreneurs, as well as internationally by some noted authors (see Maysami and Goby, 1999). Before establishing their own company, it has also been recommended that future entrepreneurs start thinking like entrepreneurs while still employed in the mainstream labor market (Kuratko et al., 1993).

The challenges faced by women entrepreneurs over the three sectors of data outlook (current study, national and international data) can also be assessed. The current study's findings indicated that, overall, women entrepreneurs faced challenges, such as an inadequate level of experience, weaker networks and a lack of access to financial capital. These challenges were even more acute for minority women entrepreneurs, whose 'doubly-disadvantaged' position placed them at even greater risk of being under compensated for their labor contributions. National and international studies done on women entrepreneurs have endorsed these particular challenges as being of key concern to the development and success of women entrepreneurial ventures.

Factors that support women's entrepreneurial success include adequate pre-business ownership experience, knowledge of the industry that one plans to operate in and a good support system that includes formal and informal affiliations that are strong in their assistance. Such success factors have been documented in numerous studies on the national front (Moore and Buttner, 1997; Smith-Hunter, 2003; Loscocco and Robinson, 1991) as well as the international front (see Maysami and Goby, 1999). Another very effective factor for the woman entrepreneur is access to a source of financial capital at the start-up stage and a continuous line of credit during the operation stage of the business.

Other miscellaneous characteristics such as the predominant industries of operation for women entrepreneurs, demographic characteristics such as age, educational levels and marital status and business characteristics such as age of the business and the number of employees remain fairly consistent across the three sectors of data (current study, national data and international data) for the most part. On average, this current study, national and international studies indicate that women entrepreneurs predominate in the services industry. They are also most likely to be in their forties, married and highly educated (compared with their male or labor market counterparts). In addition, women entrepreneurs from all three genres have been in business for an average of 12 years or less, with an average of less than 10 employees.

Exceptions to the preceding generalizations have been deduced from analysis of limited data or unusual sources. Data analyzed from targeted samples such as home-based businesses or highly successful groups of women entrepreneurs have found some slight differences. One area that remains somewhat illusive to pigeonhole is the factors leading to the financial success of women enterprises, especially in terms of the actual quantity of dimensions needed that will cause an impact. However, a sound argument could be made that such success is based primarily on having a strong network structure, especially having formal elements in one's network structure, having more males in the network structures, having a lot of pre-business ownership experiences, especially in the specific industry area of the business, management and marketing experiences and having continuous access to a source of financial capital. Evidence to support the preceding conclusion has been found in the current study and in studies done from national and international data sources.

POLICY IMPLICATIONS FOR IMPROVING WOMEN'S ENTREPRENEURIAL POSITION

One key question that resonates throughout this book is what, if anything, can be done to influence the circumstances under which women entrepreneurs operate on a local, national and international level. The following sections recommend a broad base approach to assisting women entrepreneurs overall, with a forward-thinking approach to their predicament. It covers areas such as human capital, network structures and financial capital.

In terms of human capital issues, women entrepreneurs need to have access to outlets that improve this resource for their entrepreneurial development. Such outlets could include more widespread training in development in areas related to owning one's own business. These outlets could be in the form of short-term seminars or in the form of long-term programs designed to equip women entrepreneurs in the step-by-step process of actually owning a business, what forms need to be filed, what are some useful tips that would ease the initiation process into the entrepreneurial world, etc. Training and development of women entrepreneurs, leading to human capital improvements, should also occur in the specific areas of management or supervisory experiences or marketing experiences. The glass ceiling effect in the mainstream labor market has limited women's ability to be involved in key decision-making processes for an organization. Seminars, programs or long-term development courses that are specifically geared towards addressing this oversight need to be conducted or offered on a regular basis so that women entrepreneurs can be given the opportunity to obtain this training. Such offerings should be specifically geared towards women entrepreneurs who are operating or intend to operate a business.

With the large increase in the number of women entrepreneurs in the marketplace, especially in the last decade, there is a legitimate need for such programs to be more widespread. In addition to having programs that focus on women entrepreneurs, there is also support for the idea of having programs exclusively focused on addressing the needs of minority women entrepreneurs, who through their 'doubly-disadvantaged' position have shown that they have unique needs that might not necessarily be addressed by a more general program for all women entrepreneurs.

In terms of network structures and their development for women entrepreneurs, there is a need to systematically address different aspects of this dimension, in order to adequately aid women entrepreneurs. First, women entrepreneurs need to pursue the development of smaller and more manageable network structures, so the qualities of their network structures are strengthened with very effective links.

Second, women entrepreneurs need to pursue a level of diversity in their network structures. This diversity will increase the chances of having members in the structure from different domains, for example, business contacts for professional assistance as well as members of the network structure who are customers. There is also a need for these network structures to have a mix of formal and informal affiliations. One could state further that the inclusion of more formal affiliations is beneficial to women entrepreneurs improving their access to and the level of their financial resources. Membership organizations have also been strongly linked to a woman entrepreneur's level of financial success.

Finally, women entrepreneurs need to be made aware of the need to nurture and continuously develop their network structures. This management of one's network structure involves more than attending meetings or engaging in some form of contact with the members in the structure. Instead, it should be seen as a key source of potential success or failure for the business and thus women entrepreneurs should actively engage in a 'transactional' relationship with other members of their network structure, resulting in a fair exchange of ideas, services and support.

In terms of the financial dimension, I echo the call of the Milken and National Women's Business Council 2000 report (see Chapter 8 for details), which calls for an amendment of federal laws and changes in current banking policies to include demographic information and thus allowing more personal information to be used in the assessment of granting loans to women entrepreneurs. These recommendations are specifically to accommodate women entrepreneurs who might not meet the broad-based criteria for obtaining loans because of disadvantageous occurrences or discriminatory practices they experienced in their mainstream labor market encounters. These changes would facilitate women entrepreneurs being able to obtain financial resources without the sometimes unrealistic criteria that require previous collateral development on their part. In addition to such legislative changes, there is also a need for banks and financial institutions to move to address the needs of women entrepreneurs at different stages of their development – that is, at the start-up stage, during the operational stages of the businesses and at the expansion stages of entrepreneurial ventures.

CONCLUSION

The tremendous growth in women entrepreneurs in the last three decades is nothing less than a spectacular phenomenon. The growth has forced an overall emphasis on this occurrence and a need to understand the multitude of factors that impact this extraordinary group. There is increased inspiration abounding that calls for an understanding of the motivations for women who abandon their place in the mainstream labor market to engage in entrepreneurial activities. In addition, there is the call to understand the challenges women entrepreneurs face, as well as the factors that lead to their financial success.

This book has documented the answers to these questions through the use of a national data sample. It also answers the call made by Dr Dorothy Moore 14 years ago to address the literature on women business owners with more statistical analysis (Moore, 1990). What is extraordinary about this book's findings is the fact that the analysis is being done against a backdrop across racial lines. Countless studies have analyzed women entrepreneurs and entrepreneurs in general. However, their analysis has more often than not been from the perspective of males versus females or from the perspective of summarizing the findings for all women entrepreneurs without the consideration of differences in race as an issue. This book has stepped up to the plate and answered the call for a comprehensive look at women entrepreneurs across racial lines. By holding gender constant, what emerges from this analysis is a rich description of various groups that aids our understanding of the critical factors impacting different racial groups of women.

In addition to the quantitative analysis, qualitative information is included to help clarify, explain and expand on the quantitative findings. Extensive research from a variety of national sources, with a special emphasis on statistical investigations, was also included in this study. This was followed by numerous studies done on women entrepreneurs in the international marketplace.

There is no doubt that entrepreneurship as a research and practical focus will figure prominently as a sector to be analyzed, evaluated and scrutinized throughout the coming century (Bucar and Hisrich, 2001; Busenitz, 1999; Chen et al., 1998; Daily et al., 1999; Kisfalvi, 2002; McCarthy, 2000; McDougall and Oviatt, 2000; Luthans et al., 2000). Perhaps the most meaningful direction for future research will be the areas of home-based businesses, which has received scant emphasis in the last decade (Owen et al., 1992; Parasuraman et al., 1996; Powers, 1995; Roberts, 1985; Rowe and Bentley, 1992a, 1992b; Rowe et al., 1992; Phillips, 2002; Weigel and Ballard-Reisch, 1997) and franchising, which has just begun to emerge as an option for women entrepreneurs in the last decade (Smith, 2001; Sonderup, 2001). Previously cited as a thinly researched topic (Boden, 1999b), an increased number of studies have addressed various facets of women entrepreneurs to help alleviate the deficiency.

As the body of literature in any area develops, it is useful to stop occasionally, take inventory of the work that has been done and identify new directions and challenges for future research. This reflective stance is essential in order to derive the maximum benefit from a total body of work. This book provides a solid foundation for the study of women entrepreneurs, with its emphasis on three critical areas, namely human capital, network structure and financial capital, and its groundbreaking focus on analyzing these dimensions across racial lines. By engaging in such actions, the book is applicable to a wide variety of audiences, including students, professors, institutions, organizations and others who are interested in impacting and assisting in the field of women entrepreneurship. The primary audience is of course women entrepreneurs, who are currently existing in a new era of the emerging reality of the tremendous impact they are having on their nations' economic development worldwide.

Selected references

Abelda, R. and Tully, C. 1997. *Glass Ceilings and Bottomless Pits: Women's Work, Women's Poverty*. Boston, MA: South End Press.

Acs, Z. and Audretsch, D. 1990. *Innovation and Small Firms*. Cambridge, MA: The MIT Press.

Agresti, A. and Finlay, B. 1986. *Statistical Methods for the Social Sciences*, second edition. San Francisco, CA: Dellen Publishing Company.

Ahrentzen, S. 1990. Managing Conflict by Managing Boundaries: How Professional Homeworkers Cope with Multiple Roles at Home. *Environment and Behavior*, 22, 723–52.

Alderman-Swain, W. and Battle, J. 2000. The Invisible Gender: Educational Outcomes for African American Females in Father-only Versus Mother-only Households. *Race and Society*, 3, 165–82.

Aldrich, H., Brickman, A. and Reese, P. 1995. Strong Ties, Weak Ties, and Strangers: Do Women Business Owners Differ from Men in their Use of Networking to Obtain Assistance? Washington, DC: Small Business Foundation of America.

Aldrich, H., Cater, J., Jones, T., McEvoy, D. and Velleman, P. 1985. Ethnic Residential Concentration and the Protected Market Hypothesis. *Social Forces*, 63(4), 996–1009.

Aldrich, H., Reese, P.R. and Dubini, P. 1989. Women on the Verge of a Breakthrough: Networking among Entrepreneurs in the United States and Italy. *Entrepreneurship and Regional Development*, 1, 339–56.

Aldrich, H. and Sakano, T. 1995. Is Japan Different? The Personal Networks of Japanese Business Owners Compared to those in Four Other Industrialized Nations. *KSU Economic and Business Review*, 22, 1–28.

Aldrich, H. and Tomoaki, S. 1998. Unbroken Ties: How the Personal Networks of Japanese Business Owners Compare to those in Other Nations in Networks and Markets: Pacific Rim Investigations. New York: Oxford Press.

Aldrich, H. and Waldinger, R. 1990. Ethnicity and Entrepreneurship. *Annual Review of Sociology*, 16, 111–35.

Anker, R. 2001. Theories of Occupational Segregation by Sex: An Overview, chapter 8 in *Women, Gender and Work*, edited by Martha Fetherolf Loutfi. Geneva, Switzerland: International Labor Office.

Anna, A., Chandler, G., Jansen, E. and Mero, N. 1999. Women Business Owners in Traditional and Nontraditional Industries. *Journal of Business Venturing*, 279–303.

Aronson, R. 1991. *Self-employment: A Labor Market Perspective.* Ithaca, NY: ILR Press.

Ash, M.K. 1987. *Mary Kay: The Success Story of America's Most Dynamic Businesswoman.* New York: Harper and Row Publishers.

Auster, E. and Aldrich, H. 1984. Small Business Vulnerability, Ethnic Enclaves and Ethnic Enterprise, chapter 3 in *Ethnic Communities in Business*, edited by Robin Wardand and Richard Jenkins. Cambridge: Cambridge University Press.

Ayres-Williams, R. and Brotherton, P. 1999. 5 Hot Business Fields for Women. *Black Enterprise*, September, 107–13.

Babbie, E. 1998. *The Practice of Social Research.* Belmont, CA: Wadsworth Publishing Company.

Bailey, K.B. 1994. *Methods of Social Research*, fourth edition. New York: The Free Press.

Bailey, T. and Waldinger, R. 1991. Primary, Secondary and Enclave Labor Markets: A Training Systems Approach. *American Sociological Review*, 56, 432–45.

Bailyn, Lotte. 1989. Toward the Perfect Workplace? (Social Aspects of Home-based Computing) (contains a related article on the research method used). *Communications of the ACM*, 32, 460–530.

Bannock, G. 1981. *The Economics of Small Firms: Return From the Wilderness.* Oxford: Basil Blackwell Publishers.

Bannock, G. 1986. The Economic Role of the Small Firm in Contemporary Industrial Society, chapter 1 in *The Survival of the Small Firm: The Economics of Survival of the Small Firm*, edited by J. Curran, J. Stanworth and D. Watkins. Aldershot: Gower Publishing Company.

Barrett, M. 1996. Feminist Perspectives on Learning for Entepreneurship: The View from Small Business. *Frontiers of Entrepreneurship Research 1995 Edition.* Massachusetts: Babson College.

Bates, T. 1973. *Black Capitalism: A Quantitative Analysis.* London: Praeger Publishers.

Bates, T. 1985. Entrepreneur Human Capital Endowments and Minority Business Viability. *The Journal of Human Resources*, 20(4), 540–54.

Bates, T. 1986. Characteristics of Minorities who are Entering Self-employment. *The Review of Black Political Economy*, 31–49.

Bates, T. 1987. New Data Bases in Human Resources: The Characteristics of Business Owners Data Base. *The Journal of Human Resources*, 25, 752–7.

Bates, T. 1989. The Changing Nature of Minority Business: A Comparative Analysis of Asian, Non-Minority and Black Owned Businesses. *The Review of Black Political Economy*, 18(2), 25–42.

Bates, T. 1990. Entrepreneur Human Capital Inputs and Small Business Longevity. *The Review of Economics and Statistics*, LXXII, 551–9.

Bates, T. 1991. Commercial Bank Financing of White- and Black-owned Small Business Start-ups. *Quarterly Review of Economics and Business*, 31(1), 64–80.

Bates, T. 1994. An Analysis of Korean-Immigrant-Owned Small-Business Start-Ups with Comparisons to African-American-and Nonminority-Owned Firms. *Urban Affairs Quarterly*, 30, 227–48.

Bates, T. 1995a. Self-Employment Entry across Industry Groups. *Journal of Business Venturing*, 10, 143–56.

Bates, T. 1995b. Small Businesses Appear to Benefit from State or Local Government's Economic Development Assistance. *Urban Affairs Review*, 31, 206–25.

Bates, T. 1997. Financing Small Business Creation: The Case of Chinese and Korean Immigrant Entrepreneurs. *Journal of Business Venturing*, 12, 109–24.

Bates, T. and Osborne, A.E. 1979. The Perverse Effects of SBA Loans to Minority Wholesalers. *Urban Affairs Quarterly*, 15(1), 87–98.

Becker, G. 1993. Human Capital: A Theoretical and Empirical Analysis, with Special Reference to Education. Chicago : The University of Chicago Press.

Becker, P. and Moen, P. 1999. Scaling Back: Dual-Earner Couples' Work–Family Strategies. *Journal of Marriage and Family*, 61, 995–1007.

Beech, W. 1997. Calling All Entrepreneurs. *Black Enterprise*, 28(4), 32–4.

Beesley, M. and Wilson, P. 1984a. Government and the Small Firm: Government Aid to the Small Firm since Bolton, section 5 in *Perspectives on a Decade of Small Business Research: Bolton 10 Years On*, edited by J. Stanworth, A. Westrip, D. Watkins and J. Lewis. Aldershot: Gower Publishing Company Limited.

Beesley, M.E. and Wilson, P.E.B. 1984b. Public Policy and Small Firms in Britain, chapter 9 in *Small Business Theory and Policy*, edited by Cyril Levicki. London: Croom Helm.

Beggs, J.J. 1995. The Institutional Environment: Implications for Race and Gender Inequality in the U.S. Labor Market. *American Sociological Review*, 60, 612–33.

Begley, T. 1995. Using Founder Status, Age of Firm and Company Growth Rate as the Basis for Distinguishing Entrepreneurs from Managers of Small Businesses. *Journal of Business Venturing*, 10, 249–63.

Begley, T. and Boyd, D. 1987. A Comparison of Entrepreneurs and Managers of Small Business Firms. *Journal of Management*, 13(1), 99–108.

Belcourt, M. 1990. A Family Portrait of Canada's Most Successful Female Entrepreneurs. *Journal of Business Ethics*, 435–38.

Benjamin, L. 1991. *The Black Elite: Facing The Color Line in the Twilight of the Twentieth Century*. Chicago, IL: Nelson-Hall Publishers.

Bennett, H.M. 1917. *Women and Work: The Economic Value of College Training*. New York: D. Appleton and Company.

Berger, M. 1989. The Importance of a Focus on Women: Women in the Informal Sector, chapter 1 in *Women's Ventures*, edited by Marguerite Berger and Myra Buvinic. West Hartford, CT: Kumarian Press Incorporated.

Bielby, W. and Baron, J. 1986. Men and Women at Work: Sex Segregation and Statistical Discrimination. *University of California*, 91(4), 759–99.

Biggart, Nicole. 1989. *Charismatic Capitalism: Direct Selling Organizations in America*. Chicago, IL: Chicago University Press.

Bilmoria, D. 1994. Board Committee Membership: Effects of Sex-Based Bias. *Academy of Management Journal*, 3, 341–57.

Bird, B. 1988. Implementing Entrepreneurial Ideas: The Case for Intention. *Academy of Management Review*, 13(3), 442–53.

Birley, S. 1989. Female Entrepreneurs: Are They Really Any Different? *Journal of Small Business Management*, 27(1), 32–7.

Birley, S., Moss, C. and Saunders, P. 1987. Do Women Entrepreneurs Require Different Training? *American Journal of Small Business*, 27–35.

Bitler, M.P., Robb, A.M. and Wolken, J.D. 2001. Financial Services used by Small Businesses: Evidence from the 1998 Survey of Small Business Finances. *Federal Reserve Bulletin*, 87, 183–205.

Blackwell, J.E. and Hart, P.S. 1982. *Cities, Suburbs and Blacks: A Study of Concerns, Distrust and Alienation*. New York: General Hall Incorporated Publishers.

Blalock, H.M. 1967. *Toward a Theory of Minority-Group Relations*. New York: JohnWiley and Sons, Incorporated.

Blanchflower, D. and Meyer. B. 1994. A Longitudinal Analysis of the Young Self-employed in Australia and the United States. *Small Business Economics*, 1–19.

Blau, D. 1987. A Time-series Analysis of Self-employment in the United States. *Journal of Political Economy*, 95(31), 445–67.

Bliss, R. and Garratt, N. 2001. Supporting Women Entrepreneurs in Transitioning Economies. *Journal of Small Business Management*, 39(4), 336–45.

Boden, R. 1999a. Flexible Working Hours, Family Responsibilities and Female Self-employment. *American Journal of Economics and Sociology*, 58(1), 71–84.

Boden, R. 1999b. Gender Inequality in Wage Earnings and Female Self-Employment Selection. *Journal of Socio-Economics*, 28(3), 351–64.

Boden, R. and Nucci, A.R. 2000. On the Survival Prospects of Men's and Women's New Business Ventures. *Journal of Business Venturing*, 15(4), 347–62.

Bollard, A. 1983. *Small Beginnings: New Roles for British Businesses*. London: Intermediate Technology Publications.

Bonacich, E. 1989. Inequality in America: The Failure of the American System for People of Color. *Sociological Spectrum*, 9, 77–101.

Boston, T. and Ross, C. 1996. Location Preferences of Successful African American-owned Businesses in Atlanta. *Review of Black Political Economy*, 24(2/3), 337–58.

Boucekkine, R., de la Croix, D. and Licandro, O. 2002. Vintage Human Capital, Demographic Trends, and Endogenous Growth. *Journal of Economics*, 104, 340–75.

Bowen, D. and Hisrich, R. 1986. The Female Entrepreneur: A Career Development Perspective. *Academy of Management Review*, 11(2), 393–407

Bowser, G. 1972. A Note on Success Criteria for Minority Business. *The Review of Black Political Economy*, 305–13.

Boyd, R. 1990. Black and Asian Self-employment in Large Metropolitan Areas: A Comparative Analysis. *Social Problems*, 37(2), 258–74.

Boyd, R. 1991. A Contextual Analysis of Black Self-employment in Large Metropolitan Areas, 1970–1980. *Social Forces*, 70, 409–30.

Boyd, R. 1996. Demographic Change and Entrepreneurial Occupations: African Americans in Northern Cities. *The American Journal of Economics and Sociology*, 55(2), 129–44.

Boyd, R. 1998. Race, Labor Market Disadvantage and Survivalist Entrepreneurship: The Case of Black Women in the Urban North during the Great Depression. Unpublished article.

Boyd, R.L. 2001. Ethnicity, Niches, and Retail Enterprise in Northern Cities, 1900. *Sociological Perspectives*, 44, 89–110.

Boyd, R.L. 2002a. Ethnic Competition for an Occupational Niche: The Case of Black and Italian Barbers in Northern U.S. Cities During the Late Nineteenth Century. *Sociological Focus*, 247–65.

Boyd, R.L. 2002b. A 'Migration of Despair': Unemployment, the Search for Work, and Migration to Farms During the Great Depression. *Social Science Quarterly*, 83, 554–67.

Boyd, R.L. 2002c. Urban Unemployment, the Rural Labor Market, and Southern Blacks in Farm Labor during the Great Depression: A Research Note. *The Social Science Journal*, 39, 295–9.

Bregger, J. 1996. Measuring Self-employment in the United States. *Monthly Labor Review*, 3–9.

Brodie, S. and Stanworth, J. 1998. Independent Contractors in Direct Selling: Self-employed but Missing from Official Records. *International Small Business Journal*, 16, 95–101.

Brophy, B. 1989. The Truth about Women Managers. *U.S. News & World Report*, 106(10), 57.

Brotherton, P. 1999. Get Financing Now. *Black Enterprise*, August, 77–84.

Brown C.M. 1995. A Network of Opportunities. *Black Enterprise*.

Brown, S. and Segal, P. 1989. Female Entrepreneurs in Profile. *Canadian Banker*, 96(4), 32–5.

Browne, K. 2001. Female Entrepreneurship in the Caribbean: A Multisite, Pilot Investigation of Gender and Work. *The Human Organization*, 326–42.

Bruderl, J., Preisendorfer, P. and Ziegler, R. 1992. Survival Chances of Newly Founded Business Organizations. *American Sociological Review*, 57, 227–42.

Brush, C.G. 1990. Women and Enterprise Creation: Barriers and Opportunities, chapter 3 in Enterprising Women: Local Initiatives for Job Creation, edited by the Organization for Economic Co-operation and Development. Head of Publication Services, Washington, DC: OECD.

Brush, C.G. 1992. Research on Women Business Owners: Past Trends, a New Perspective and Future Directions. *Entrepreneurship Theory and Practice*, 16(4), 5–30.

Brush, C. 1997. Women-Owned Businesses: Obstacles and Opportunities. *Journal of Developmental Entrepreneurship*, 2, 1–24.

Brush, C., Carter, N., Gatewood, E., Greene, P. and Hart, M. 2001. The Diana Project: Women Business Owners and Equity Capital: The Myths Dispelled. Sponsored by Kauffman Center for Entrepreneurial Leadership, US Small Business Administration and National Women's Business Council.

Brush, C., Greene P., and Hart, M. 2001. From Initial Ideas to Unique Advantage: The Entrepreneurial Challenge of Constructing a Resource Base. *The Academy of Management Executive*, 15(1), 64–80.

Brush, C. and Hisrich, R. 1986. Characteristics of the Minority Entrepreneur. *Journal of Small Business Management*, 24(4), 1–9.

Brush, C. and Hisrich, R.D. 1991. Antecedent Influences on Women-owned Businesses. *Journal of Managerial Psychology*, 6(2), 9–16.

Bucar, B. and Hisrich, R.D. 2001. Ethics of Business Managers vs. Entrepreneurs. *Journal of Developmental Entrepreneurship*, 6, 59–82.

Burkett, J.P. 2000. Marx's Concept of an Economic Law of Motion. *History of Political Economy*, 381–94.

Burr, Sara G. and Strickland, Mary. 1992. Creating a Positive Business Climate for Women: An Approach to Small Business Development. *Economic Development Review*, 10, 63–70.

Busenitz, L.W. 1999. Entrepreneurial Risk and Strategic Decision Making: It's a Matter of Perspective. *The Journal of Applied Behavioral Science*, 35, 325–40.

Butler, J.S. 1991. *Entrepreneurship and Self-help among Black Americans: A Reconsideration of Race and Economics*. Albany, NY: State University of New York Press.

Buttner, E.H. 2001. Examining the Female Entrepreneurs' Management Style: An Application of a Relational Frame. *Journal of Business Ethics*, 29, 253–69.

Buttner, E.H., and Moore, D. 1997. Women's Organizational Exodus to Entrepreneurship: Self-reported Motivations and Correlates with Success. *Journal of Small Business Management: Milwaukee*, 35, 34–46.

Buttner, E.H. and Rosen, B. 1988. Bank Loan's Officers' Perceptions of the Characteristics of Men, Women, and Successful Entrepreneurs. *Journal of Business Venturing*, 3(3), 249–58.

Buttner, E.H. and Rosen, B. 1989. Funding New Business Ventures: Are Decision Makers Biased against Women Entrepreneurs? *Journal of Business Venturing*, 4(4), 249–61.

Buttner, E.H. and Rosen, B. 1992. Rejection in the Loan Application Process: Male and Female Entrepreneurs' Perceptions and Subsequent Intentions. *Journal of Small Business Management: Milwaukee*.

Buzzanell, P.M. 1995. Reframing the Glass Ceiling as a Socially Constructed Process: Implications for Understanding and Change. *Communications Monographs*, 62, 327–50.

Bygrave, W.D. 1989. The Entrepreneurship Paradigm (I): A Philosophical Look at its Research Methodologies. *Entrepreneurship Theory and Practice*, Fall, 7–25.

Bygrave, W. and Hofer, C. 1991. Theorizing about Entrepreneurship. *Entrepreneurship, Theory and Practice*, 16(2), 13–22.

Caputo, R. and Dolinsky, A. 1998. Women's Choice to Pursue Self-employment: The Role of Financial and Human Capital of Household Members. *Journal of Small Business Management: Milwaukee*, 8–17.

Carland, J.W., Hoy, F., Bolton, W. and Carland, J. 1984. Differentiating Entrepreneurs from Small Business Owners. *Academy of Management Review*, 9, 254–59.

Carroll, G. and Mosakowski, E. 1987. The Career Dynamics of Self-employment. *Administrative Science Quarterly*, 570–89.

Carter, N. M., Williams, M. and Reynolds, P.D. 1997. Discontinuance among New Firms in Retail: The Influence of Initial Resources, Strategy, and Gender. *Journal of Business Venturing*, 12, 125–45.

Catalyst Guide, 1998. *Advancing Women in Business*. San Francisco, CA: Josey-Bass Publishers.

Cauthorn, R. 1989. *Contributions to a Theory of Entrepreneurship*. New York: Garland Publishing Incorporated.

Chaganti, R. 1986. Management in Women-owned Enterprises. *Journal of Small Business Management*, 24(4), 18–30.

Chaganti, R. and Parasuraman, S. 1996. A Study of the Impacts of Gender on

Business Performance and Management Patterns in Small Businesses. *Entrepreneurship Theory and Practice*, 73–5.

Charboneau, F.J. 1981. The Woman Entrepreneur. *American Demographics*, 21–3.

Chatterjee, P. 2001. Encountering 'Third World Women': Rac(e)ing the Global in a U.S. Classroom. *Pedagogy*, 2(1), 79–108.

Chen, C.C., Greene, P.G. and Crick, A. 1998. Does Entrepreneurial Self-efficacy Distinguish Entrepreneurs from Managers? *Journal of Business Venturing*, 295–316.

Chen, G. 1986. Minority Business Development: An International Comparison. *The Review of Black Political Economy*, 15, 93–111.

Choi, T.Y. and Hong, Y. 2002. Unveiling the Structure of Supply Networks: Case Studies in Honda, Acura, and DaimlerChrysler. *Journal of Operations Management*, 20, 469–93.

Christopher, J. 1998. Minority Business Formation and Survival: Evidence on Business Performance and Viability. *The Review of Black Political Economy*, 26(1), 37–72.

Christou, C. 2001. Differential Borrowing Constraints and Investment in Human Capital. *Journal of Macroeconomics*, 23, 277–95.

Chung, L. and Gibbons, P. 1997. Corporate entrepreneurship: The Roles of Ideology and Social Capital. *Group & Organization Management*, 22(1), 10–31.

Cianni, M. and Romberger, B. 1995. Perceived Racial, Ethnic, and Gender Differences in Access to Development Experiences. *Group and Organization Management*, 20(4), 440–59.

Clain, S. 2000. Gender Differences in Full-time Self-employment. *Journal of Economics and Business*, 499–513.

Clark, T. and James, F. 1992. Women-owned Businesses: Dimensions and Policy Issues. *Economic Development Quarterly*, 6, 25–40.

Clarke, R. 1999. An Office of Her Own. *Black Enterprise*, August, 59–63.

Cliff, J. 1998. Does One Size Fit All? Exploring the Relationship between Attitudes towards Growth, Gender, and Business Size. *Journal of Business Venturing*, 523–42.

Cobas, J.A. 1989. Six Problems in the Sociology of the Ethnic Economy. *Sociological Perspectives*, 32(2), 201–14.

Coleman, M. and Pencavel, J. 1993. Trends in Market Behavior of Women since 1940. *Industrial and Labor Relations Review*, 46(4), 653–76.

Coleman, S. 2000. Access to Capital and Terms of Credit: A Comparison of Men- and Women-owned Small Businesses. *Journal of Small Business Management*, 38, 37–52.

Collerette, P. and P. Aubry. 1990. Socio-economic Evolution of Women Business Owners in Quebec. *Journal of Business Ethics*, 417–22.

Collins, S. 1993. Blacks on the Bubble: The Vulnerability of Black Executives in White Corporations. *The Sociological Quarterly*, 34(3),429–47.

Connelly, R. 1992. Self-employment and Providing Child Care. *Demography*, 29(1), 17–29.

Cook, R., Belliveau, P. and VonSeggern, K. 2001. A Case Study of Microenterprise Training: Beta Test Findings and Suggestions for Improvement. *Journal of Developmental Entrepreneurship*, 6, 255–67.

Cooper, A.C. 1981. Strategic Management: New Ventures and Small Business. *Long Range Planning*, 14(5), 39–45.

Cooper, A.C. and Dunkelberg, W. 1987. Entrepreneurial Research: Old Questions, New Answers and Methodological Issues. *American Journal of Small Business*, 11–23.

Coughlin, J. and Thomas, A. (2002). *The Rise of Women Entrepreneurs: People, Processes and Global Trends*. Westport, CN: Quorum Books.

Covin, J. and Slevin, D. 1994. Corporate Entrepreneurship in High and Low Technology Industries: A Comparison of Strategic Variables, Strategy Patterns and Performance in Global Markets. *Journal of Euro-Marketing*, 3(34), 99–138.

Cox. T. 1994. Cultural Diversity in Organizations: Theory, Research and Practice. San Francisco, CA: Berrett-Kohler Publishers.

Cressy, R. 1996. Are Business Startups Debt-Rationed?. *The Economic Journal*, 1253–70.

Cromie, S. 1987. The Aptitudes of Aspiring Male and Female Entrepreneurs, chapter 2 in *Small Business Development: Some Current Issues*, edited by K. O'Neill, R. Bhambri, T. Faulkner and T. Cannon. Aldershot: Gower Publishing Company Limited.

Cromie, S. and Hayes, J. 1988. Towards a Typology of Female Entrepreneurs. *The Sociological Review*, 36(1), 87–113.

Crowder, K. 2000. The Racial Context of White Mobility: An Individual-level Assessment of the White Flight Hypothesis. Department of Sociology, Western Washington University, 223–57.

Cuba, R., Decenzo, D. and Anish, A. 1983. Management Practices of Successful Female Business Owners. *American Journal of Small Business*, 8(2), 40–46.

Cummings, S. 1999. African American Entrepreneurship in the Suburbs: Protected Markets and Enclave Business Development. *Journal of American Planning Association*, 65(1), 50–61.

Curran, J. and Blackburn, R. 1991. Changes in the Context of Enterprise: Some Socioeconomic and Environmental Factors facing Small Firms in the 1990's, chapter 9 in *Paths of Enterprise: The Future of the Small Business*, edited by J. Curran and R. Blackburn. London: Routledge, Chapman and Hall Incorporated.

Curran, J., Stanworth, J. and Watkins, D. 1986. *The Survival of the Small Firm: The Economics of Survival of the Small Firm.* Aldershot: Gower Publishing Company.

Daily, C., Certo, S. and Dalton, D. 1999. Entrepreneurial Ventures as an Avenue to the top?: Assessing the Advancement of Female CEOs and Directors in the Inc. 100. *Journal of Developmental Entrepreneurship,* Spring, 4(1), 19–33.

Dallalfar, A. 1994. Iranian Women as Immigrant Entrepreneurs. *Gender and Society,* 8(4), 541–61.

Dannhauser, C.L. 1999. Who's in the Home Office? *American Demographics,* 21, 50–56.

Dant, R., Brush, C. and Iniesta, F. 1996. Participating Patterns of Women in Franchising. *Journal of Small Business Management,* April, 14–28.

Daunis, L. 1992. The Immigrants: How They're Helping to Revitalize the U.S. Economy. *Business Weekly,* 114–22.

DeCarlo, J.F. and Lyons, P.R. 1979. A Comparison of Selected Personal Characteristics of Minority and Non-minority Female Entrepreneurs. *Journal of Small Business Management,* 17, 22–9.

de Groot, T. 2000. Challenges Faced by Women in Industrial Development, section III in *Women Entrepreneurs in Africa: Experience From Selected Countries.* New York and Geneva: United Nations Publications.

DeLollis, B. 1997. Today's Female Passion for Entrepreneurship. *The American Enterprise,* 8, 42–5.

Deng S., Hassan, M. and Jivan, S. 1995. Advertising in Malaysia – A Cultural Perspective. *International Journal of Advertising,* 13(2), 153–67.

DeSimone, M. 2002. Latina-owned Businesses are Fast-growing Sector. *National Underwriter,* 106, 12.

Devine, T. 1994a. Changes in Wage-and-salary Returns to Skill and the Recent Rise in Female Self-employment. *Economic Issues for Work and Family,* 84(2), 108–13.

Devine, T. 1994b. Characteristics of Self-employed Women in the United States. *Monthly Labor Review,* 20–34.

Dhaliwal, S. 1998. Silent Contributors: Asian Female Entrepreneurs and Women in Business. *Women's Studies International Forum,* 21(5), 463–74.

DiPrete, T. and Sourle, W. 1998. Gender and Promotion in Segmented Job Ladder Systems. *American Sociological Review,* 54.

Dolinsky A., Caputo R., Pasumarty, K. and Quazi, H. 1993. The Effects of Education on Business Ownership: A Longitudinal Study of Women. *Entrepreneurship Theory and Practice,* 18(1), 43–54.

Dominguez, J.R. 1976. *Capital Flows in Minority Areas.* Lexington, MA: Lexington Books.

Dugan, I.J. 1996, Small Business is Big Business. *Business Week*, September 30, p. 117.

Dumas, C. 2001. Evaluating the Outcomes of Microenterprise Training for Low Income Women: A Case Study. *Journal of Developmental Entrepreneurship*, 6, 97–128.

Dunn, T. and Holtz-Eakin, D. 2000. Financial Capital, Human Capital, and the Transition to Self-employment: Evidence from Intergenerational Links. *Journal of Labor Economics*, 18, 282–305.

Easter, G.M. 1996. Personal Networks and Postrevolutionary State Building: Soviet Russia Reexamined. *World Politics*, 48, 551–78.

Edwards, L. and Field-Hendrey, E. 1996. Home-based Workers: Data from the 1990 Census of Population. *Monthly Labor Review*, 119(11), 26–35.

Ehlers, T. and Main, K. 1998. Women and the False Promise of Microenterprise. *Gender and Society*, 12, 424–40.

England P., Christopher, K. and Reid, L.L. 1999. Gender, Race, Ethnicity and Wages, chapter 4 in *Latinas and African American Women at Work: Race, Gender and Economic Inequality*, edited by Irene Browne. New York: Russell Sage Foundation.

Etzkowitz, H., Kemelgor, C., Neuschatz, M. and Uzzi, B. 1992. Athena Unbound: Barriers to Women in Academic Science and Engineering. *Science and Public Policy*, 19(3),157–79.

Evans, D.S. and Jovanovic, B. 1989. An Estimated Model of Entrepreneurial Choice under Liquidity Constraints. *Journal of Political Economy*, 97(4), 808–27.

Evans, D. and Leighton, L. 1989. Some Empirical Aspects of Entrepreneurship. *The American Economic Review*, 519–35.

Fabowale, L., Orser, B. and Riding, A. 1995. Gender, Structural Factors, and Credit Terms between Canadian Small Businesses and Financial Institutions. *Entrepreneurship Theory and Practice*, 19(4), 41–65.

Fairlie, R. 1999. The Absence of the African-American Owned Business: An Analysis of the Dynamics of Self-employment. *Journal of Labor Economics*, 17(1), 80–108.

Farkas, George, England, Paula, Vicknair, Keven and Kilbourne, Barbara Stanek. 1997. Cognitive Skill, Skill Demands of Jobs, and Earnings among Young European American, African American, and Mexican American Workers. *Social Forces*, 75(3).

Feagin, J. and Imani, N. 1994. Racial Barriers to African American Entrepreneurship: An Exploratory Study. *Social Problems*, 41(4), 562–85.

Field-Hendrey, E. 1990. Home-based Workers. *Data from the 1990 Census of Population Monthly Labor Review*, 119, 26–34.

Finnerty, J. and Krzystofik. A. 1986. Barriers to Small Business Formation. *Journal of Small Business Management*, 50–58.

Firestone, S. 1994. The Dialectic of Sex, part 6 in *Social Stratification: Class, Race and Gender in Sociological Perspective*, edited by David B. Grusky. San Francisco, CA and Oxford: Westview Press.

Fischer, E.M., Reuber, A.R. and Dyke, L.S. 1993. A Theoretical Overview and Extension of Research on Sex, Gender and Entrepreneurship. *Journal of Business Venturing*, 8(2), 151–68.

Fratoe, F. 1986. A Sociological Analysis of Minority Business. *The Review of Black Political Economy*, 15, 5–29.

Fratoe, F. 1988. Social Capital of Black Business Owners. *The Review of Black Political Economy*, Spring, 33–50.

Fried, J. 2002. From Modest Business Loans, the Fulfillment of Modest Dreams. *New York Times*, 1(37).

Fried, L.I. 1989. A New Breed of Entrepreneur – Women. *Management Review*, 78(12), 18–25.

Frost, P.J. and Stablein, R.E. 1992. *Doing Exemplary Research*. Newbury Park, London: Sage Publications.

Fukuyama, F. 2002. Social Capital and Development: The Coming Agenda. *SAIS Review*, 22, 23–37.

Furry, M. and Lino, M. 1992. An Overview of Home-based Work: Results from a Regional Research Project. *Family Economics Review*, 5, 2–8.

Furry, M. and Radhakrishna, R. 1992. *Home-based Workers in Pennsylvania: Implications for Educational Programming*. Department of Agricultural and Extension Education: The Pennsylvania State University, 20–27.

Garland, S. 2000. Work at Home? First, Get Real; Often, Visions of Time and Freedom are Quickly Dashed. *Business Week*, September 18, p. 112.

Gartner, W. 1985. A Conceptual Framework for Describing the Phenomenon of New Venture Creation. *Academy of Management Review*, 10(4), 696–706.

Gartner, W. 1989. Some Suggestions for Research on Entrepreneurial Traits and Characteristics. *Entrepreneurship Theory and Practice*, 26–37.

Gartner, W. and Bhat, S. 2000. Environmental and Ownership Characteristics of Small Businesses and their Impact on Developments. *Journal of Small Business Management*, 38(3), 14–27.

Gassenheimer, J., Baucus, D., and Baucus, M. 1996. Cooperative Arrangements among Enterpreneurs : An Analysis of Opportunism and Communication in Franchise Structures. *Journal of Business Research*, 36, 67–79.

Gilbertson, G. 1995. Women's Labor and Enclave Employment: The Case of Dominican and Columbian Women in New York City. *The International Migration Review*, 29(3), 657–67.

Gimeno J., Folta T., Cooper A. and Woo, C. 1997. Survival of the Fittest? Entrepreneurial Human Capital and the Persistence of Underperforming Firms. *Administrative Science Quarterly*, 42(4), 750–83.

Glover, H.D., Mynatt, P.G. and Schroeder, R.G. 2000. The Personality, Job

Satisfaction and Turnover Intentions of African-American Male and Female Accountants: An Examination of the Human Capital and Structural/Class Theories. *Critical Perspectives on Accounting*, 11, 173–92.

Godbout, T.M. 1993. Employment Change and Sectoral Distribution in 10 Countries, 1970–90. *Monthly Labor Review*, 3–20.

Godfrey, J. 1995. *No More Frogs To Kiss: 99 Ways to Give Economic Power to Girls*. New York: HarperBusiness.

Godoy R., O'Neill K., McSweeney, K. and Wilkie, D. 2000. Human Capital, Wealth, Property Rights, and the Adoption of New Farm Technologies: The Tawahka Indians of Honduras. *Human Organization*, 59(2), 222–34.

Goffee, R. and Scase, R. 1983a. Business Ownership and Women's Subordination: A Preliminary Study of Female Proprietors. *The Sociological Review*, 31, 625–48.

Goffee, R. and Scase, R. 1983b. Class Entrepreneurship and the Service Sector: Towards a Conceptual Clarification. *The Services Industries Journal*, 146–60.

Goffee, R. and Scase, R. 1985. *Women in Charge: The Experiences of Female Entrepreneurs*. London: George Allen and Unwin Limited.

Goldenberg, S. and Kline, T. 1999. An Exploratory Study of Predicting Perceived Success and Survival of Small Businesses. *Psychological Reports*, 85(2), 365–77.

Goldsmith, William W. and Edward J. Blakely. 1992. Separate Assets: Race, Gender, and Other Dimensions of Poverty. *Separate Societies: Poverty and Inequality in U.S. Cities*, 14–55.

Goo, S. 2001. Mixed Story on Minority Businesses. *The Washington Post*, July 13, E2.

Gould, S. and Parzen, J. 1990. Recommendations, Conclusions and Plans of Action, chapter 6 in *Enterprising Women: Local Initiatives for Job Creation*, edited by the Organization for Economic Co-operation and Development. Head of Publication Services, Washington, DC: OECD.

Green, S. and Pryde, P. 1990. *Black Entrepreneurship in America*. London: Transaction Publishers.

Greenfield, W. M. 1989. *Developing New Ventures*. New York: Harper and Row Publishers.

Greenfield, S.M. 1979. Entrepreneurs, Choices and Decisions, chapter 2 in *Entrepreneurs in Cultural Context*, edited by Sidney M. Greenfield, Arnold Strickon and Robert T. Aubey. Albuquerque, NM: University of New Mexico Press.

Gregg, G. 1985. Woman Entrepreneurs: The Second Generation. *Across the Board*, 10–18.

Greller, M. and Stroh, L. 2002. Variations in Human Capital Investment Activity by Age. *Journal of Vocational Behavior*, 61, 109–38.

Griffiths, S. 1996. *Beyond the Glass Ceiling: Forty Women whose Ideas Shape the Modern World*. New York: Manchester University Press.

Greenwood, A. 2001. Theories of Occupational Segregation by Sex: An Overview, chapter 5 in *Women, Gender and Work*, edited by Martha Fetherolf Loutfi. Geneva: International Labor Office.

Grogan, P. 2000. Can the Cities Come Back?. *Journal of Housing and Community Development*, 57, 19.

Guaitoli, D. 2000. Human Capital Distribution, Growth and Convergence. *Research in Economics*, 54, 331–50.

Gunderson, M. 1994. Pay and Employment Equity in the United States and Canada. *International Journal of Manpower*, 15(7), 26–43.

Gundry L., Ben-Yoseph, M. and Posig, M. 2002. The Status of Women Entrepreneurship: Pathways to Future Entrepreneurship Development and Education. *New England Journal of Entrepreneurship*, 5(1), 39–50.

Haberfeld, Y. 1992. Pay, Valence of Pay and Gender: A Simultaneous Equation Model. *Journal of Economic Psychology*, 13(1), 93–109.

Hacker, Andrew. 1995. Dividing American Society. *Two Nations*, 3–54

Haddleston-Mattai, B. 1995. The Black Female Academician and the 'Superwoman Syndrome'. *Race, Gender and Class*, 3, 49–64.

Hannan, M.T. and Freeman, J. 1977. The Population Ecology of Organizations. *American Journal of Sociology*, 82(5), 929–64.

Haskins, G. and Gibb, A. 1987. Support for Small Business Development in Europe, chapter 3 in *Small Business Development: Some Current Issues*, edited by Ken O'Neill, Ransit Bhambri, Terry Faulkner and Tom Cannon. Aldershot: Gower Publishing Company.

Haynes, P. and Helms, M. 2000. A Profile of the Growing Female Entrepreneur Segment. *Bank Marketing*, 32(5), 28–35.

Heck, Ramona K.Z. 1992. The Effects of Children on the Major Dimensions of Home-based Employment. *Journal of Family and Economic Issues*, 13, 315–46.

Heck, Ramona K.Z., Winter, Mary and Stafford, Kathryn. 1992. Managing Work and Family in Home-based Employment. *Journal of Family and Economic Issues*, 13, 187–212.

Heckman, J.J. 2000. Policies to Foster Human Capital. *Research in Economics*, 54, 3–56.

Heckman, J.J. and Payner, B. 1989. Determining the Impact of Federal Antidiscrimination Policy on the Economic Status of Blacks: A Study of South Carolina. *The American Economic Review*, 70, 138–78.

Hemenway, K. 1995. Human Nature and the Glass Ceiling in Industry. *Communication of the ACM*, 38, 55–61.

Henderson, C.C. 1999. The Economic Performance of African-American

Owned Banks: The Role of Loan Loss Provisions. *Financial Services in the Black Community*, 89, 372–6.

Hendricks, L. 2001. How Do Taxes Affect Human Capital? The Role of Intergenerational Mobility. *Review of Economic Dynamics*, 4, 695–735.

Hennon, C.B., Jones, A. and Roth, M. 1998. Family-enterprise Initiatives as a Response to Socioeconomic and Political Change in Eastern and Central Europe. *Journal of Family and Eonomic Issues*, 19, 235–53.

Hennon, C. and Locker, S. 2000. Gender and Home-based Employment in a Global Economy. *Gender and Home-Based Employment*, edited by Charles B. Hennan, Suzanne Lotur, and Rosemary Walker. Westport, CN.: Auburn House, pp. 18–43.

Henry, S. 2002. Women Fighting for Venture Capital; Study Cites Entrepreneur Networks. *The Washington Post*, February 13, E5.

Herring, C., Horton, H. and Thomas, M. 1993. Feminization of Poverty or Pauperization of Women?: Clarifying the Sources of Change in the Impoverishment of Women and Their Families. *National Journal of Sociology*, 7(1).

Higginbotham, E.B. 1995. African-American Women's History and the Metalanguage of Race, chapter 1 in *We Specialize in the Wholly Impossible: A Reader in Black Women's History*, edited by Darlene Clarke Hine, Wilma King and Linda Reed. New York: Carlson Publishing Incorporated.

Highman, E. 1985. *The Organization Woman: Building a Career – An Outside Report*. New York: Human Science Press Inc.

Himelstein, L. and Anderson, S. 1997. Breaking Through. *Business Week*, February 17, 64–70.

Hisrich, R. 1986. The Woman Entrepreneur: Characteristics, Skills, Problems and Prescriptions for Success, chapter 3 in *The Art and Science of Entrepreneurship*, edited by Donald Sexton and Raymond W. Smilor. Cambridge, MA: Ballinger Publishing Company.

Hisrich, R. and Brush, C. 1984. The Woman Entrepreneur: Management Skills and Business Problems. *Journal of Small Business Management*, 22, 30–37.

Hisrich, R. and Brush, C. 1985. *The Woman Entrepreneur: Starting, Financing and Managing a Successful Business*. Boston, MA: Lexington Books.

Hisrich, R. and Brush, C. 1986. Characteristics of the Minority Entrepreneur. *Journal of Small Business Management*, 1–8.

Hoffman, C. and Marger, M. 1991. Patterns of Immigrant Enterprise in Six Metropolitan Areas. *SSR*, 75, 144–57.

Hogan, J. M. 2001. Social Capital: Potential in Family Social Sciences. *Journal of Socio-Economics*, 30, 151–5.

Hogarty, D.B. 1993. Beating the Odds: Avoid these Mistakes at all Costs. *Management Review*, 16–21.

Horst, L. and Merino, K. 1982. Perceptions of Sex Discrimination: University, Sex and Major Field Differences. Portions presented at American Psychological Association Annual Convention, 1982.

Horton, H. 1988. Occupational Differentiation and Black Entrepreneurship: A Sociodemographic Analysis. *National Journal of Sociology*, 187–201.

Horton, H. and De Jong, G. 1991. Black Entrepreneurs: A Sociodemographic Analysis. *Research in Race and Ethnic Relations*, 6, 105–20.

House, B. 2000. Does Economic Culture and Social Capital Matter?: An Analysis of African-American Entrepreneurs in Cleveland, Ohio. *Western Journal of Black Studies*, 24, 183.

Hovey, J. 2001. Financing and Insurance; Growing Network of lenders help Minority Entrepreneurs. *The Los Angeles Times*, March 12, C4.

Huff, P. 2003. Home-based Business Myths. *Moms Business Magazine*, June, 11–13.

Humphreys, M. and McClung, J. 1981. Women Entrepreneurs in Oklahoma. *Review of Regional Economics and Review*, 6(2), 13–20.

Hundley, Greg. 2000. Male/Female Earnings differences in Self-employment: The Effects of Marriage, Children, and the Household Division of Labor. *Industrial and Labor Relations Review*, 54, 95–114.

Hundley, G. 2001. Why Women Earn Less than Men in Self-employment. *Journal of Labor Research*, 22(4), 817–29.

Hurtado, A. 1989. Relating to Privilege: Seduction and Rejection in the Subordination of White Women and Women of Color. *Signs: Journal of Women in Culture and Society*, 14, 833–55.

Hustedde, R. and Pulver, G. 1992. Factors Affecting Equity Capital Acquisition: The Demand Side. *Journal of Business Venturing*, 7, 363–74.

Hyden G. 2001. The Social Capital Crash in the Periphery. *Journal of Socio-Economics*, 30, 161–3.

Ibarra, H. 1993. Personal Networks of Women and Minorities in Management: A Conceptual Framework. *Academy of Management Review*, 18(1), 56–87.

Inman, K. 2000. *Women's Resources in Business Start-up: A Study of Black and White Women Entrepreneurs*. New York and London: Garland Publishing.

Ireland, R.D. and Van Auken, P.M. 1987. Entrepreneurship and Small Business Research: An Historical Typology and Directions for Future Research. *American Journal of Small Business*, Spring, 9–20.

Jackson, B. 2001. Chicago Start-Up Aims Solely at Hispanics. *American Banker*, 166, 6.

Jenkins, R. 1985. Black Workers in the Labor Market: The Price of Recession, chapter 8 in *New Approaches to Economic Life: Economic Restructuring, Unemployment and the Social Division of Labor.* London: Manchester University Press.

Jessup, C. and Chippe, G. 1976. *The Women's Guide to Starting A Business*. New York: Holt, Rinehart and Winston.

Johnson, B. 1990. Toward a Multidimensional Model of Entrepreneurship: The Case of Achievement, Motivation and the Entrepreneur. *Entrepreneurship Theory and Practice*, 39–54.

Johnson, P. 1996. 1996 Essence Awards. *Essence*, 27, 61.

Johnson, S. 1991. Small Firms and the UK Labor Market: Prospects for the 1990's, chapter 5 in *Paths of Enterprise: The Future of the Small Business*, edited by J. Curran and R. Blackburn. London: Routledge, Chapman and Hall Incorporated.

Jones, G. and George, J. 2003. *Contemporary Management*, third edition. Boston: McGraw-Hill Irwin Publishers.

Joyce, J.P. 1988. *The Economic Activities of Business: An Analysis of the Modern Corporation*. New York: Praeger Publishers.

Jurik, Nancy C. 1998. Getting Away and Getting By: The Experiences of Self-Employed Homeworkers. *Work and Occupations*, 25, 7–28.

Kallenberg, A. and Leicht, K. 1991. Gender and Organizational Performance: Determinants of Small Business Survival and Success. *Academy of Management Journal*, 34(1), 136–62.

Kao, J. 1989. *Entrepreneurship, Creativity and Organization*. Englewood Cliffs, NJ: Prentice Hall.

Kay, Fiona M. and Hagan, John. 1995. The Persistent Glass Ceiling: Gendered Inequalities in the Earnings of Lawyers. *British Journal of Sociology*, 46, 279–305.

Kazemipur, A. and Halli, S. 2001 The Changing Colour of Poverty in Canada. Abdolmohammad Kazemipur, Shiva S Halli. *The Canadian Review of Sociology and Anthropology*, 38(2), 217–39.

Kean, R., Van Zandt, S. and Maupin W. 1993. Successful Aging: The Older Entrepreneur (the Woman, from Retired Employee to Businesswoman). *Journal of Women & Aging*, 5, 25.

Keefe, B. 2002. Blacks Confront a Digital Divide Despite Progress, the World of Technology is White-dominated. *The Atlanta Journal*, 1.

Kerber, L.K. and Matthews, J. 1982. *Women's America: Refocusing the Past*. New York: Oxford University Press.

Kerlinger, F. 1986. *Foundations of Behavioral Research*. New York: Holt, Rinehart and Winston.

Kessler, A. 2001. The Market in Women: Small Entrepreneurs. *Bank Marketing*, 33(9), 12–13.

Kessler-Harris, A. 1982. *'Out of Work': A History of Wage-earning Women in the United States*. New York: Oxford University Press.

Kim, K. and Hurh, W. 1996. Ethnic Resources Utilization of Korean Immigrant Entrepreneurs in the Chicago Minority Area. Immigrants and Immigration

Policy: Individual Skills, Family Ties, and Group Identities. *Contemporary Studies in Economic and Financial Analysis*, 79, 149–73.

King, D.K. 1988. Multiple Jeopardy, Multiple Consciousness: The Context of a Black Feminist Ideology. *Signs: Journal of Women in Culture and Society*, 14, 42–73.

Kirby, C. 2001. California Top U.S. in Minority Firms. *San Francisco Chronicle*, July 13, B3.

Kisfalvi, V. 2002. The Entrepreneur's Character, Life, Issues, and Strategy Making: A Field Study. *Journal of Business Venturing*, 17(5), 489–518.

Kloosterman, R.C. and Van Der Leun, J.P. 1999. Just for Starters: Commercial Gentrification by Immigrant Entrepreneurs in Amsterdam and Rotterdam Neighbourhoods. *Housing Studies*, 14, 659.

Kottak, C. and Kozaitis, K. 1999. *On Being Different: Diversity and Multiculturalism in the North American Mainstream*. Boston, MA: McGraw-Hill Publishers.

Krackhardt, D. and Kilduff, D. 2002. Structure, Culture and Simmelian Ties in Entrepreneurial Firms. *Social Networks*, 24(3), 279–90.

Kroll, L. 1998. Entrepreneur Moms. *Forbes*, May 18, 161(10), 84–92.

Krueger, N.F., Jr. and Brazeal, D.V. 1994. Entrepreneurial Potential and Potential Entrepreneurs. *Entrepreneurship Theory and Practice*, 90–105.

Krueger, N.F., Jr., Reilly, M.D. and Carsrud, A.L. 2000. Competing Models of Entrepreneurial Intentions. *Journal of Business Venturing*, 15, 411–32.

Kuratko, D.F, Hornsby, J.S., Naffziger, D.W. and Montagno, R.V. 1993. Implement Entrepreneurial Thinking in Established Organizations. *Sam Advanced Management Journal*, 28–33.

Lachman, L. and Brett, D. 1997. The Immigration Factor. *Mortgage Banking*, 57(10), 68–74.

Lan, N. 2001. Training to aid women entrepreneurs in Vietnam. United Nations Development Programme Vietnam, www.undp.org/dpa.

Langan-Fox, J. and Roth, S. 1995. Achievement Motivation and Female Entrepreneurs. *Journal of Occupational and Organizational Psychology*, 68, 209–18.

Laverdy, M. 1995. Affirmative Action Works for Hispanic Entrepreneurs. *Hispanic*, 8(5), 84.

Learned, K.E. 1992. What Happened Before the Organization? A Model of Organization Formation. *Entrepreneurship Theory and Practice*, 17(1), 39–48.

Lee, C.K. 1995. Engendering the Worlds of Labor: Women Workers, Labor Markets, and Production Politics in the South China Economic Miracle. *American Sociological Review*, 60, 378–97.

Lee, J. 1999. Retail Niche Domination among African American, Jewish and

Korean Entrepreneurs: Competition, Coethnic Advantage and Disadvantage. *The American Behavioral Scientist*, 42(9), 1398–416.

Lee, V. and Croninger, R. 2001. The Elements of Social Capital in the Context of Six High Schools. *Journal of Socio-Economics*, 30, 165–7.

Leibow, C. 1991. Necessity Mothers a Child-Care Invention – Child-Care Referral Service. Column in *Nation's Business*, June.

Lerner, M. and Almor, T. 2002. Relationship among Strategic Capabilities and the Performance of Women-owned Small Ventures. *Journal of Small Business Management*, 40(2), 109–25.

Lerner M., Brush, C. and Hisrich, R. 1997. Israeli Women Entrepreneurs: An Examination of Factors affecting Performance. *Journal of Business Venturing*, 12(4), 315–40.

Levine, D. 1996. Hatching Success Stories: Oakland to Help Entrepreneurs give Birth to Future Stars. *San Francisco Business Times*, January 19, 1.

Lewis, L. 1995. The Glass Ceiling. *The Economist*, 33(6), 59.

Lewis, S. 2001. Restructuring Workplace Cultures: The Ultimate Work–Family Challenge. *Women in Management Review*, 16, 21–29.

Light, I.H. 1972. *Ethnic Enterprise in America: Business and Welfare among Chinese, Japanese and Blacks*. Berkeley, CA: University of California Press.

Light, I.H. 1979. Disadvantaged Minorities in Self-employment. *International Journal of Comparative Sociology*, 20, 31–45.

Light I., Bernard, R. and Kim, R. 1999. Immigrant Incorporation in the Garment Industry of Los Angeles. *The International Migration Review*, 33(1), 5–25.

Light, I. and Rosenstein, C. 1995. *Race, Ethnicity and Entrepreneurship in America*. New York: Walter de Gruyter, Incorporated.

Light, I. and Sanchez, A.A. 1987. Immigrant Entrepreneurs in 272 SMSAs. *Sociological Perspectives*, 30, 373–99.

Lisowska, E. 2002. Women's Entrepreneurship: Trends, Motivations and Barriers, part one, no. 2 in *Women's Entrepreneurship in Eastern Europe and CIS Countries*. New York and Geneva: United Nations Economic Commission for Europe.

Littnen, H. 2000. Entrepreneurship and the Characteristics of the Entrepreneurial Personality. *International Journal of Entrepreneurial Behaviour and Research*, Volume 6, 295–302.

Loscocco, K. 1997. Work–Family Linkages among Self-employed Women and Men. *Journal of Vocational Behaviour*, 50, 204–26.

Loscocco, K. and Cozzens, K. 2000. The Upstate New York Small Business Project Preliminary Report. University at Albany, State University of New York.

Loscocco, K. and Leicht, K. 1993. Gender, Work–Family Linkages and Economic Success among Small Business Owners. *Journal of Marriage and Family*, 55, 875–87.

Loscocco, K. and Robinson, J. 1991. Barriers to Women's Small Business Success in the United States. *Gender and Society*, 5(4), 511–32.

Loscocco, K., Robinson, J., Hall, R.H. and Allen J.K. 1991. Gender and Small Business Success: An Inquiry into Women's Relative Disadvantage. *Social Forces* 70(1), 65–83.

Loscocco, K. and Smith-Hunter, A. 2004. Women Home-based Business Owners: Insights from Comparative Analyses. *Women in Management Review*, 19(3), 164–73.

Low, M.B. and Macmillan, I.C. 1988. Entrepreneurship: Past Research and Future Challenges. *Journal of Management*, 14(2), 139–61.

Lucas, J., Youngs, W., Lovaglia, M. and Markovsky, B. 2001. Lines of Power in Exchange Networks. *Social Forces*, 80(1), 185–214.

Luthans, F., Stajkovic, A.D. and Ibrayeva, E. 2000. Environmental and Psychological Challenges Facing Entrepreneurial Development in Transition Economies. *Journal of World Business*, 95–110.

MaCurdy, T. 1999. An Essay on the Life Cycle: Characterizing Intertemporal Behavior with Uncertainty, Human Capital, Taxes, Durables, Imperfect Capital Markets, and Non-separable Preferences. *Research in Economics*, 53, 5–46.

Maffezzoli, M. 2000. Human Capital and International Real Business Cycles. *Review of Economic Dynamics*, 3, 137–65.

Malveaux, J. and Wallace, P. 1987. Minority Women in the Workplace, in *Working Women: Past, Present, Future*. Industrial Relations Research Association Series. Washington, DC: Bureau of National Affairs, pp. 265–98.

Marger, M.N. 2001. Social and Human Capital in Immigrant Adaptation: The Case of Canadian Business Immigrants. *Journal of Socio-Economics*, 30, 169–70.

Marger, M.N. and Hoffman, C.A. 1992. Ethnic Enterprise in Ontario: Immigrant Participation in the Small Business Sector. *Ethnic Enterprise in Ontario*, 968–81.

Mason, C. and Harrison, R. 1995. Developing the Informal Venture Capital Market in the UK: Is there Still a Role for Public Sector Business Angel Networks? *Frontiers of Entrepreneurship Research*.

Mason-Draffen, C. 2001. The Entrepreneurs' Toolbox: Practical Resources to Plan for Small-business success. *Essence*, 32, 108–86.

Maxwell, J.R. and Westerfield, D.L. 2002. Technological Entrepreneurism Characteristics Related to the Adoption of Innovative Technology. *Sam Advanced Management Journal*, 9–21.

Maysami, R. and Goby, V. 1999. Female Business Owners in Singapore and

Elsewhere: A Review of Studies. *Journal of Small Business Management*, 37(2), 96–105.

Mazumdar S., Mazumdar S., Docuyan, F. and Mclaughlin, C. 2000. Creating a Sense of Place: The Vietnamese-Americans and Little Saigon. *Journal of Environmental Psychology*, 20, 319–33.

McCarthy, B. 2000. Researching the Dynamics of Risk-taking and Social Learning: An Exploratory Study of Irish Entrepreneurs. *Irish Marketing Review*, 13, 46–60.

McCrea, B. 2001. Boosting Black Female Entrepreneurs. *Black Enterprise*, 32, 45–6.

McDougall, P. and Oviatt, B. 2000. International Entrepreneurship: The Intersection of Two Research Paths. *The Academy of Management Journal*, 43(5), 902–8.

McGrath, R.G. 1999. Falling Forward: Real Options Reasoning and Entrepreneurial Failure. *The Academy of Management Review*, 24(1), 13–30.

McGrath, R.G. and Macmillan, I.C. 1992. More Like Each Other than Anyone Else? A Cross-cultural Study of Entrepreneurial Perceptions. *Journal of Business Venturing*, 7(5), 419–30.

McGuire, G.M. and Reskin, B.F. 1993. Authority Hierarchies at Work: The Impacts of Race and Sex. *Gender and Society*, 7, 487–501.

Mier, R. and Giloth, R. 1986. Hispanic Employment Opportunities: A Case of Internal Labor Markets and Weak-tied Social Networks. *Social Science Quarterly*, 66(2), 296–309.

Mills, R., Duncan, K. and Amyot, D. 2000. Home-based Employment and Work-Family Conflict: A Canadian Study, in *Gender and Home-Based Employment*, edited by Charles Hennon, Suzanne Loker, Rosemary Walker. Westport, CT: Greenwood Press, pp. 137–64.

Milne, T. and Thompson, M. 1986. Patterns of successful business start-up, chapter 3 in *Readings in Small Business*, edited by T. Faulkner, G. Beaver, J. Lewis and A. Gibb. Aldershot: Gower Publishing Company Limited.

Min, P. 1988. Problems of Korean Immigrant Entrepreneurs. *International Migration Review*, 26(1), 437–55.

Miner, J. 1997. The Expanded Horizon for Achieving Entrepreneurial Success. *Organizational Dynamics*, 54–67.

Minkes, A.L. 1987. *The Entrepreneurial Manager: Decisions, Goals and Business Ideas*. Middlesex, England: Penguin Books Limited.

Minniti, M. and Bygrave, W. 1999. The Microfoundations of Entrepreneurship. *Entrepreneurship Theory and Practice*, 41–52.

Minor, J.B. 2000. Testing a Psychological Typology of Entrepreneurship using Business Founders. *The Journal of Applied Behavioral Science*, 36, 43–69.

Misra, J. 1999. Latinas and African-American women in the Labor Market: Implications for Policy, chapter 13 in *Latinas and African-American Women at Work: Race, Gender and Economic Inequality*, edited by Irene Browne. New York: Russell Sage Foundation.

Model, S. 1985. A Comparative Perspective on the Ethnic Enclaves: Blacks, Italians, and Jews in New York City. *International Migration Review*, 19(1), 64–81.

Molm, L.D., Peterson, G. and Takahashi, N. 2001. The Value of Exchange. *Social Forces*, 80, 159–84.

Monk-Turner, E. 1992. Sexual Nuances Within Internal Labor Markets: 'The Politics of Being Known'. *The Social Science Journal*, 29, 227–32.

Moore, D. 1990. An Examination of Present Research on the Female Entrepreneur – Suggested Research Strategies for the 1990's. *Journal of Business Ethics*, 9(4/5), 275–81.

Moore, D. 2000a. *Careerpreneurs: Lessons from Leading Women Entrepreneurs on Building a Career Without Boundaries*. California: Davies-Black Publishing.

Moore, J. 2000b. Placing Home in Context. *Journal of Environmental Psychology*, 207–17.

Moore, D. and Buttner, H. 1997. *Women Entrepreneurs: Moving Beyond The Glass Ceiling*. Thousand Oaks, CA: Sage Publication.

Moore, M.E., Parkhouse, B.L. and Konrad, A.M. 2000. Women in Sport Management: Advancing the Representation through HRM Structures. *Women in Management Review*, 16, 51–61.

Morrison, A. 2000. Entrepreneurship: What Triggers It? *International Journal of Entrepreneurial Behaviour and Research*, 6, 59.

Moses, C.G. 1998. 'French Feminism' in Academia. *Feminist Studies*, 24(2), Summer, 241–74.

Mueller, S.L. and Thomas, A.S. 2001. Culture and Entrepreneurial Potential: A Nine Country Study of Locus of Control and Innovativeness. *Journal of Business Venturing*, 16, 51–75.

Naffziger, D., Hornsby, J. and Kuratko, D. 1994. A Proposed Research Model of Entrepreneurial Motivation. *Entrepreneurship Theory and Practice*, 29–43.

National Association of Women Business Owners. 2000. Annual Report. Mclean, VA: National Association of Women Business Owners.

National Women's Business Council. 2000. *Annual Report: Economic Prosperity, Women and Access to Credit, Best Practices in the Financial Markets*. Sponsored by the Milken Institute and the National Women's Business Council, Washington, DC.

National Women's Business Council. 2002. Getting to Success: Helping Women Business Owners Gain Access to Capital: A Study of Best Practices in Access to Capital Training Programs for Women Business Owners.

Neese, T. 2000. Little Known Latina Firms are Booming, Study Shows. *Long Island Business News*, 47(45), 32–3.

Neider, L. 1987. A Preliminary Investigation of Female Entrepreneurs in Florida. *Journal of Small Business Management*, 22–9.

Nelton, S. 1989. The Age of the Woman Entrepreneur. *Nation's Business*, 22–30.

Nelton, S. 1997. Woman Entrepreneurs Make Credit Gains. *Nation's Business*, January, 57.

Nelton, S. 1999. Women-owned Firms Lag in Winning Federal Contracts. *Nation's Business*. March, 87(3), 12.

Nichols, N. 1994. *Reach for the Top: Women and the Changing Facts of Work Life*. Boston, MA: Harvard Business Review.

Nicholson, P. 1996. *Gender, Power and Organization: A Psychological Perspective*. New York: Routledge Publishers.

O'Hare, W.O. and Suggs, R. 1986. Embattled Black Businesses. *American Demographics*, April, 27–49.

Ohlott P., Ruderman, M. and McCauley, C. 1994. Gender Differences in Managers' Developmental Job Experiences. *Academy of Management Journal*, 37(1), 46–58.

Ojito, M., Musibay, O., Pena, A., Radelat, A. and Dominguez, F. 2001. Hispanics at the Top of their Game. *Hispanic*, 14, 24–34.

Oliver, S. 1996. How Katherine Hammer Reinvented Herself. *Forbes*, August 12, 158(4), 98–103.

Olsen, S.F. and Currie, H.M. 1992. Female Entrepreneurs: Personal Value Systems and Business Strategies in a Male-dominated Industry. *Journal of Small Business Management*, 30(1), 49–56.

Olson, P. 1997. Are the Floors Less 'Sticky' at Home? Pay Equity in Home-Based Work. *Consumer Interests Annual*, (43), 239–51.

Ong, P. 1981. Factors Influencing the Size of the Black Business Community. *The Review of Black Political Economy*, 11, 313–19.

Oppedisano, J. 1998. Having Wits and Taking Risks: American Women Entrepreneurs 1776–1976. *A Leadership Journal: Women in Leadership – Sharing the Vision*, Fall, 3(1), 87–94.

Oppedisano, J. 2000. *Historical Encyclopedia of American Women Entrepreneurs: 1776 to Present*. New York: Garland Publishing Group.

Orhan, M. and Scott, D. 2001. Why Women Enter into Entrepreneurship: An Explanatory Model. *Women in Management Review*, 16, 232–43.

Orser, B., Hogarth-Scott, S. and Riding, A. 2000. Performance, Firm Size and Management Problem Solving. *Journal of Small Business Management*, 38(4), 42–58.

Owen, A., Carsky, M. and Dolan, E. 1992. Home-based Employment: Historical and Current Considerations. *Journal of Family and Economic Issues*, 13, 121–38.

Palme, M. 2000. Comments on James Heckman's 'Policies to Foster Human Capital'. *Research in Economics*, 54, 65–9.

Parasuraman, S., Purohit, Y. and V. Godshalk. 1996. Work and Family Variables, Entrepreneurial Career Success, and Psychological Well-being. *Journal of Vocational Behavior*, 48, 275–300.

Pellegrino, E. and Reece, B. 1982. Perceived Formative and Operational Problems Encountered by Female Entrepreneurs in Retail and Service Firms. *Journal of Small Business Management*, 15–24.

Pendakur, K. and Pendakur, R. 2002. Language as Both Human Capital and Ethnicity. *The International Migration Review*, 36, 147–77.

Perkov, A. 2002. Selected Aspects of Women's Position in Croatia, part two, no. 4 in *Women's Entrepreneurship in Eastern Europe and CIS Countries*. New York and Geneva: United Nations Economic Commission for Europe.

Phillips, B.D. 2002. Home-based Firms, E-commerce, and High-technology Small Firms: Are they Related? *Economic Development Quarterly*, 16, 39–48.

Phizacklea, A. 1988. Entrepreneurship, Ethnicity and Gender, chapter 2 in *Enterprising Women: Ethnicity, Economy and Gender Relations*, edited by Sallie Westwood and Parminder Bhachu. New York: Routledge Publishers.

Phizacklea, A. and Wolkowitz, C. 1995. *Homeworking Women: Gender, Racism and Class at Work*. London, Thousand Oaks, CA and New Delhi: Sage Publications.

Politova, O. 2002. Women Entrepreneurs in the Russian Federation: Key Problems and Trends, part two, no. 1 in *Women's Entrepreneurship in Eastern Europe and CIS Countries*. New York and Geneva: United Nations Economic Commission for Europe.

Pope, H. 2002. For Saudi Women, Running a Business Is a Veiled Initiative – In a Nation of the Strictest Islam, Discretion is the Vital Trait in a Female Entrepreneur. *The Wall Street Journal*, January, A1.

Popielarz, Pamela A. 1999. Organizational Constraints on Personal Network Formation. *Research in the Sociology of Organizations*, (16), 263–81.

Portes, A. and Zhou, M. 1992. Gaining the Upper Hand: Economic Mobility among Immigrant and Domestic Minorities. *Ethnic and Racial Studies*, 15(4), 491–522.

Powers, M. 1995. Home is Where the Work is. *Human Ecology*, 23, 8–12.

Priesnitz, W. 1989. Running a Business Out of Your Home. *Women and Environments*, 4–8.

Putnam, R. 1995. Bowling Alone: America's Declining Social Capital. *Journal of Democracy*, 6(1), 65–78.

Putnova, A. 2002. Women Entrepreneurs in the Czech Republic, part two, no.

2 in *Women's Entrepreneurship in Eastern Europe and CIS Countries*. New York and Geneva: United Nations Economic Commission for Europe.

Radhakishun, C. 2000. Women Entrepreneurs in Least Developed Countries: Profile, Problems and Policies, section II in *Women Entrepreneurs in Africa: Experience from Selected Countries*. New York and Geneva: United Nations Publications.

Raijman, R. 2001. Mexican Immigrants and Informal Self-employment in Chicago. *Human Organization*, 60(1), 47–55.

Ramierez-Beltran, N. 2002. Neural Networks to Model Dynamic Systems with Time Delays. *IIE Transactions*; *Norcross*, 34, 313–27.

Raymo, J.M. and Xie, Y. 2000. Income of the Urban Elderly in Postreform China: Political Capital, Human Capital, and the State. *Social Science*, 29, 1–24.

Reilly, M.L. 2001. Investing in Inner-city Neighborhoods. *Journal of Housing and Community Development*, 58, 28.

Renzulli, L., Aldrich, H. and Moody, J. 2000. Family Matters: Gender, Networks and Entrepreneurial Outcomes. *Social Forces*, 79(2), 523–46.

Reskin, B. and Roos, P. 1990. *Job Queues, Gender Queues: Explaining Women's Inroads into Male Occupations*. Philadelphia: Temple University Press.

Reynolds, P., Bygrave, W., Autio, E., Cox, L. and Hay, M. 2002. Global Entrepreneurship Monitor: 2002 Executive Report. The Ewing Marion Kauffman Foundation.

Riding, A. and Swift, C. 1990. Women Business Owners and Terms of Credit: Some Empirical Findings of the Canadian Experience. *Journal of Business Venturing*, 5(5), 327–40.

Riley, J. 1999. Latinas: Natural-born entrepreneurs?. *Hispanic*, 12, 86.

Roberts, C. 1985. Research on Women in the Labor Market: The Context and Scope of the Women and Employment Survey, chapter 12 in *New Approaches to Economic Life, Economic Restructuring, Unemployment and the Social Division of Labor*, edited by Bryan Roberts, Ruth Finnegan and Duncan Gallie. Manchester, England: Manchester University Press.

Robinson, J.G. and McIlwee, J.S. 1991. Men, Women and the Culture of Engineering. *The Sociological Quarterly*, 32(3), 403–21.

Robinson, P. and Sexton, E. 1994. The Effect of Education and Experience on Self-employment Success. *Journal of Business Venturing*, 9(2), 141–57.

Robinson-Jacobs, K. 2002. Black-owned Businesses Blossoming in the Suburbs; Survey: Firms find Room to Grow in Outlying Valleys and Better Access to Tech Resources in Orange County. *The Los Angeles Times*, February 21, C1.

Rowe, B. and Bentley, M. 1992a. At-home Income Generation – Part Two: Introduction. *Journal of Family and Economic Issues*, 13, 241–3.

Rowe, B. and Bentley, M. 1992b. The Impact of the Family on Home-based Work. *Journal of Family and Economic Issues*, 13, 279–97.

Rowe, B., Stafford, K. and Owen, A. 1992. Who's Working at Home: The Types of Families Engaged in Home-based Work. *Journal of Family and Economic Issues*, 13, 159–72.

Ruminska-Zimny, E. 2002. Women's Entrepreneurship and Labour Market Trends in Transition Countries. Part One, Number One in *Women's Entrepreneurship in Eastern Europe and CIS Countries*, New York and Geneva: Economic Commission for Europe, United Nations.

Russell, C. 1981. The Minority Entrepreneur. *American Demographics*, 3, 18–23.

Sabirianova, K. 2001. The Great Human Capital Reallocation: A Study of Occupational Mobility in Transitional Russia. *Journal of Comparative Economics*, 30, 191–217.

Sanders, J.M. and Nee, V. 1996. Immigrant Self-employment: The Family as Social Capital and the Value of Human Capital. *American Sociological Review*, 61, 231–49.

Scase, R. and Goffee, R. 1980. *The Real World of the Small Business Owner*. London: Croom Helm Limited.

Scheinberg, S. and MacMillan, I. 1988. An 11 Country Study of Motivations to Start a Business. *Frontiers of Entrepreneurship Research: Proceedings of the Eighth Annual Babson College Entrepreneurship Research Conference*. Wellesley, MA.: Center for Entrepreneurial Studies, Babson College, pp. 669–87.

Scherer R., Adams J., Carley, S. and Wiebe, F. 1989. Role Model Performance Effects on Development of Entrepreneurial Career Preference. *Entrepreneurship Theory and Practice*, 13(3), 53–73.

Scherr F., Sugrue, T. and Ward, J. 1993. Financing the Small Firm Start-up: Determinants of Debt Use. *Journal of Small Business Finance*, 3(1), 17–36.

Schollhammer, H. and Kuriloff. 1979. *Entrepreneurship and Small Business Management*. United States of America: John Wiley and Sons.

Schreiner, M. 1999. Self-employment, Microenterprise, and the Poorest Americans. *The Social Service Review*, 73, 496.

Schwartz, E.B. 1976. Entrepreneurship: A New Female Frontier. *Journal of Contemporary Business*, 5(1), 47–76.

Scott, W. 1983. Financial Performance of Minority versus Non Minority-owned Businesses. *Journal of Small Business Management*, 42–8.

Sexton, D. and Bowman-Upton, N. 1990. Female and Male Entrepreneurs: Psychological Characteristics and their Role in Gender-Related Discrimination. *Journal of Business Venturing*, 5(1), 29–37.

Sexton, D. and Smilor, R. 1986. *The Art and Science of Entrepreneurship.* Cambridge, MA: Ballinger.

Shabbir, A. and Di Gregorio, S. 1996. An Examination of the Relationship between Women's Personal Goals and Structural Factors Influencing their Decisions to Start a Business: The Case of Pakistan. *Journal of Business Venturing*, 507–29.

Shane, S., Kolvereid, L. and Westhead, P. 1991. An Exploratory Examination of the Reasons Leading to New Firm Formation across Country and Gender (Part 1). *Journal of Business Venturing*, 6(6), 431–46.

Shaver, K. and Scott, L. 1991. Person, Process, Choice: The Psychology of New Venture Creation. *Entrepreneurship Theory and Practice*, 16(2), 23–46.

Smart, G. 1999. Management Assessment Methods in Venture Capital: An Empirical Analysis of Human Capital Valuation. *Venture Capital*, 1, 59–82.

Smith, A.S. 1998. The American Community Survey and Intercensal Population Estimates: Where are the Crossroads? US Bureau of Census, Population Division Technical Working Paper, no. 31. Washington, DC.

Smith, A.W. and Moore, J.V. 1985. East-West Differences in Black Economic Development. *Journal of Black Studies*, 16, 131–53.

Smith, E.L. 1996. Is Black Business Paving the Way? *Black Enterprise*, 26, 194.

Smith, G. 2001. Franchise Growth through Diversity: IFA's Role. *Franchising World*, 33, 21–3.

Smith, P., Smits, S. and Hoy, F. 1992. Female Business Owners in Industries Traditionally Dominated by Males. *Sex Roles*, 26, 485–96.

Smith, S. and Tienda, M. 1988. The Doubly Disadvantaged: Women of Color in the U.S. Labor Force, in *Women Working: Theories and Facts in Perspective*, edited by Ann Helton Stromberg and Shirley Harkness. Mountain View, CA: Mayfield Publishing Company, pp. 61–80.

Smith-Hunter, A. 2000. Oligopolistic Discrimination: A New Theory on Women and Minority Business Ownership. *The Journal of International Business and Entrepreneurship*, 8(2), 47–64.

Smith-Hunter, A. 2003. *Diversity and Entrepreneurship: Analyzing Successful Women Entrepreneurs*. Lanham, MD: University Press of America.

Smith-Hunter, A. and Nolan, J. 2003. Funding New Business Ventures: Differences in Minority and Non Minority Family-owned Business Access to Start-up Capital. *Journal of Business and Economic Research*, 1(2), 43–57.

Sonderup, L. 2001. Are Minorities the Future of Franchising?. *Franchising World*, 33, 26–7.

Sorger, Gerhard. 2001. A Spatial-temporal Model of Human Capital Accumulation. *Journal of Economic Theory*, 96, 153–79.

Stanfield II, J.H. 1993. Methodological Reflections: An Introduction, chapter 1 in *Race and Ethnicity in Research Methods*. California, London and India: Sage Publications.

Stanfield II, J.H. and Dennis, R. 1993. *Race and Ethnicity in Research Methods*. California, London and India: Sage Publications.

Stearns, T. and Hills, G. 1996. Entrepreneurship and New Firm Development: A Definitional Introduction. *Journal of Business Research*, 36(1), 1–5.

Steinmetz, G. and Wright, E. 1989. The Fall and Rise of the Petty Bourgeoisie: Changing Patterns of Self-employment in the Postwar United States. *American Journal of Sociology*, 94(5), 973–1018.

Stevens, J. 1992. *Applied Multivariate Statistics for the Social Sciences*. Hillsdale, NJ: L. Erlbaum Associates.

Stevenson, L.A. 1986. Against all Odds: The Entrepreneurship of Women. *Journal of Small Business Management*, October, 30–6.

Strauss, A. and Corbin, J. 1990. *Basics of Qualitative Research: Grounded Theory, Procedures and Techniques*. Newbury Park, CA London and New Delhi: Sage Publications.

Stuart, T.E. 1999. Interorganizational Endorsements and the Performance of Entrepreneurial Ventures. *Administrative Science Quarterly*, 44, 315–49.

Stuart, T., Hoang, H. and Hybels, R. 1999. Interorganizational Endorsements and the Performance of Entrepreneurial Ventures. *Administrative Science Quarterly*, 44(2), 315–50.

Sullivan, T. and McCracken, S. 1988. Black Entrepreneurs: Patterns and Rates of Return to Self-employment. *National Journal of Sociology*, 167–85.

Takyi-Asiedu, S. 1993. Some Socio-cultural Factors Retarding Entrepreneurial Activity in Sub-Saharan Africa. *Journal of Business Venturing*, New York, March (2), 91–98.

Tang, J. 1995. Differences in the Process of Self-employment among Whites, Blacks and Asians: The Case of Scientists and Engineers. *Sociological Perspectives*, 38(2), 273–309.

Taniguchi, H. 2002. Determinants of Women's Entry into Self-employment. *Social Science Quarterly*, 83(3), 875–94.

Teixeira, C. 2001. Community Resources and Opportunities in Ethnic Economies: A Case Study of Portuguese and Black Entrepreneurs in Toronto. *Urban Studies*, 38(11), 2055–78.

Teo, S. 1996. *Women Entrepreneurs in Singapore*. Singapore Business Development Series: Entrepreneurs, Entrepreneurship and Enterprising Culture, edited by A. Low and W. Tan. Singapore: Addison-Wesley Publishing Company.

Terpstra, D.E. and Olson, P. 1993. Entrepreneurial Start-up and growth: A Classification of Problems. *Entrepreneurship Theory and Practice*, Spring, 5–20.

The Center for Women's Business Research. (2004a). Privately-held 50% or more Women-owned Businesses in the US, 2004. Retrieved June 1, 2004, from www.womensbusinessresearch.org/nationalnumbers.html

The Center for Women's Business Research. (2004b). Minority Women-owned businesses in the United States, 2001: A Fact Sheet. Retrieved June 1, 2004, from www.womensbusinessresearch.org/minorityreports.html

The Center for Women's Business Research. (2004c). African American Women-owned Businesses in the United States, 2002: A Fact Sheet. Retrieved June 1, 2004, from www.womensbusinessresearch.org/minorityreports.html

The Center for Women's Business Research. (2004d). Hispanic Women owned Businesses in the United States, 2002: A Fact Sheet. Retrieved June 1, 2004, from www.womensbusinessresearch.org/minorityreports.html

The Center for Women's Business Research. (2004e). Asian and Pacific Islander Women-owned Businesses in the United States, 2002: A Fact Sheet. Retrieved June 1, 2004, from www.womensbusinessresearch.org/minorityreports.html

The Center for Women's Business Research. (2004f). Native American and Alaska Native Women-owned Businesses in the United States, 2002: A Fact Sheet. Retrieved June 1, 2004, from www.womensbusinessresearch.org/minorityreports.html

Tian, Q. and Cox, D.C. 2002. Optimal Replication Algorithms for Hierarchical Mobility Management in PCS Networks. *Computer Networks*, 38, 447–59.

Trent, E. 2000. Industry and Self-employment Analysis by Gender. *Gender and Home-based Employment*, 167–87.

Turk, M. 2002. Entrepreneurship as a Challenge and an Opportunity in Slovenia, part two, no. 3 in *Women's Entrepreneurship in Eastern Europe and CIS Countries*. New York and Geneva: United Nations Economic Commission for Europe.

United States Census Bureau. 2000. US Census Bureau, Statistical Abstract of the United States.

United States Small Business Administration. 1978. Women's Handbook: How SBA can Help you go into Business. Small Business Administration, Office of Management Assistance.

Utsch, A., Rauch, A., Rothfufs, R. and Frese, M. 1999. Who Becomes a Small Scale Entrepreneur in a Post-Socialist Environment: On the Differences between Entrepreneurs and Managers in East Germany. *Journal of Small Business Management*, 37, 31–42.

Uzzi, B. 1999. Embeddedness in the Making of Financial Capital: How Social Relations and Networks Benefit Firms Seeking Financing. *American Sociological Review*, 64(4), 481–505.

Van Auken, H. and Horton, H. 1994. Financing Patterns of Minority-owned Small Business. *Journal of Small Business Strategy*, 31–43.

Van Horn, R.L. and Harvey, M. 1998. The Rural Entrepreneurial Venture: Creating the Virtual Megafirm. *Journal of Business Venturing*, 13, 257–74.

Vesper, K.H. 1990. *New Venture Strategies*. Englewood Cliffs, NJ: Prentice-Hall Incorporated.

Villemez, W. and Beggs, J. 1984. Black Capitalism and Black Inequality: Some Sociological Considerations. *Social Forces*, 63(1), 117–44.

Waldinger, R., Aldrich, H., Bradford, W.D., Boisssevain, J., Chen, G., Korte, H., Ward, R. and Wilson, P. 1998. Conclusion and Policy Implications, chapter 7 in *Ethnic Entrepreneurs: Immigrant Business in Industrial Societies*, edited by Roger Waldinger, Howard Aldrich and Robin Ward. Newbury Park, CA and London: Sage Publications.

Warbington, R. 2000. Women Entrepreneurs Make Large Gains. *Women in Business*, 52(2), 10–11.

Watkins, J.M. and Watkins, D. 1986. The Female Entrepreneur: Her Background and Determinants of Business Choice – Some British Data, chapter 12 in *The Survival of the Small Firm: The Economics of Survival and Entrepreneurship*, edited by James Curran, John Stanworth and David Watkins. England: Publishing Company Limited.

Weigel, Daniel J. and Deborah S. Ballard-Reisch. 1997. Merging Family and Firm: An Integrated Systems Approach to Process and Change. *Journal of Family and Economic Issues*, 18, 7–31.

Weiler, S. and Bernasek, A. 2001. Dodging the Glass Ceiling? Networks and the New Wave of Women Entrepreneurs. *The Social Science Journal*, 38(1), 85–103.

Weiling, E., Winter, M., Morris, E.W. and Murphy, A.D. 2001. Women Working for Pay of Profit in Oaxaca de Juarez, Mexico, 1987–1992: Integration, Marginalization, or Exploitation? *Women's Policy Journal*, 1, 48–66.

Weiss, C. 1990. The Role of Intermediaries in Strengthening Women's Self-employment Activities, chapter 4 in *Enterprising Women: Local Initiatives for Job Creation*, edited by the Organization for Economic Co-operation and Development. Head of Publication Services, Washington, DC: OECD.

Wen, U., Wu, T. and Shyur, C. 2002. Bi-directional Self-healing Ring Network Planning. *Computers and Operations Research*, 29, 1719–37.

Westwood, S. and Bhachi, P. 1988. *Enterprising Women: Ethnicity, Economy and Gender Relations*. London and New York: Routledge Publishers.

White, L.J. 1982. The Determinants of the Relative Importance of Small Business. *The Review of Economics and Statistics*, 64, 42–9.

Wilkins, D. 1980a. The Financing of Small Firms. in *Policy Issues in Small Business Research*, edited by A. Gibb and T. Webb. England: Teckfield Limited.

Wilkins, D. 1980b. Large Company/Small Company Relations, theme IV in

Policy Issues in Small Business Research, edited by Allan Gibb and Terry Webb. England: Teckfield Limited.

Wilkinson, I. and Young, L. 2002. On Cooperating: Firms, Relations, and Networks. *Journal of Business Research*, 2, 123–32.

Williams-Harold, B. 1998. Up the Mountain: Securing Capital Remains a Steep Challenge for Female Entrepreneurs. *Black Enterprise*, August, 24.

Wilson, K. and Martin, W. 1982. Ethnic Enclaves: A Comparison of the Cuban and Black Economies in Miami. *American Journal of Sociology*, 134–57.

Wilson, P. 1984. Black Business in Britain: A Survey of Afro-Caribbean Businesses in Brent, chapter 6 in *Success and Failure in Small Business*, edited by J. Lewis, J. Stanworth and A. Gibb. England: Gower Publishing Company Limited.

Wilson, P. and Stanworth, J. 1987. The Social and Economic Factors in the Development of Small Black Minority Firms: Asian and Afro-Caribbean Business in Brent 1982 and 1984, chapter 4 in *Small Business Development: Some Current Issues*, edited by K. O'Neill, R. Bhambri, T. Faulkner and T. Cannon. Aldershot: England: Gower Publishing Company Limited.

Woodard, M.D. 1997. *Black Entrepreneurs in America: Stories of Struggle and Success*. New Brunswick, NJ: Rutgers University Press.

Woodcock, C. 1986. The Financial and Capital Environment of the Small Firm, chapter 3 in *The Survival of the Small Firm: The Economics of Survival and Entrepreneurship*, edited by James Curran, John Stanworth and David Watkins. England: Gower Publishing Company Limited.

Woodson, R. 1988. Black America's Legacy of Entrepreneurship. *National Journal of Sociology*, 204–24.

Woolcock, M. 2001. Microenterprise and Social Capital: A Framework for Theory, Research, and Policy. *Journal of Socio-Economics*, 30, 193–8.

Wong, L.L. and Ng, M. 1998. Chinese Immigrant Entrepreneurs in Vancouver. A Case Study of Ethnic Business Development. *Canadian Ethnic Studies*, 30, 64–85.

World Bank Group. 2004. World Development Indicators 2003. Washington, DC.

Wortman Jr., M. S. 1986. A Unified Framework, Research Typologies and Research Perspectives for the Interface between Entrepreneurship and Small Business, chapter 10 in *The Art and Science of Entrepreneurship*, edited by D. Sexton and R. Smilor. Cambridge, MA: Ballinger.

Wright, E., Baxter, J. and Birkelund, G. 1995. The Gender Gap in Workplace Authority: A Cross-national Study. *American Sociological Review*, 60(3), 407–35.

Wu, X. 2002. Work Units and Income Inequality: The Effect of Market Transition in Urban China. *Social Forces*, 80(3), 1069–99.

Index

and obtaining capital 131, 143
Loscocco, K. 3, 4, 28, 36, 38, 48, 50, 56, 61, 62, 71, 73, 74, 77, 83, 86, 100, 127, 140, 143, 213
Low, M.B. 41, 43
Lucas, J. 41
Luthans, F. 216
Luxembourg, wage gap in 5*t*
Lyons, P.R. 30, 62, 64, 73, 77, 78, 100, 143

MacMillan, I. 69
MacMillan, I.C. 41, 43, 170
McCarthy, B. 216
McCauley, C. 11
McClung, J. 28, 56, 134
McCrea, B. 203, 209
McDougall, P. 216
McGrath, R.G. 170
McGuire, G.M. 210
McIlwee, J.S. 9
Macao, China, self-employed women, percent 19*t*
MaCurdy, T. 211
Madagascar 189, 190*t*, 192*t*, 194*t*
Maffezzoli, M. 211
Main, K. 29, 77
Maine 151, 159
Malaysia, wage gap in 5*t*
Mali 189, 191
Malveaux, J. 3
Marger, M.N. 41, 42, 199
marginalization, of women 169
marital status
   Canadian entrepreneurs 199
   cross-cultural comparisons 176*t*, 177
   and experience 118, 119
   and obtaining capital 113–14
   of survivalist entrepreneurs 113
marital status, of entrepreneurs 63–5
   and obtaining capital 101
Martin, W. 37
Martinique 171
Maryland 151, 154
Mason, C. 27, 142
Mason-Draffen, C. 71, 121, 206, 212
Massachusetts 156
Matthews, J. 2
Maupin, W. 2
Maxwell, J.R. 212

Maysami, R. 10, 14, 25, 71, 90, 142, 175, 176*t*, 177, 178*t*, 179*t*, 180*t*, 212, 213
Mazumdar, S. 17
memberships, organizational 91–2, 112, 113, 114, 115, 168
Merino, K. 8
Mexico 184
   self-employed women, percent 19*t*
Meyer, B. 203
Michigan 154
Michigan sample 55, 56*t*
Mier, R. 41
migration network theory 121
Milken Institute 163, 164, 165, 168, 215
Milne, T. 212
Min, P. 66, 212
Miner, J. 212
Minkes, A.L. 206
Minnesota 156
Minnesota Women's Business Center 165
Minniti, M. 206
minorities *see also* African Americans; Asians; Hispanics; Native Americans
   as doubly disadvantaged 205, 210–11, 212, 214
   inclusion in sample 50, 54–8
   as percentage of entrepreneurs 151–2
   race, definitions of 21
   United Kingdom 20
   women-owned firms, by race 9, 9*t*
Misra, J. 210
mobility, career *see also* glass ceiling
   expectations 3
   lack of 4, 10
Model, S. 141
Moen, P. 10, 69
Mohdova, Republic of 197
Molm, L.D. 41, 103
Monk-Turner, E. 42
Montana 151, 159
Moore, D. 1, 10, 17, 28, 30, 43, 44, 52, 60, 63, 65, 66, 69, 77, 84, 86, 92, 100, 105, 120, 122, 145, 146, 207, 213, 216
Moore, Dorothy 216
Morocco 189, 191
Morrison, A. 206
Mosakowski, E. 203
Moses, C.G. 32